111 Years Waldhaus Sils

The Curious Tale and Incomplete History of an Alpine Grand Hotel and Its People

111 Years
Waldhaus Sils

The Curious Tale and Incomplete History of an Alpine Grand Hotel and Its People

by Urs Kienberger

Including conversations with eye witnesses
by Andrin C. Willi
and texts by Rolf Kienberger

New photos by Stefan Pielow

Scheidegger & Spiess

Contents

111 years Waldhaus Sils. Why?

Why? That is is the favorite word of my six-year-old great nephew Elias, member of the Waldhaus's youngest generation. Why did our ancestors build this hotel? Why in this very spot, why just so and not any different? Why is our family still obsessed with it, why do we continue to work here after all these years, as if our life depended on it? What does it mean to its guests? Why is it still around in the first place? Does it justify such a hefty book? And, why celebrate "111" years?

None of the answers are obvious. Our ancestors did not have nearly enough money. And they built for a world that ceased to exist in 1914. And that was just the beginning of our troubles. Looking around, you can easily find bigger and grander hotels, older, more architecturally interesting, spectacularly more expensive hotels or ones that are far easier on your budget and, of course, more famous ones. Nothing is obvious. That is what's best about our hotel and our story: its magic, its fascination and its very essence are not obvious, but they are potent. Let's call it the power of the seemingly inconspicuous.

Ages ago, my father Rolf Kienberger, who died in 1994, and I made a first attempt to tell the story with *Waldhaus Sils-Maria. The first 75 years* (1983). This volume incorporates much of that book, particularly the lovely chapters written by my father, but also goes far beyond. And yet, much remains untold. So much more and, especially, so many who have helped shape this hotel should also have been included. The omissions would have been more glaring yet had it not been for my talented co-authors: Andrin C. Willi talked to “eye witnesses,” and these interviews make a substantial contribution to the tone and contents of this book. And, photographer Stefan Pielow has deftly and precisely captured the present in a book often focused on the past.

Why “1-1-1”? That’s easy to answer. We simply did not have the patience to wait for the 200-year anniversary.

Urs Kienberger, Waldhaus Sils

This book also lends a voice to David R. Bon, Christian Zuan, Marietta Tschander, Beat Birchler, Guido Schmidt, Quintus Miller, Karl Baedeker, Annatina Pinösch, Claudia Duschletta, Christina and Maria Godly, Amalia Giger, Aldo Balzer, Peter Hefti, Rose-Marie Hunziker, Walter Natsch, Tino Conrad, Annalisa Cavelti, Michael Matantos, Walter Nana, Signor X, Claudia Klotz, Adeline Burger, Donata Willi, Felix Dietrich, Kurt Röösli, Hartly Mathis, Maria Dietrich, Marcella Maier, John Kirchheimer, Erwin Brunschwiler, Jürg Kienberger, Alexander Kluge, Martin Müller, Claudio Dietrich, Patrick Dietrich and Patrick Ghielmetti.

The beginning

On a fine spring day in 1905, the scene in the woods of Laret above the village of Sils must have been more than a little puzzling to the townspeople. In the middle of the forest, workmen had erected a wooden scaffold with a ladder leading up to a platform on top: something one might expect to find on a children's playground or in the exercise yard of an army camp. But instead of children or recruits, a group of dignified gentlemen now stood there, climbed all over the scaffold and looked around, unfolded blueprints and held earnest discussions. The one who clearly had the last word was an elderly man with stern features and a beard, Josef Giger, who wanted to build a hotel here. With him were his 27-year-old son Gustav, Karl Koller, a prominent and successful hotel architect, and Christian Zuan, head of the "commons," the public lands of Sils and Giger's local trustee; Oskar Kienberger, the young reception manager of the large St. Moritz hotel which Josef Giger had managed for 17 years, had also come along.

The scaffold was meant to give the gentlemen a good look at the view above the tree tops so that they could decide exactly how to place the planned hotel—for which the very appropriate, if unimaginative name of "Waldhaus" (House in the Forest) had already been chosen. The rest is history—a history that we want to tell you a little about. Let's begin by introducing the oldest member of the little group, the initiator of this whole undertaking.

← Josef and Amalia Giger's descendants at the Waldhaus

Josef and Amalia Giger

Josef Giger (1847–1921)

Josef Giger's parents were farmers in Murg, a small village on the Walensee halfway between Zurich and Graubünden, and later took over an inn, the Zum Ochsen in the up-and-coming spa of Ragaz, some 15 miles north of Chur. They were on the move. So was their son, who decided on a career in the hotel business. By 1872, when he was 25, Ragaz tsar Bernhard Simon had entrusted Josef Giger with the management of a large resort hotel with many and illustrious guests, the Hof Ragaz. Josef Giger managed it for the next 17 years, very ably and diligently seconded by his wife Amalia Giger, nee Nigg. They got married in the same year of 1872. She was two years his junior, the daughter of a builder and mayor of nearby Pfäfers.

Right across the street from the Hof Ragaz was the Quellenhof Hotel, and it was run by the parents of Oskar Kienberger, whom we have just met.

In 1889, Josef and Amalia Giger, who by then had four children, moved to the Engadine, to the Du Lac Hotel in St. Moritz-Bad, which was in full bloom at the time. They ran this hotel with great success until the Waldhaus was built. The Du Lac, owned by a stock company, was an elegant resort hotel which could accommodate as many as 350 guests—"une grande maison fort chère," to quote the 1876 Baedeker. It was torn down in 1974 and replaced by a public parking lot (more about the Du Lac on p. 155).

About 1914: Amalia Giger (1849–1924) and her husband Josef with their daughter Helen Kienberger (standing) and their granddaughter of the same name (b. 1912)

In contrast to St. Moritz-Dorf, there was only a summer season in St. Moritz-Bad in those years. During the rest of the year, though, Giger did not simply retire to Neuhof, his house in Ragaz, but he managed other hotels which had their main season in winter. At one point, for instance, he was in Sestri Levante on the Italian Riviera. The winter of 1900/01 even brought him to the Russian capital St. Petersburg, to take charge of the Grand Hotel Europe with its 200 rooms and just as many employees.

Josef and Amalia's four children were born between 1873 and 1882: Amalia (Mali or Malli), Fanny, Gustav and Helen. To them, Josef Giger was a conscientious and caring father, but otherwise he lived entirely for his profession, which he practiced with single-minded dedication and great skill and a tremendous amount of experience. He knew the hotel business from top to bottom and concerned himself with even the tiniest of details. And woe if something was not exactly to his liking! Then he could be a difficult boss. Oskar Kienberger told the story of how Giger once had the executive chef of the Du Lac come see him on account of a plate of gnocchi Parisienne, which had not turned out right. Giger first calmly pointed out the mishap, but then gradually worked himself into such a state that he dressed down the chef—a grand master of his art who divided his time between the Du Lac in summer and the Hotel de Paris in Monte Carlo in winter, as if he had been a schoolboy.

The Giger siblings, around 1950. From left Gustav Giger, Helen Kienberger, Amalia Woflisberg and Fanny Lutz

What could have driven this successful hotelier couple to want to open a big hotel of their own? At its opening, he would after all be 61 years old and rendered so near-sighted by cataracts that he could only read with a magnifying glass and was forced to dictate all his letters; and his wife had, for years already, been confined to a wheelchair, suffering from gout. It is unlikely that Giger's main motivation was to make a ton of money in his old age. He wasn't that kind of person. Of course, he did hope that the new undertaking would be profitable, especially for the next generation. "The Waldhaus should support my children," he wrote in 1904, apparently thinking of Gustav and of Josef Wolflisberg, Mali's husband, who was already a successful hotelier in his own right. It was likely, though, that he was mainly driven by a different ambition. For decades this born perfectionist had been running hotels for others, where he must have found many things to be unsatisfactory, impractical or inelegant. It is no surprise that he finally wanted to build a hotel that would fulfill his own ideals in every respect!

The part about "supporting the children" did not exactly work out, or at least not until several generations later. In fact, Josef and Amalia Giger's descendants would probably have been far better off if they had not built the hotel. But if their main ambition was to translate their talent and experience into mortar and stone and thus preserve them for future generations, then—with the help of an outstanding architect—they succeeded brilliantly.

"I am perplexed ..."

David R. Bon

"I am perplexed by Josef Giger's obsession with details. Patton, the famous tank general in World War II, said, 'Never tell people *how* to do things. Tell them *what* to do and they will surprise you with their ingenuity.' In my professional career I always followed the chain of command, i.e. told the boss of the 'victim' what to do in principle but never how. When we prepared to celebrate the completion of the Albigna dam, with the last bucket of concrete being poured, I told the foreman of the carpenters where which booth should go and for what purpose (shooting gallery, etc.), but nothing else. When I came by, I was humbled to see how ingeniously he had set things up. I would just have made a mess of it."

David Bon, quite attached to the Waldhaus and also a distant relative of the family, took part in the construction of the Albigna power plant in the Bregaglia valley, in the late 1950s, as a civil engineer. As a grandson of the founders of the Suvretta in St. Moritz, Anton and Marie Bon, and son of the legendary entrepreneur Primus Bon of the Zurich main-station restaurants, he has given a lot of thought to these old grand hotels as a family's legacy and burden. Used to precise calculations, the levelheaded engineer takes a critical view of what he sees as the outsized professional and entrepreneurial ambitions of the hotel pioneers of old and of subsequent generations, which often led them to fail to do their sums; time and again, they let themselves get caught up in irresponsible visions and investments, tightrope acts without a net.

"He may well have a point," thinks the Waldhaus chronicler, who may have some of these same tendencies. But he cannot stop muttering under his breath, "Reason has its limits, too. The experts who told Columbus that India was much too far away, had a point as well. But they would have never discovered America."

Choosing a location

What makes the Waldhaus special in the first place is its unique location—even in a country like Switzerland, where a great many hotels justifiably boast of an attractive location. (Merely "attractive"? "Unique," "incomparable," "splendid," "ideal," or at the very least "privileged" are words you can find in almost any hotel brochure.) Not only does the Waldhaus lie amid a fantastically beautiful landscape, it also occupies the equivalent of the royal box in it: high on a hill, but still in the axis of the valley, with unimpeded views on all four sides. The painstaking choice bears all the marks of an experienced hotelier: it saves him and his guests the endless aggravation of having to deal with a popular lake front, but an unpopular street side, or a splendid view of the valley but with the back against a steep hillside. While the views from the rooms are delightful, even better, you can step outside and be right in the midst of those views. That, too, is not something to take for granted.

This superb location is by no means a matter of simple chance. Giger had very clear ideas of a good location for a resort hotel, and searched for it with his own brand of stubborn thoroughness and care. The episode with the scaffolding in the Laret woods with which this book begins was only the final step in this search. He had been living in the Engadine for a long time now and had had time to look around. Three construction sites were shortlisted: in addition to the site he finally chose, there was the Suvretta area of St. Moritz (where Anton Bon, brother-in-law of Giger's wife, would eventually build) and a spot above Silvaplana near the Julier pass road. By 1904, he had definitively decided on Sils and the Laret heights (pronounced: Lar*e*t), perhaps even sooner, as he had apparently owned a plot in the woods behind and above the hotel, where the Chesa Laret (originally Villa Spitzer) now stands.

The next question was exactly where and how to place the hotel. The original plan had been to build where the Villa Spitzer came to be located, but it had the drawback that one of the façades would have risen straight above the cliffs of the Fex canyon. Only guests with absolutely no fear of heights could have been expected to take the rooms atop this spectacular drop. (Even at our present location our more exposed rooms sometimes make guests from the plains feel a bit queasy.) Josef and Amalia Giger were also worried that the precipice could be dangerous for children. And there was the practical problem that the water pressure from the town's water supply would not have been sufficient to reach that height. The hotel would have had to pipe in its own water from the Fex valley.

In the fall of 1904, Josef Giger therefore acquired an adjacent and somewhat lower site. It was forest land which had been part of the commons of Sils. That in itself is remarkable and symbolic. The villagers of Sils evidently reacted to Giger's big plans as self-confident partners, rather than viewing it with suspicious caution. The land sale itself was a good indication (followed step-by-step, in the next few years and the

Around 1910: panorama with Lake Sils and the Waldhaus

Sils Maria with Piz Margna (3,159 m; 10,400 ft)

short-lived boom of the 1920s, by further transactions until all the land the hotel needed for its operations had been acquired), as was, by the standards of its time, the rather substantial price. Even the first lots went for a hefty ten francs per square meter. In addition, the enterprising villagers also contracted with the new venture to supply the necessary stone, sand and wood from the commons. Josef Giger arrived as a stranger, but, from the beginning, his and our Waldhaus stood firmly on Sils ground and had a solid Sils core.

Josef Giger had his trusted local representative, Christian Zuan, carefully measure and record the hours of sunlight at the planned location throughout the seasons, notably also in winter, for even then there were plans to eventually introduce a winter season. These records and the scaffolding were instrumental in determining the exact placement of the building and its façades.

So far, we have an experienced hotelier eager to build a hotel, and an excellent construction site. To realize the project, however, two more elements were needed: a good architect and plenty of money.

The very first overnight guest: "22 Lügl 1907, durmit eau per la prüma vouta nel nouv Hotel Waldhaus."

Christian Zuan

Josef Giger's trusted intermediary came from an old and important Sils family. His father Paul had opened the Edelweiss Hotel in 1876, although it later changed hands. Christian Zuan himself, like so many other young men from the valley, went abroad to become a confectioner in foreign lands when he was just 16 years old, working for the Klainguti family from the Engadine in Nice and Genoa. By the time he returned for good, fifteen years later, he was an accomplished man; he bought a house and began an active and enterprising life as a "burgher," a farmer, fisherman, ski instructor, mountain guide, shopkeeper and much more. Zuan was one of the first in Sils to try out skis; the tourist office listed him as a mountain guide and ski instructor for many years. Henry Hoek, the mountain and ski pioneer and book author (p. 255), reported that as early as 1895, Zuan (presumably on "home leave") and two other Silsers, Johann Eggenberger and Toni Fümm, were the first to cross on skis from Sils via the Longhin Pass to Bivio. Later, Zuan opened a store for "colonial goods," as the old expression went, where he also rented out skis and ice skates. And when in 1925, private cars were allowed into Graubünden, he promptly installed a gasoline pump at the corner of his house.

His private records illustrate his key role during the period when the Waldhaus was being built, and confirm and supplement Josef Giger's own notes. *Suot la peidra grossa gniro eret ün Hotel, 200 lets, e sün Laret Höhe gniro fat üna villa,* he wrote when the Sils "commons" sold the first two plots of land to *Sigr. J. Giger da Ragaz* in December 1904: "A hotel with 200 beds is to be built below the large boulder on the Laret heights, and a villa above it." He duly recorded the hours of sunshine at the site of the future "Giger Hotel" (which soon became

Christian Zuan's house and store in Sils Maria around 1930, with the gas pump at the corner (Photo: Emil Meerkämper)

the "Waldhaus" in his notes), for example on February 5, 1905: *Il sulagl arriva a l'hotel Giger allas uras 9 ¼ fin la saira allas 5*, with further data for March 20 and 28.

Work began in late August of 1905. The stones and the sand came from the "commons" of Sils, and Christian Zuan proudly noted that he had personally located the deposits and organized deliveries. A temporary quarry for the stone was opened about 1 kilometer west of the hotel and rails were laid directly to the hotel. Even today the track, obviously minus the rails, is a popular promenade, the "Ebene Weg" or "level way." Sand ("4,000 m^3," Christian Zuan recorded) came from a pit in the Fex Valley.

On March 4, 1906, a town meeting approved the rerouting of the Fex Road in the area of the hotel. At the end of November 1906, the shell of the building had already been roofed: *Glivro cuvrir il tet del Waldhaus Laret,* he wrote on November 29. After July 18, 1907, he noted: *Durmit eu per la prüma vouta nel nouv Hotel Waldhaus*, "I slept at the new hotel for the first time." In all probability, this makes Christian Zuan, by a long shot, the hotel's very first overnight visitor, as it only officially opened eleven months later. During the extremely hectic month of that opening, June 1908, he noted that he had been too busy even to keep up with his regular, meticulous records of the weather and such: *Siand controlleur al Waldhaus schi nun avet temp da remarcher correctamaing l'ora etc.*

There were also tragic moments to record. In September 1907, he reported: *Di 17, crudet ün toller F. Lehmann dal tet del Hotel Waldhaus giò sün üna terrazza e zieva ca. 2 uras spiret el, per fortüna, siand tuot fracascho.* "On the 17th a roofer named F. Lehmann fell from the roof of the Waldhaus Hotel onto a terrace, and after 2 hours he passed away, fortunately for him, as he had broken every bone in his body."

We owe these excerpts from Christian Zuan's records to his grandson Reto Zuan (b. 1947). He, too, has Waldhaus connections. Who wouldn't, in Sils? He confesses that he would have loved to be the miniature-golf cashier at the hotel during his summer vacations, but never got the chance. But Reto Zuan has positive memories of the Waldhaus, too, e.g. from New Year's Eve in 1965 or 1966, when Rolf Kienberger hired him to perform on guitar at the ball. And then there was his wedding, on October 14, 1978. Almost exactly 71 years after the day, on October 22, 1907, when his grandfather had drily recorded: *Fet nozzas con Anna Pedrun, ad eiran 98 persunas e bell'ora.* "Celebrated my wedding with Anna Pedrun. There were 98 guests, and the weather was lovely."

Every child at the Waldhaus, at least those who visit in summer, will know what large boulder (or "fat boulder," in Romansh) Christian Zuan was talking about. It is the one which appears in the background of the two photos of the fifth Waldhaus generation on p. 304 taken in 1985 and 2015 on the children's playground.

In an essay much quoted by lovers of Sils and of Nietzsche, Theodor Adorno wrote that an old Silser had told him how, in the 1880s, he and other young rascals would conjure pebbles into Nietzsche's umbrella on his walks, so that when the thinker opened the umbrella the stones fell on his head (Th. Adorno, "Ohne Leitbild"). That old man (and rascal), too, was Christian Zuan.

← Perfect to enjoy, perfect to work with: Karl Koller's mastery still shows

The architect: Karl Koller

In those years, more new hotels were built in Switzerland than ever before or since. Some architects designed dozens of large hotels, becoming outright experts. When the time came for Giger to select the right one from among these experts, he once again made a very inspired and fortunate choice: Karl Koller (1873–1946), based in St. Moritz. Koller's designs already included the Schweizerhof in Vulpera (see p. 76), the Parkhotel in Vitznau on Lake Lucerne, which Anton Bon had opened in 1903, and the castle-like extension which turned the Enderlin Hotel in Pontresina into the newly and appropriately named Schlosshotel, or "castle hotel," around the same time when the Waldhaus was taking shape. After the Waldhaus, he drew up plans for the magnificent Suvretta House, the imposing St. Moritz hotel which opened in December, 1912. In the archives of the Chantarella in St. Moritz, Rolf Kienberger even came across blueprints by Koller for a hotel in Prague.

Architect Karl Koller (1873–1946) continued to supervise all of the renovations and additions at the Waldhaus until his death (Photo: Albert Steiner)

That the long-gone Grand Hotel in St. Moritz was also one of his creations may at first glance seem less of a recommendation. Huge and ostentatious, the Grand Hotel opened in 1905 on the site of what would later be—but no longer is—the main post office of St. Moritz. On period photographs, it makes the Palace Hotel next door appear almost slender and delicate in comparison. In June 1944, the Grand Hotel burned down to its foundations; few mourned its passing. In the architect's defense, however, it must be said that the investors abruptly decided to double the volume of the building when construction was already well under way, leaving him with the unenviable task of designing a hotel for 450 guests on foundations meant for a hotel half that size.

In any case, Karl Koller was a very lucky choice for the Waldhaus.

"There's no such thing as typical Koller"

Marietta Tschander

MARIETTA TSCHANDER comes from a family of architects and is an architect in her own right, a partner of Tschander.Keller Architekten in Zurich, and the great-granddaughter of Karl Gottlieb Koller (1873–1946). After the death of her grandmother, who lived in the Villa Berna in St. Moritz, Marietta Tschander began transferring, cataloguing and archiving Koller's papers for the Graubünden State Archives in Chur.

"There are architects who celebrate their signature style. My great-grandfather was not one of them. His buildings took into account the client, the surroundings and the location, which means that each one is different. There's no such thing as typical Koller. When I look at his projects from the early 1900s, I notice how carefully the chosen building sites also incorporated the availability of local building materials and factors such as site logistics and the supply of water and electricity. My mother found my great-grandfather to be an imposing man. She was seven when he died, and she remembered stories about the 'ladder,' or really a scaffold, which he set up in 1905 to determine the exact placement of the Waldhaus. The original plans were drawn up in 1906. The hotel opened two years later. Isn't it crazy that I have found practically no documentation, no letters, no notes about building permits? To get a building of this size, on such a highly visible site, approved and built in such a short time would be inconceivable today. Even just getting a building permit so quickly would be absolutely impossible nowadays.

The blueprints are quite simple. For example, there are no cross-sections or plans of details and no technical drawings. There are drawings for the interior appointments, i.e. plans which show the desired results, but none about how to get there. I assume that much was decided and made right on site. I am fascinated by this pioneering model. All the processes, the exchange of letters, everything proceeded in a rush. The courier and postal system must have functioned extremely well as projects of this size had an international dimension and correspondence with firms in Brussels or Berlin were not uncommon. In addition, my great-grandfather simultaneously worked in different locations and could not be everywhere at once.

"The visible woodwork creates much atmosphere. If you replaced it by marble, for example, you would drive away the building's spirit. Wood records history, stores it and relinquishes it. Marble is like a mirror, it doesn't take up anything, it just reflects everything directly."

If you consider it carefully, the Waldhaus would have to be turned by 180 degrees, but then they would have had to deal with constructing a driveway around the building and through the rocks. As it is, the Waldhaus is oriented like a church, facing east, with the entrance in the west. My great-grandfather also built a church, he was fascinated by churches and would go to Italy to buy church furnishings which were no longer needed, antique structural elements or lamps which he simply used in another context.

The name Waldhaus, House in the Woods, is an apt choice. You can always see the forest, yet you get a sense of distance and openness. But not everywhere, which I also think is a good thing. When a building is the same all over, it becomes boring. The Waldhaus does not have a front or a back, but it stands there with a kind of natural assurance. As if it had always been there. Koller's client did not want anything ostentatious, but something handsome, solid and practical, I think it succeeded, as Koller divided up the volume from the beginning. For me, the Waldhaus is like a stand-alone village. Externally and internally, diverse and yet a whole. I would call the style 'historicism': it has a little bit of everything and this mix retains its visual tension; inside, too, the rooms are deliberately different. The staircase is oriented towards Maloja, an organizational design which includes a large open well. When I use the stairs, I can discover things, I can linger, look out at nature, the staircase becomes an experience, a kind of *promenade architecturale*. But the most important thing for me is that when I enter the hotel I feel welcome. It is like coming home."

Capital matters

Unfortunately, the funding, the fourth important element of the Waldhaus plans, was not resolved nearly as elegantly as the other three. In his own records (perhaps for tax purposes?), Josef Giger stated his private net worth in 1904 to be about CHF 440,000–CHF 500,000 in assets and CHF 60,000 in liabilities—much of it in land and real estate. Although that was impressive for someone who had probably started off with nothing, it was not near enough for erecting a large luxury hotel. Much less for two hotels! Just before embarking on the Waldhaus project, our great-grandfather had in fact been the leading partner in Giger, Bon & Co., established to build the 100-bed Bristol Hotel which opened in 1906 near the train station in Ragaz. (The "Bon" in the partnership was Primus Bon, Sr., husband of one of Josef Giger's sisters and brother of the Suvretta founder, Anton Bon; not to be confused with Anton Bon's son of the same name, who became an industry legend as the proprietor of the Zurich station restaurants.) From the start, Ragaz proved to be a bad investment and put a strain on Giger's finances. His motives for taking an interest in that hotel are not clear, as he was already working intensively on his plans for the Engadine by 1903/04, if not earlier. Was he pushed into it by the ambitions of another sister, Veronika Huber, whose family had taken over their parents' inn in Ragaz?

In Sils, as his 1904 letters to architect Koller and to friends and relatives show, Josef Giger wanted a hotel with at least 180 to 200 beds, "modern and comfortable enough that it may still satisfy the demands of guests 20 or 30 years hence." "I envisage about four floors of guest rooms in addition to an attic, where guests could also stay. Of course, it would be nice to have an apartment for the manager's family on the main floor. As the guests who stay here will be on their own, enough public rooms for social activities will have to be provided." "We ought to build something beautiful, solid and practical, but to make it profitable we are forced to think carefully about every expense. Building in the Engadine is very expensive, the tourist season is short, the guests arrive with great expectations, even if also willing to pay good prices."

His worries about cost were justified: these were expensive plans, the more so in the Engadine, as Giger knew. Even St. Moritz was rather remote, although the Rhaetian Railways had started service in 1903/04, but horse-drawn coaches and carts were still the only means of reaching Sils. (As late as the 1970s and 1980s, depending on the state of the economy, we still had to reckon with building costs 15 to 30 percent higher than in the Swiss midlands.) The hotel's cost, initially estimated at CHF 1.6 million, ultimately exceeded two million: about 1.6 million for the structure itself and CHF 425,000 to furnish it. Added to this were CHF 127,000 for the land and another CHF 100,000 for the Waldhaus's share of the construction costs for a small power plant, built jointly with the Barblan Hotel (the Schweizerhof). Within a few years, the power plant was sold (at a loss) to the then Madulain power company.

How was this amount raised? First of all, as had been the case for the Bristol in Ragaz, a partnership, a Kollektivgesellschaft, was set up under the name of "Giger & Co." Its capital of CHF 560,000 originated as follows:

Josef Giger	CHF 355 000	Fanny Giger	CHF 5000
Josef Wolflisberg	CHF 160 000	Helen Giger	CHF 5000
Gustav Giger	CHF 30 000	Anton Bon	CHF 5000

We know, however, from Giger's personal records that a part of his own share was financed by a private bank loan. On the other hand, several partners and other family members contributed additional capital to the project in the form of loans: CHF 102,000 from Anton Bon (whom, in return, Giger had lent CHF 100,000 in 1903 for his project in Vitznau), 58,000 from Giger's brother-in-law Primus Bon, about 50,000 from Josef Wolflisberg, 25,000 each from the brothers, Oskar and Josef Kienberger, and smaller amounts from other relatives. Even if we count these loans from family members as a sort of equity, the raised capital covered only about a third of the financial requirements, at most. That was quite a gamble, considering that even some of the family loans were apparently meant as mere bridge financing.

Two possible sources were available to cover the large gap: banks or outside investors. It would probably have been easy for Josef Giger with his sterling reputation as a hotelier and his many contacts with prosperous guests from decades of hosting them, to interest some wealthy investors in his project, at a time when European economies were booming. A little later, Anton Bon did indeed partly follow this route in financing the construction of the Suvretta. The fact that Giger did not (only a very small share of all the funds came from outside individuals, probably personal friends), again shows just how determined he was to be his own boss where the Waldhaus project was concerned.

In fact, most of the remaining funds, except for what supplier credits and the earnings from the first years of operation could cover, were borrowed from banks. The personal loan Giger had taken up to raise a part of his own share in the partnership came from Bank in Ragaz. Giger & Co did business with Bank für Graubünden, with which later Waldhaus generations fought many a battle ere it ran into economic difficulties in the 1930s, morphed into Bündner Privatbank and was finally bought up by Union Bank of Switzerland, today's UBS.

From Bank für Graubünden, Giger & Co took out a mortgage, but also borrowed money with the hotel furnishings as collateral, and had a large overdraft facility. These three loans were consolidated into a single mortgage of CHF 1.1 million in 1912.

The young enterprise thus began its life with a heavy burden, even if at the time wars and major crises may have seemed to be a thing of the past. But now the project was finally ready to start!

← 111 years later, we haven't stopped building: our spa, which opened in 2016

Construction

After the Fex Road had been rerouted (it had run through the middle of the construction site), construction began late in the summer of 1905. Two and a half years later, on June 15, 1908, the hotel was opened. An amazing pace, especially considering that most of the work stopped in winter.

Architect Koller was in charge of supervising construction, and a younger architect, Johann Ulrich von Salis from Malans, handled the day-to-day site management. Josef Giger himself was, of course, intimately involved. He rented a house in Sils-Maria, but in the summer of 1906, he again managed the Du Lac, and he generally spent the winters in Ragaz. During his absence, he relied heavily on Christian Zuan to represent his interests in Sils.

The hotel which opened in 1908 was largely the hotel as we know it today. In many ways, it was a remarkable work.

The time was not long past when the design of such hotels primarily wanted to convey the impression of a palace furnished with fairytale splendor: operatic settings for regal vacations. The result was then often named "Palace." Admittedly, the Waldhaus, too, has decidedly castle-like features on the outside—"Scottish baronial," as an English author somewhat disapprovingly called it (Vivian H. Green, *The Swiss Alps*). However, you can see this as a clever architectural response to the selected site, which it is easy to imagine as a medieval castle hill. It would hardly have been the spot for erecting a Renaissance palace, a baroque monastery with Victorian-Oriental touches or a ten-story moun-

The premises (partly labeled backwards)

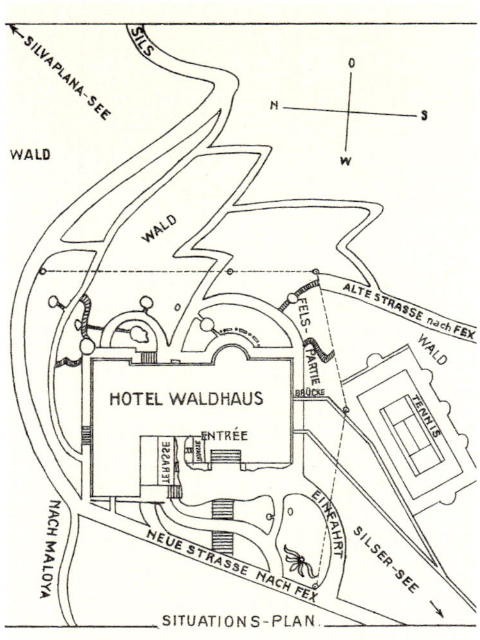

tain chalet. At any rate, the structure and proportions of the large and prominently placed building show considerable skill. The Schweizerhof Hotel (a 1980s reconstruction, roughly with the same roofline and in the same dimensions, of the original 1907 structure), probably has about half the volume of the Waldhaus, yet dominates the village at least as much.

While the Waldhaus's exterior does hint at a castle or a palace, the interior has few palatial touches. Giger wanted and obtained elegance and luxury, "something beautiful, practical and solid"; but he was not interested in marble bathtubs with golden fixtures or other such gimmickry. In its style the result had, as far as is possible in a building of this size, more of the discrete elegance of a well-appointed private home than the splendor of a palace. I am not sure to what extent you can speak of "art nouveau" in the case of the Waldhaus, perhaps more in spirit than in form. Its interiors were at least as eclectic as they are today. Chesterfield sofas, "American" easy chairs and "cane-backed Louis XVI" chairs (to quote the inventory) were peacefully united in the lounge. The private sitting rooms, in turn, variously featured what the inventory describes as "Adam," Empire, Louis XVI, Biedermeier, English and Modern.

The Waldhaus was distinguished by a carefully thought-out layout, designed to facilitate a smooth and efficient operation, and by the most up-to-date technical installations, which would have been unthinkable even just a few years earlier. In fact, Giger's constant push to include the latest technical advances was probably one of the main reasons for the cost overruns. Again and again, he would think of something else that he just had to have.

There was electric lighting throughout the building, with over 1,300 lamps; the light fixtures in the main dining room and in the Empire room as well as the lamps in the corridors and main staircase, for example, are still the original ones. We have already mentioned the small power plant built by the Waldhaus and the Hotel Barblan (Schweizerhof) in 1907. Sils already had a power line from Silvaplana, but Giger did not think it was reliable enough. So, they erected a power house at the east end of Sils-Maria, on the lane that leads to the Furtschellas cable car and to Lake Silvaplana, for two diesel generators and storage batteries. From there an underground cable led to the two hotels. The gray masonry building later became a farm, still in place until a few years ago. The descendants of the farmers have now replaced it with a building of similar dimensions containing seven apartments for local residents.

Winter 1906/07: not quite done yet

With the exception of a few remote corners, the entire hotel was centrally heated from the start. The system came from Sulzer Winterthur—just one example from a surprisingly long list of firms and suppliers with whom we continued to do business for many years. The public rooms and some guest rooms which were especially exposed had steam radiators, while the rest of the hotel had hot-water radiators. The furnaces were fired with coal. The public rooms on the main floor even

The south tower (which went up in flames in 1927) under construction, seen from the southeast

As eclectically furnished as today: the lounge in the 1920s (Photo: Emil Meerkämper)

had a rough-and-ready ventilation system. It was ingeniously simple. Under the window ledges and behind the radiators, there were vents to let in outside air. Other vent openings in the ceiling led to shafts which reached up to the roof. Radiators at the bottom of the shafts, just above the ceiling, were meant to heat the air and cause it to rise. This, in turn, drew new outside air into the rooms underneath. This system worked only too well, creating such a draft that the vents under the windows soon had to be boarded up.

The remarkably large number of nearly 40 private bathrooms, a feature which just a few years earlier had been regarded as little more than another folly from Albion, was one of the hotel's most important innovations. Connecting doors allowed the guest rooms to be combined into individual suites or "apartments" of several rooms each, if needed. One of the rooms might serve as a private sitting room; there would be one or more bedrooms, and a bathroom. But it was also possible to rent out each room separately, with the exception of the few which only had one shared entrance from the corridor. To enhance the flexibility, most of the sitting rooms were not permanently furnished as such, but could be converted from bedrooms as needed, most notably the 14 guest rooms which had and still have their own decorative open fireplace. The built-in versatility has largely survived and is yet another good illustration for the supreme "hotel savvy" of the hotel's founder and his architect.

The large display panels of the original electric bell system can still be seen in the guest hallways. Guests used it to summon the chambermaids, who saw on the display which room had rung. In the days before personal pagers, which, in our case, meant all the way until 1976, it also served for in-house communication. From his desk, the concierge could activate the bells on every floor: one ring for the floor porter, two for the head housekeeper, three for the manager. When the hotel was busy with many arrivals and departures, the ringing never stopped. Much more quietly, the old Magneta system of centrally controlled wall clocks continues its march through time. The wind-up grandfather clock with weights and a pendulum, near the cashier's office, is the master clock for the hotel's wall clocks, nine of which remain in operation. Minute after minute (unless we forget to wind it), it charges a magnet and then discharges it to send a faint electric impulse to all the wall clocks through a closed circuit, making their hands move forward in unison and reminding us of the passage of time.

By contrast, the built-in "dust-extractor" has not survived. It consisted of a network of pipes which reached all the corridors and public rooms and an electric motor in the basement which created a vacuum. Outlets to which hoses could be hooked up were located on every floor—a 1908 vintage vacuum cleaner. The system was in use for more than 40 years, finally abandoned when increasingly leaky pipes made it ever noisier and ever less effective.

Besides connections with the outside world—Sils had become part of the Swiss telephone network in 1902—an extensive in-house phone system linked the kitchen, the pantry, the wine cellar, etc. already in 1908. The fanciest and most expensive guest rooms also had their own phones; it was even possible to set up a permanent connection between a guest room and the courier room where that guest's personal maid or

Room no. 51 as private sitting room

manservant was staying. A modern convenience that was probably less popular with the servants than the guests.

Two elevators already ensured easy access to the upper floors, although it took quite a while for their presence to change the guests' thinking and habits. Many guests continued to prefer rooms on the lower floors, which is why the lowest of the guest-room floors was grandly named the "bel etage," and it as well as the so-called first floor immediately above it were more expensive than the upper floors with their fantastic views. Of the two elevators, the service elevator was powered by electricity and served us well for 68 years before it had to be replaced. The guest elevator was hydraulic. Water flowed into a counterweight until it was heavy enough to pull the elevator up; to go down, the water was emptied. Each time the elevator descended, a water fountain shot up in a basin on the east side of the hotel under the dining room windows. As an unintended side-effect, the water rumbled noisily through the neighboring Villa Spitzer (see p. 19) whenever the Waldhaus elevator ran. In 1923, the Spitzers, worn out by a lack of sleep, actually helped finance the conversion to an electric elevator.

"The Waldhaus is full of surprises"

Beat Birchler

"I have worked on many building projects at the Waldhaus. From a professional point of view, the craziest were the entrance and the kitchen. In both cases, we had to put up a steel framework to support the floors above, that was tricky. The Waldhaus is full of surprises, as the 1906 construction plans are rudimentary and at the time it was common practice to make changes during construction. The basics are clear, but the details ... This means that it is always possible to come across an unexpected structural situation in a wall. That is why I always examine the walls carefully. I usually have to do this during the season, when it is not possible to drill probing holes. I have developed a simple technique. I tap on the wall with my fist and listen, trying to hear where the wooden beams are.

BEAT BIRCHLER was born in Zurich and became a draftsman before studying civil engineering at the ETH and then moving to the Engadine in 1986. He worked at an engineering firm in Silvaplana until 1992, when he became self-employed. In 2009, he moved to Ardez in the Lower Engadine. His first small job at the Waldhaus was in 1992. "They wanted to break out a door and combine two rooms, but a thick wooden beam ran diagonally through the wall," he remembers. A good thing that he stepped in.

Sometimes I am amazed, believe me. The good thing is that the hotel stands on firm bedrock. The lowest three floors, underneath the kitchen, have solid stone walls. That continues on the main floor, where the public rooms are. Here we have quarry-stone walls 60 to 70 centimeters, 24 to 28 inches thick. There are no bricks at the Waldhaus; the material, i.e. the stone, comes from nearby, and it was probably all cut to size on the spot. The upper floors have a timbered framework filled with stones. The transition between the public rooms and the bel étage, where the span between the walls dividing the rooms is 10 to 16 feet or 3 to 5 meters, is interesting. On the main floor, there is a much wider span between the load-bearing pillars. Steel beams were installed above these pillars, and the walls of the corridors are placed on them. I can't imagine that these beams, which stretch along the entire length of the kitchen, for instance, certainly 50 feet or 15 meters, were transported in one piece. How were they raised into place? They would have been transported to St. Moritz by train, but then, by horses to Sils? They are like heavy bridge girders, I imagine they must have been riveted together on the site, as transporting them would have been crazy.

If I had to make an estimate, I would say that 100 people worked at the construction site, as they had to make everything on their own. There was no trader of building materials to call up and say, please, bring me 20 cubic meters of cement at 11 a.m. For the wooden beams, someone first had to cut down trees, cut them to the exact length and haul them to the construction site. That would involve many people, perhaps my estimate of a hundred is even too small.

"Thinking of the construction of the Waldhaus, we should put things in perspective: the Eiffel Tower in Paris, which was built from 1887 to 1889, was a much greater technical challenge. The challenges in the case of the Waldhaus were the circumstances. It takes courage to build in such a remote place and in this climate. I do not think they were able to work in the winter, which makes the short construction period even more remarkable."

Back to the transition from the large public rooms to the smaller structure of the bedroom floors. In my professional opinion, this was extremely challenging. Above the main floor, all of the dividing walls between the rooms are load-bearing. They did not put in massive ceilings, but instead had the individual partition walls bear the load, and they ran a corridor down the middle. Nowadays we would pour slabs of reinforced concrete on which you could place the walls so that you could lay out the rooms at will on each floor. In 1908, that wasn't possible, as reinforced concrete only started to be used widely in residential construction in the 1950s or so. For that reason, we have to think twice before tearing down just any old wall at the Waldhaus."

Furnishings

View of the original reading room (today's bar)

Of course, it took more than just technical wizardry to accommodate the guests. Also needed were beds (205 master beds, 12 iron children's beds, 160 beds for employees and servants), 566 tables and 1,129 chairs of all kinds, as well as 129 arm chairs, 24 sofas, 111 chaises longues, and outdoor furniture for the garden and the terraces (218 pieces); as well as 291 chamber pots, 4 plant stands and the books for the hotel library (220 in German, 104 in English and 56 in French), not to mention a stuffed eagle for the reading room, today's bar; the aspergillum for the chapel, a hammock, three upright pianos, a grand piano, two chess sets, and on and on.

We have already introduced Josef Giger as a man for whom there was no such thing as an unimportant detail. This trait was nowhere more obvious than in the selection and purchase of the extensive and diverse hotel furnishings. Take, as an example, a passage from his correspondence with Berndorf's of Lucerne, purveyors of silverware. "In particular, we want to point out that the two large soup ladles should hold at most 17 centiliters, better only 16, the handles should match the size of the 10-liter soup bowls in length, should have a nicely rounded end and be comfortable to hold. It is important that the soup ladles be practical and comfortable, not too large and not too small."

The reader will now understand why Josef Giger's great-grandson, who writes these lines, also has a certain penchant for details!

Welte-Mignon

One of the most interesting pieces in the inventory was the electric Welte-Mignon piano in the Empire Room, a mechanical marvel which later lay dormant and hidden for generations.

The "Mignon," named for a female character full of charm and mystery in a Goethe novel, was invented and built by the German firm of M. Welte & Söhne in Freiburg, Germany. Ours was purchased in 1910. The instrument, built of mahogany wood "with bronze chase-work in the Empire-style, simple, but flawlessly encased" (as Josef Giger insisted), was bought for the Music or Empire room in which it now stands. A guest who was annoyed when there was no live orchestra at the beginning of the season, apparently suggested the purchase.

After many letters and much bargaining, the price for two instruments —the second one intended for the Bristol in Bad Ragaz—was set at 4,200 German marks, i.e. 2,100 per piano. With an exchange rate, at the time, of CHF 1.23 for 1 Reichsmark, each instrument cost about CHF 2,600, plus another CHF 1,000 for freight charges and customs duties.

The Welte-Mignon. Not everything was simpler in the past

Welte originally provided the perforated paper rolls, on which the music was recorded, on a lending basis. Like books from a library they could be exchanged every few weeks. Later, the rolls were apparently purchased; in any case, we now own about 100 of them. They had a hefty price. On one of them, it says in pencil: CHF 30. This price corresponded to the hotel's average daily income from one guest. Just imagine, the entire daily income from one guest, for ten minutes of music!

The large instrument with its confoundingly intricate mechanism fell silent some time in the 1920s. After many more years in its original location, it was finally relegated to a storeroom in the basement. There simply wasn't anyone who could repair it. Piano technicians just shrugged. So, it stayed there, half-forgotten, until it was rediscovered in 1978 by our enterprising house engineer, Guido Schmidt. In three years of patient and painstaking work, he brought it back to life to the great delight of our family and guests, and especially of Rolf Kienberger, who had been hoping to hear it again ever since his childhood.

"It's really simple, if you know how it works"

Guido Schmidt

"The project closest to my heart at the Waldhaus continues to be the Welte-Mignon reproducing piano. While cleaning up the former bakery, in around 1980, I found a bunch of perforated paper rolls, labeled with the names of composers and works. A total of 93 original rolls. I couldn't figure out what they were for but decided not to throw them away just yet. Then we had to clean out chairs and tables from another storage space, and there it was: in total disarray, hidden away in a corner at the very back of the room, a Welte-Mignon piano in mahogany. Rolf Kienberger knew about the instrument, but he told me that he had never really heard it play. It had been purchased by Josef Giger in 1910 and had stood in the Empire room (the *salon bleu*). I hesitantly asked if I could have a look at it. Rolf Kienberger didn't hesitate, he said he would be glad if I wanted to try, as up to now all attempts to

GUIDO SCHMIDT has been the chief engineer at the Waldhaus for 41 years, with a wide range of duties (see p. 196). Now he is retiring. He has promised to return from time to time to take us back musically to the Waldhaus of 1910, in collaboration with Urs Kienberger.

put it back together had failed. Piano technicians had advised him not to bother. A piano builder cannot really do much of anything with such a mechanical marvel, since it combines mechanics, electrical engineering and pneumatics. All subjects in which I had been trained, now I just needed to combine them. It's really simple, if you know how it works. Still, there was no Google yet and professional literature was scarce, so I had to try to figure it out on my own.

I began by building a model. After about three years, the piano produced a few notes and I knew that I was on the right track. In 1998, a specialist thoroughly restored the piano part and charged us CHF 13,000 for it. In hundreds of hours of work, I repaired the entire vacuum system, renewed the bellows, restored the membranes, the valves, the motor and everything else to their original condition. The instrument had been purchased for the guests' enjoyment, but I am sure that it did not work for very long as the Engadine air is much too dry. The manufacturer insisted on 60 percent humidity, which is why even now we can only run it in summer. It's too bad that we can't locate any letters of complaint to the manufacturer, as there surely must have been some. It was an expensive purchase and the rolls also cost a small fortune in those days.

I am especially fascinated by the fact that we can now hear the Welte-Mignon in the exact place where it originally stood, and we can listen to the same pieces of music that the hotel founder selected for his guests. Given enough money, anyone can set an old instrument tinkling, but in the case of our specimen, it is history brought back to life. Since the 75th anniversary of the Waldhaus, we have presented the Welte-Mignon five or six times each summer. Objectively speaking, the restoration was a crazily difficult project, but in my career, I have made it a habit to keep myself and my accomplishments in the background."

Built-in efficiency

What constitutes a good hotel? There is a lot that will catch your eye, either by its presence or its absence. You might think of the comforts it offers. Or you might judge it by what you can see: how imposing and inviting is its exterior, how elegant, how generous, how welcoming are its public spaces? What a casual observer will hardly ever think about is the efficiency of its layout or of its amenities. Yet, such questions, though largely hidden from sight, can make or break how a hotel works—and thus, ultimately, how it will work for you as a guest.

By the time they embarked on their Waldhaus adventure, Josef and Amalia Giger had spent a lifetime working with and in hotels. And their architect, Karl Koller, was just as firmly focused on hotels as a working organism. It shows. The Waldhaus is certainly designed to be comfortable and inviting, but at the same time it is masterfully designed to work. That may not even have seemed all that important when it opened. After all, labor was cheap and abundant. If a waiter or a chambermaid costs you no more per *month*, in cash wages, than a guest will pay you in a *day* (see p. 90), why go to any great length to make its operations as smooth and efficient as possible? Yet, remarkably, it is precisely what the Waldhaus builders did. It was almost as if they had a premonition of the many hard and very lean times that were to follow, in the hotel's long and varied history. For you can truly say that this concern for efficiency and practicality, and the masterful answers they found, were a key element in making the Waldhaus survive—if often

Once upon a time, all this was state-of-the-art, now it's in the Waldhaus Museum (Photo: Irene Haberthür)

only by a thread. An inept design can easily make a significant and, in times of crisis, critical difference in terms of staff requirements, just to provide the same level of service; and how many hotels—especially if (unlike the Waldhaus) they were built in stages—had and have to spend large sums to correct inefficient work flows and past mistakes.

Their careful thinking can best be illustrated by an example that at first glance seems to prove the exact opposite. Of all the rooms on the main floor, it is the kitchen which has the best view and most sunlight. While this might at first appear to be a grave mistake, or at least reflect a way of thinking far from our own, a closer look reveals the excellent reasoning behind it. First, the kitchen is on the same floor as the two dining rooms and is directly connected to them. Second, it is positioned on the side of the hotel where the ground drops away most steeply, making room for three floors underneath. This made it possible to place the wine cellar, the storerooms and all the other related facilities (such as, until 1939, our own bakery) and the dining halls for the hotel staff and the guests' servants directly underneath the kitchen, greatly shortening internal distances. Third, it happens to be the side of the hotel where prevailing winds nearly always carry cooking odors away from the roof—where, even at that time, the kitchen ventilation led—rather than back to the building and into open bedroom windows.

Even after all these years, we would be ill-advised to move the kitchen to a different location!

In his efforts to make hotel operations more efficient, Josef Giger went for every conceivable labor-saving device. The inventory lists them: for the kitchen, appliances for potato peeling, chopping meat, grating almonds, grating cheese and slicing cured meat, "Bündnerfleisch"; in the pastry kitchen, a device for peeling oblong fruit (whatever that was); in the breakfast kitchen, an electric coffee grinder and a "butter curler"; in the pantry, a mechanical bread cutter as well as an electric knife-cleaning machine; in the wine cellar, an electric bottle-washing machine and another for capsuling bottles; in the laundry, a foot-powered sewing machine and an electric sheet presser for bed linen, and so on.

My Dear Mr. Koller

Before we elevate Josef Giger and Karl Koller to the pantheon of perfect hotel builders, we concede that they, too, produced some blunders. Otherwise, the following chapters on renovations and additions would be somewhat shorter.

The fact that they gave pride of place to the east and north sides for the placement of guest rooms, rather than to the west and south sides so much in demand in our own times, can fairly be attributed to shifting preferences; it is conceivable that future generations will come to see it their way again. In any case, more than 60 percent of the guest rooms faced east or north, while the two staircases and all the public facilities (the toilets, as we bluntly say in German) offered spectacular views towards Maloja.

What was pretty bad by anybody's standards was that a couple of staff bedrooms ended up having, as their only window, a skylight opening right into a public bathroom. And the flat roofs and terraces were a problem almost from the start. After just a few years there was trouble with leaking terraces over the public rooms, and ever since, the water—be it rain or snowmelt—has found its way in with faithful regularity. Living in an alpine climate takes its toll!

And finally, with all due respect for Josef Giger's judgement: was it really smart to open the Bristol in Ragaz just before taking on a major project in Sils? The money might have been put to better use by giving the Waldhaus a sounder financial footing or, say, by building a funicular from the village to the hotel. And while we are on the subject, why not install 160 private bathrooms instead of 40?

On the whole, though, the Waldhaus is a wonderful achievement. "Not so fast!" the stern Josef Giger might have told us. He was not easily mollified if something was not quite right, and the construction work with all its pressures and worries was exceptionally hard on him who took everything so seriously, thus making him very distrustful and irritable. The Brussels firm of Lowe & Serin, which had installed the bathrooms, could testify to that: two years after the Waldhaus opened, Giger managed to have them replace 16 of the 40 tubs, at their expense, as he was not satisfied with the quality! More than one supplier met him before the district judge in Samedan, and the law did not always side with Josef Giger's view of the case.

Even his cordial relationship with the architect became increasingly fraught as construction proceeded. One incident that actually had little to do with Giger himself did not help matters. In the winter of 1907, son-in-law Josef Wolflisberg as partner in Giger & Co. had his own favorite architect, Karl Mackensen, draw up a complete counterproposal for the interior design of all the public rooms. Mackensen, a German who was very en vogue in St. Petersburg at the time, had extensively remodeled Wolflisberg's hotel in Russia. Wolflisberg probably found Koller's design much too sober and restrained (precisely the qualities which would stand the Waldhaus in such good stead, once the exuberance of the Belle Epoque fell out of fashion): a reproach that could not be made to Mackensen's flamboyant art nouveau interiors that were still all the rage in St. Petersburg. Surprisingly there is hardly any echo of this episode in the thousands of pages of Giger's correspondence from the construction period. In the end, though, it was Koller's version and, we presume, Giger's own sense of style and restraint, which carried the day.

But Koller, too, got his share of Josef Giger's displeasure. In the fall of 1908, Giger fired off a sharply worded letter to "Mr. Koller," (whom he had not so long ago addressed as "My dear Mr. Koller," or at least "Dear Mr. Koller"), in which he listed his grievances.

The blueprints were, "with few exceptions, too superficial, causing great cost and damage." The laundry was "completely botched, although there would have been more than enough room." "The design of the main staircase on the third floor is a complete failure, architecturally speaking" and "the tiny windows of the fourth-floor courier rooms could have been turned into regular dormer windows, at little additional expense, and the value of these rooms would have risen by at least 2 francs per room per day." And so on, for pages on end.

While it is true that after 20 years a larger laundry was added (designed by Koller), that regular dormer windows on the fourth floor would have been welcome, and that Koller, who always had several large projects going at the same time, probably could not always devote enough time and attention to each project, those details pale in relation to the thousands of matters which were solved with great skill—except, alas, in the eyes of an absolute perfectionist like Josef Giger. Luckily, Gustav and his sisters dissuaded Josef Giger from insisting on an arbitrator. For 30 more years, Karl Koller would design nearly every renovation and addition at the Waldhaus, much to the hotel's advantage.

"What does the Waldhaus need?"

Quintus Miller

"You can't create good buildings without good clients. Debates are a stepping stone to quality. Quality obtains if, as an architect, you can capture a building's soul, know and understand the clients and their needs and find a suitable architectural expression of both. The architect's signature only comes much later in the process. A hotel is primarily there for its guests and not for its architects. Our first question then is: "What does the Waldhaus need?" Based on the answers, we plan the next steps, and thus continue to shape a hotel which already has a long history and gains a future through its structural modifications. Guests need change, and so the Waldhaus is no longer the same it was 111 years ago, it is constantly being transformed. If, like me, you have grown up with resort hotels, you know that a hotel needs a mix of the familiar and the new. If everything always stays the same, the guests evolve away from the hotel as their needs also evolve and change. And if too much changes too fast, guests no longer feel at home. The hotel has to constantly improve without the guests noticing. Proceeding cautiously in a sequence of steps both large and small makes it possible to successfully adapt a resort hotel to the present without driving away its guests.

QUINTUS MILLER (58) grew up in the legendary Schatzalp Hotel in Davos and studied architecture at the ETH Zurich. In 1990, he and his wife Paola Maranta started the architectural firm Miller & Maranta in Basel, which now has a staff of 40. He has been a full professor at the Accademia di Architettura of the Università della Svizzera Italiana since 2009.

To be more specific, the atmosphere, the tone of every room and space is a key reference plane for designing a hotel, as space, color, smell and much more generate an overall experience, a feeling of familiarity, creating a sense of being at home. In formal terms, our own interventions are recognizable, rather than impersonating history; the intervention stands for the moment when it occurred. Nevertheless, what already exists should not be changed, so that the traditional way of dealing with a hotel as an architect always remains present to a certain degree. In each project, our job is to find an appropriate way to complement and reinforce the quality of what already exists, where it is relevant, or make a clear and visible new statement where that quality is no longer relevant. Take, as an example, the new temporal strata clearly visible in the bar, in the red (rather than green) color of the walls, in the bar counter, or in the large light fixtures.

For close to 30 years, we have been working with the Kienberger and Dietrich family. It is clear that we have both gone through a process. From the family's point of view, we architects have missed the mark hundreds of times; we have had hundreds of discussions and sometimes the results were more convincing and sometimes less so. This readiness to engage with each other shows courage and a healthy culture of debate on both sides. The family who palpably and visibly love their hotel, now know that I, too, fight for the Waldhaus. We have thus grown closer and have gradually matched each room and space to its specific situation. This only works with people who take a stand and have opinions of their own and an interest in architecture, who have the desire and the passion to create rooms with which they can work and through which they can offer new experiences. You can ruin a building with character if you just strictly follow the rules and leave no disruption, no discrepancy anywhere in sight. In turn, the owners have to be prepared to live with that character and all its contradictions. The Waldhaus is full of contradictions, but with the right attitude behind it, its quirks can be kept alive. This requires people with a passion, people willing to stand by something other than their own opinions and willing to accept responsibility for the result. It is rare anymore to find such people, which is why I am grateful that I can still work with the Waldhaus, despite all the challenges. I am happy to go there frequently, to work through its history and to continue to push forward. This calls for passion and vigor, nothing else will do.

"In the late 1980s, I spent a November day driving from hotel to hotel in the Upper Engadine. A gentleman came towards me in the empty Waldhaus. After three hours, we said good-bye. Years later, Urs Kienberger wrote me that he remembered our conversation and asked if we could meet again. That is how we began working together in 1993."

With fifteen years' distance, I can say that I am particularly proud of our reworking of the entrance. It was very challenging to try to do justice to the hotel and its users. Urs Kienberger's obsession was to have a view in all four directions and also have the sun shine far into the foyer and the lounge. Obviously, placing a canopy in front is a contradiction to that aim, but it allows those arriving to alight and enter the hotel with dry feet. The canopy, as it is, has the shape of a crown and juts out a hefty 4.6 meters, 15 feet—and you hardly notice it from inside! Those who wish can see all of the connections, those who are not interested will not notice anything. I think that good architecture has to be able to tell good stories. Karl Koller was capable of doing that. He and his client Josef Giger carefully placed the Waldhaus on a specific spot, on a rocky ridge, an orientation point in the landscape, at the entrance to the Fex Valley. The building marks this spot in the landscape, making it visible from afar. In terms of landscape design, this is masterful, Koller added a cultural, man-made aspect to the landscape and made it possible for us to experience it spatially."

"For years now, we have been transforming a hotel from the past into one for the future."

A sense of place

We should not picture Josef Giger arriving in Sils the way Columbus came to America. By the time Giger started drawing up his grand plans, the Upper Engadine, and Sils with it, had already found a firm place on the map of international tourism. For an idea of how things had been earlier, when it was truly only on the verge of being discovered and changed by tourists, we have to look back a little further. Here is, extensively quoted, what the famous German Baedeker guide had to say in 1864 (*Switzerland and the Adjacent Portions of Italy, Savoy, and the Tyrol, 2nd English-language edition*). It still has a nice ring about it, of travelling to wondrous and unexplored lands.

> *"The climate of the Upper Engadine between Sils and Puntota is very inclement, resembling that of the N. of Sweden or Finland. The cultivation of corn is almost unknown, and tillage generally very uncommon, except at Maria and Pontresina, where a few small gardens, miserable potato fields, a few patches of oats, and in very favourable seasons a little rye, is all that greets the eye of the traveller. In consequence of the almost entire want of straw, the natives have to use long grass, moss, or the dried branches of pine trees as litter for the cattle in winter. Manure is spread on the meadows starting in mid-August.*
>
> *The atmosphere is so dry, that meat may be preserved solely by its influence from October to May between St. Moritz and Soglio, and so remarkably clear, even in warm weather, that objects are*

distinctly visible at great distances. The sky in the intensity of its blue vies with that of southern climes. "Nine months winter and three months cold" is the laconic, if somewhat exaggerated account the natives give of their climate. White frosts and snow are by no means uncommon in August.

One striking peculiarity of the mountains of this valley is the perfect silence which exists there. The songs of birds and the rustling of leaves are scarcely ever heard. At first sight the bottom of the valley resembles a vast meadow, in which the eye in vain searches for a tree. The pasturage is excellent, but is seldom in the hands of the inhabitants, being let by them to the Bergamasque shepherds, or to speculators [leaseholders] who engage reapers from the Tyrol or the Valtellina to collect the hay. During the hay harvest nearly 1,000 day labourers repair to the valley; it is regarded as a fête in which all classes participate.

The inhabitants of the Engadine usually leave their native country in early life and migrate to all parts of Europe. They seem to have a special aptitude as sugar-bakers, confectioners, coffee-house keepers, and manufacturers of liqueurs and chocolate, and in these avocations they frequently amass considerable fortunes; they then return to their native valley to pass their remaining days. To this class belong the picturesque habitations, with windows made small (to exclude the cold) and gilded lattices. These abodes are most comfortably furnished, whilst their owners are generally well-educated and respectable men, who have acquired in their cosmopolitan pursuits a knowledge of most of the continental languages, sometimes to the partial forgetfulness of their native "Ladin." Many well-known names, evoking sweet memories, can be found in the patrician families of the Upper Engadine, in Sils Josty and Giovanoli, in Silvaplana Stehely, in the Bregaglia valley the Spargnapani and Pomati and others.

The native of the Engadine is sober, industrious, frugal and intelligent, learning with facility all the kindred dialects of his native tongue. Poverty is rare, though there is not that eager pursuit of wealth so common to the age.

Almost all the inhabitants belong to the reformed faith. Sermons are usually delivered in the Romansch dialect, German being occasionally employed. The government of this valley is a pure democracy. "Next to God and the sun, the poorest inhabitant is the chief magistrate," says an old Engadine proverb; nevertheless certain noble families, such as the Planta, have for centuries enjoyed a considerable influence, which is still far from being extinct."

The living conditions were probably not quite as harmonious and untroubled as Herr Baedeker makes them sound, considering that so many had to emigrate in order to find a livelihood. We therefore do not need to regard the beginning tourist boom too starkly and exclusively as the intrusion of a foreign and possibly dubious civilization into an idyllic mountain world. In addition, the Engadiners' cosmopolitanism resulting from their economic history put them in a good position to handle the new "invasion," to actively participate in it, rather than be overrun by the onslaught and relegated to the role of helpless bystanders, as may have happened, more typically, in other alpine regions.

St. Moritz

When we turn to the details of this development, even we Silsers have to admit: tourism really got its start in St. Moritz! We have neither time nor space for a complete history here, but we do want to highlight one aspect, the emergence of the grand hotels, as this in turn puts Josef and Amalia Giger's Waldhaus project in context.

Taking the waters at the St. Moritz mineral springs had been a tradition for centuries, but the first real hotel, the Kurhaus, only opened in 1855, initially with 70 guest rooms. It was so successful that a much larger addition was already built in 1864 (today's Kempinski). It was followed ten years later by the Du Lac and the similar Victoria. In 1892, the last of the grand spa hotels, Grand Hôtel des Nouveaux Bains or

Stahlbad, was built. In a very short time, St. Moritz Bad had become a world-renowned spa. (Indeed, "Bad" stands for baths, or spa.)

Meanwhile, in 1856, the enterprising Johannes Badrutt (1819–89) from Samedan leased an inn which he purchased shortly thereafter in uptown St. Moritz (St. Moritz Dorf, then just a small village). He renamed the twelve-room property the Engadiner Kulm and started to expand it at a breakneck pace, eventually turning it into a huge and glamorous grand hotel. Over time, he and his descendants also acquired a lot of real estate throughout the region; for example, they owned the Margna Hotel in Sils-Baselgia for a while as well as fishing rights to a part of Lake Sils. A son of Johannes Badrutt's opened the Palace in St. Moritz in 1896. Unlike the Kulm, which gradually became a corporation no longer directly associated with the family, the Palace remained in the founder's family and under their management almost until the present. The last of the principal owners made hotelier Hans Wiedemann their heir, so that it is still a very personal and private operation.

This success story and the rise of St. Moritz Dorf are inextricably tied to the famous bet that Johannes Badrutt is said to have made to convince several British summer guests to come in winter as well in 1864/65. Their visit was so much fun that a regular and ever-growing winter season developed. In reality, Badrutt's bet is no easier to prove historically than Wilhelm Tell's existence; but it is undeniably true that in the last few years before World War I, St. Moritz already had more overnight stays in winter than in summer.

The corollary of this was that St. Moritz-Bad, which continued to have only a summer season, started to meet with somewhat harder times after the turn of the century. By contrast, with completion of the Albula line of the Rhaetian Railway (reaching Samedan in 1903 and St. Moritz in 1904), St. Moritz Dorf was gripped by another building boom. Counting luxury hotels alone, the Grand Hotel (1905), the Suvretta (1911) and the Carlton (1913) were built, each more opulent and luxurious than the last, which in turn caused existing hotels to renovate, rebuild, add on. Along with the nine luxury palaces (today there are still five, possibly more than in any other alpine resort town), there were two dozen hotels in other categories and some 50 inns or *pensions*. By 1914, St. Moritz and the entire region already had as many, if not more hotel rooms than today.

The boom soon spread to the surrounding towns; there, too, the old Engadine houses were joined and often overshadowed by more and more hotels, inns, and all the other accessories of tourism. Substantial hotels appeared in Pontresina (Kronenhof, Saratz, Schlosshotel and Palace, today's Walter), Celerina (Cresta Palace) and Zuoz (the Castell). Nowhere, though, were the undertakings quite as extravagant, monumental and urban in scale as in St. Moritz. Except in Maloja! It was there, of all places, that what was probably the boldest and most improbable project in the history of tourism in our region came about.

The Maloja Palace

In 1880, Maloja was not yet even a permanently settled village, and it could only be reached by a seven-hour stagecoach ride from Chiavenna, or a ride twice as long from Chur; the most remote corner in our remote valley. And that is where, from 1882 to 1884, a grand hotel went up that was said to be the third largest building in the Switzerland of its time, second only to the abbey of Einsiedeln and the main building of the Swiss Federal Institute of Technology in Zurich. A Belgian entrepreneur, Count Camille de Renesse, had come up with the plan, inspired by the success of St. Moritz. With little capital of his own, he managed to raise share capital of CHF 3.5 million and an equal amount in bonds and loans in the shortest of times. He bought up virtually all of Maloja, 140 hectares, 350 acres, of land (we have about 2.5 ha.) and began building. After an unbelievably short construction period of just two years, including winter breaks, the hotel was opened right on schedule on July 1, 1884: 300 rooms and 450 beds, everything of the highest quality, plus the complete infrastructure of a tourist destination, a park, sports facilities, private villas, the Schweizerhaus inn for pseudo-Swiss local color, two churches (one Catholic and one Anglican) for spiritual salvation and, later, a golf course. For the Count's own use, a proper neo-gothic castle, the Belvédère, was built. Its tower still peers down into the Bregaglia Valley from above the village. Marketing for the new hotel was already underway throughout Europe. De Renesse had boldly promised his creditors that the hotel would be fully occupied, at least in the two best summer months and no less than four winter months. Unimpressed by the extensive gambling ban in the Swiss constitution of 1874, de Renesse apparently also speculated that in due time Maloja could become an alpine Monte Carlo or Baden-Baden. In any case, he named the entire complex the Maloja "Kursaal"; it would only become the "Palace" in later years.

The fact that Count Renesse succeeded in financing his monumental project, in building it in this remote spot and in opening it on schedule, is an entrepreneurial achievement of such magnitude that the same man, quite possibly, could also have made a success of its operations if he had only had a bit more luck.

It was not to be. In the summer of its opening a cholera epidemic broke out in southern Europe. Switzerland's border to Italy remained closed for months. Unfortunately, Chiavenna—or (initially) Colico—was the nearest train station, and most of the guests were expected to travel that way. So that was a very major setback. What's more, the economic outlook was darkening; several bank collapses and stock-market crashes had given the world of international finance the jitters. The count was dealt another blow in autumn, when his 38-year-old wife died unexpectedly. De Renesse gave up, declaring bankruptcy before the year was out. The main creditor, a Belgian bank, took over the business. A succession of other owners managed to keep the hotel open until World War I; the guest list included some prominent names, but success remained elusive. The winter season was abandoned in 1889, and only resurrected briefly in 1913/14. Sir Henry Lunn, the great English travel

"Make no little plans!", advised Daniel Burnham, architect of the 1893 World's Fair in Chicago. Camille de Renesse took him at his word, ten years before he said it.
Since we are jumping from language to language (in German I quoted Burnham in English and called Maloja "Chicago avant la lettre"), I am reminded here of a very special Waldhaus guest, Mrs. Ida Legler (1888–1987) from Ponte di San Pietro near Bergamo, who had the habit of always mixing all the languages in which she was fluent, Swiss German, Italian and French, often in the same sentence. The Waldhaus was another of her habits. She came more than fifty times, between 1930 and 1983, usually for many weeks.

operator, brought some new life to the hotel in the 1920s, in winter and summer, but that ended with the Great Depression. After World War II, the huge building which would by then have been very hard to use as a regular hotel, luckily found a good and practical reincarnation as a holiday home for up to 700 young people or families with children under the wings of Mutualités Chrétiennes de Belgique, Belgium's biggest mutual health fund, which offered its members affordable alpine vacations.

History is written by the winners; losers have a hard time finding a good chronicler. For a long time, people simply shook their heads about the Maloja Palace, really knowing very little about it. Georges Baggerman, long-time manager of the Palace for the Mutualités Chrétiennes, finally collected a wealth of interesting details about the hotel and its history in a private printing for the 100-year anniversary of the hotel in 1982: "Maloja entre cimes et lacs – cent ans d'histoire d'un hôtel"; but it did not gain wide circulation. Things only changed when a prominent legal expert and corporate lawyer, Peter Böckli, took it upon himself to write an excellently documented and highly readable history of the hotel and its fate, *Bis zum Tod der Gräfin* (NZZ Libro, 1998; also published in French as *Jusqu'à la mort de comtesse*), which has rightly remained a bestseller. Those interested in our region and its history should read it.

Böckli's book is full of intriguing details and observations. For example, that the Countess de Renesse came from a very rich family, and that her husband carefully kept her inheritance separate from the risky project in Maloja, but had on the other hand insured her life to the tune of CHF 1.5 million (!) before her untimely death. That he bought up all the land in Maloja on his own account, for a total of about CHF 100,000, and then brought it into the company in exchange for about ten times that amount in shares and bonds. To put it mildly, de Renesse was no saint. Böckli, though, also convincingly shows that the count's original vision, as well as the intermittent entrepreneurial success of the complex in Maloja until its final demise in 1934/1935, were much more solid than what the bad press it got over the years—influenced, perhaps, by its gloating competitors—made us believe.

And Maloja today? A visionary Italian real-estate entrepreneur, Amedeo Clavarino, bought the Palace from the Belgians, or more specifically from their Swiss partners, Intersoc, in 2006, with the dream of resurrecting it as a truly grand hotel. Reality quickly and painfully caught up with him. The hotel continues to await a future which may never materialize. But then, with Maloja, who knows?

Sils. The thinker and the tourist office

While Maloja in the days before the "Kursaal" was mostly just a temporary base for the inhabitants of the Bergell and their cattle on their annual migrations to different altitudes, the stately old houses and pretty little churches in Sils Baselgia, Sils Maria and in the Fex Valley show that Sils, even before tourism, was a well-established little village in its own right. The 1864 Baedeker did not have much to say about it yet. Sils lies "in a very bleak district" and Lake Sils, though abounding in trout, is "frozen so hard from the end of September (really??) until May that loaded carts can cross it." Interested readers will find more reliable details about Sils past and present in a modest publication, *Sils im Engadin*, by Rudolf Boppart (1980, 2nd ed. 1994, Zollikofer, St. Gallen). It is a village chronicle without literary ambitions but with a wealth of information about the town and its history. The author, who passed away in 1999, owned a vacation home in Sils and was the first person to seriously work his way through all the sources and particularly the village archive. We still have a few copies for sale at the Waldhaus, and it can also be found at the Sils library.

The chronicle reveals, for example, that in 1860 Sils had 50 inhabited houses and a little over 200 residents. By 1980, there were nearly twice as many, a figure that may have already been equaled in earlier centuries. Today we have about 800 residents. The fact that in 1860, there were 127 female but only 88 male villagers shows the extent to which the Silsers of those years, like everyone else in the Engadine, had to go abroad to find a livelihood. Nevertheless, the Sils of the time leaves the impression of a viable and active community with connections to the outside world.

The Waldhaus hill without the Waldhaus: Sils Maria around 1850

The development of Sils differs in another way from Maloja, but particularly from St. Moritz. When tourism started here, it was generally on a more modest scale so that the transformation of Sils into a resort area took place gradually and without turning everything upside down. This was probably more accidental than intentional, but it stood Sils in good stead.

As early as 1865, a first small hotel, the Alpenrose, joined the ranks of the traditional inns—the Pension Chastè may have been around for some time. Ten years later a second hotel was built, the Edelweiss. Friedrich Nietzsche took his meals in these two hotels during his much-cited summer stays in Sils (1881–89). Ah, Nietzsche! While there is little evidence that the uncommon visitor made much of an impression on the villagers, the Sils tourist office posthumously came to hold him in very high regard—a rare case of such appreciation of a philosopher by a tourist office, if mostly based on a tiny part of Nietzsche's work, his wonderfully apt and enthusiastic comments about the place and its scenery.

Irony aside, Sils Maria's Nietzsche connection is largely responsible for the fact that the guest lists of the Waldhaus and all of Sils are dominated to this day by names of writers, musicians and intellectuals rather than the “fashionable set” (although that is not missing, either). While travelling both in North and Latin America, I was repeatedly surprised that even people who scarcely knew Switzerland, when I said “Sils-Maria,” would immediately respond with: “Oh: Nietzsche!” As patron saint of our village, the great thinker continues to have an impact. The Sils of today would be very different if, back then, somebody like Bismarck, the Rockefellers or, say, members of the Japanese imperial family had taken his place.

In any case, growth continued at a measured pace. The tourist office we just talked about was founded in 1883. In 1874, 1894 and 1907, the inconspicuous Alpenrose of the early days was expanded into a very handsome vacation hotel with 100 beds. (Sadly, it folded in 1974. Rebuilt in 1999, it is now limited to condos and a restaurant.) The Edelweiss also continued to grow, expanding to hold 150 guests. In 1869, Johannes Badrutt acquired the impressive residence that Johann Josty, a Silser who had prospered as a confectioner and coffee house owner in Berlin, had built in Sils Baselgia 50 years earlier. From about 1871 to 1885, and again starting from 1901, it served as an inn, first with such names as “Hôtel de la Grande Vue”; in 1901, it became the “Margna,” was enlarged into a proper hotel in 1905/06 and expanded again in 1913.

In connection with the power station built with the Waldhaus, we have mentioned the Barblan Hotel, completed in 1907. It was built at the initiative of a local family, whose name it bore, just as the other hotels we have named were built by locals or people from nearby, i.e. not with capital from far away. The same is true of the smaller hotels such as the Sonne in the Fex and the Silserhof between Maria and Baselgia.

When the Waldhaus was built, Sils was already a lively mid-size summer resort, not radically different from what it is today. But what was now being built on the Laret hill was bigger and grander than anything Sils had seen. To be sure, elsewhere in the Engadine, even if not in Sils itself, there already were at least a dozen hotels of a similar caliber, and others were about to be built. What was truly special about this new hotel was less its size than the many modern ideas and the immense

Sils with the Barblan, Alpenrose and Waldhaus hotels

care and expertise with which it was planned and carried out. And above all, it became special because of what followed: 111 uninterrupted years (so far) of the Waldhaus simply remaining what it has always been, with the descendants of the founders welcoming—sometimes quite literally—the grandchildren and great-grandchildren of the original guests.

In 1908, Sils did not have much of a winter business. The Margna and Silserhof were open for a modest winter season, and possibly the Barblan was open in the winter at some point before 1914 as well. We know that Josef Giger's daughters Fanny and Helen came from Ragaz to take part in a ski course in Sils in December 1908. Most of the hotels and inns, though, were only open in summer.

Further reading

Interested readers have a wealth of information about the past and present of the Engadine and Sils available at their fingertips (though, sadly, not so much in English). Choices range from home-grown chronicles such as Rudolf Boppart's, to the masterful and knowledgeable report by Peter Böckli, and the entertaining *St. Moritz – Die Geschichte des mondänsten Dorfs der Welt* written with a light touch by Curt Riess (1968, Classen in Zurich and Stuttgart, republished in 2013 by Karl Lüönd at Europa Verlag in Zurich). The Wega bookshop in St. Moritz, worth a visit in any case, offers a good selection. The charming library in Sils-Baselgia, the Biblioteca Engiadinaisa, counts among its many treasures hundreds of titles of every description on Sils, the Engadine and Graubünden, as well as such rarities as a Romansch Bible from 1745 printed in Scuol.

If you enjoy reading about the history of tourism, we also recommend searching the internet for the beautifully presented and researched *Schweizer Pioniere der Hotellerie* or, in French, *Pionniers suisses de l'hôtellerie* by Louis Gaulis and René Creux (Editions de Fontainemore in Paudex/ Switzerland, 1970). Unfortunately, it has been out of print for a long time.

"With all the ups and downs, somehow it keeps going"

Annatina Pinösch

"My great-grandfather Duri Pinösch from Ardez was, like Josef Giger, a pioneer of tourism in the Engadine. In about 1880, he and his brother Caspar bought land and farms in Vulpera and began building resort hotels on a grand scale. Incidentally, Karl Koller, the architect of the Waldhaus in Sils, built one of them, the Schweizerhof. The Grand Hotel Waldhaus Vulpera, on the other hand, was designed by Nicolaus Hartmann Senior. After the First World War a golf course was added. Our forefathers were visionaries without blinders. They farsightedly recognized the opportunities for growth in tourism in the Engadine, which led to the realization of one project after another. The clientele from Britain also gave impetus to their optimistic undertakings. The guests included the aristocracy, even the tsar's family came. From St. Petersburg to Vulpera, just think about that for a minute. It must have been an incredible boom. Even after World War I, in the Roaring '20s, life in the Engadine must have been something like a long party.

ANNATINA PINÖSCH grew up in a hotel dynasty, in Pontresina in winter and in Vulpera in summer. The oldest of four children, she actually wanted to be a veterinarian, but then decided to follow in her parents' footsteps and became a celebrated hotel manager in Switzerland and abroad. The "nomadic hotelier," as food critic Daniel Eggli called her, is still active as a consultant and member of various boards. "History connects me with the Waldhaus Sils," she says; the two families knew each other for a long time and a variety of historical circumstances continue to connect them.

The momentum, the huge success of the first hotels was catching. Suddenly others had the idea of building hotels as well. Our forefathers saw the big picture. I don't see this spirit today, when hotel managers are often only kings of their own castles. What I admire about our predecessors is their spirit of working for the common good. The incredible way the Waldhaus in Sils was financed is a good example. When somebody wanted to build a hotel, others underwrote shares. People went along instead of trying to stop them. They wanted to be part of something new, see how others succeeded and have a hand in what happened. My family held shares of the Edelweiss Hotel in Sils and participated in diverse other projects.

"A hotel has to be functional in how it is designed and built, otherwise it won't work. That was true yesterday. That is true today."

The guests came and continue to come to the Engadine because of the special light, the unique landscape of lakes and mountains—the pioneers of tourism knew this and put it to good use. But there had to be other attractions, even if it was cost-intensive to provide entertainment, sports or cultural activities. That was no different in the early years, and yet they did it. If I have learned anything from our ancestors, it is that with all the ups and downs, somehow it keeps going. I miss the courageous, visionary spirit of that time. The bold bellwethers of old are missing in today's Engadine."

"I admire how the Waldhaus has been managed by siblings from generation to generation and how dedicated the young generation is to the hotel."

Besides the imposing Waldhaus of 1897 and the Schweizerhof (its first stage from 1900 was architect Karl Koller's first independent hotel commission), as well as the Kurhaus Val Sindestra (1912) also designed by Koller, much land, villas, a golf course and one of Switzerland's first and loveliest outdoor pools were all part of the Pinösch family's hotel empire in the Lower Engadine. From 1900–01, Waldhaus-Sils shareholder Josef Wolflisberg (p. 14, 32, 57, 98, 116) managed the Waldhaus Vulpera, destroyed by fire in 1989. In the boom year of 1928, Alfred Kienberger (pp. 127, 209), who would become chairman of our own family corporation, was its Chef de Réception. Around 1942, Rolf Kienberger had a job there for a few months between his long stretches of military service. And in 1977, after the Pinösch family had sold out, Alfred's son Georg Kienberger was hired to run it for a summer.

1908–18: peaks and valleys

The two diagrams on the right are both a preview of the following chapters and a summary of the first 111 years of the hotel's operation. They show in a nutshell how things were going in summer and winter, for every year, measured in what we call "guest-nights." (For example, if a couple stays for two weeks, that results in 28 guest-nights.)

It is often fortunate that we are not able to look into the future. Would Josef Giger have built the hotel if he had anticipated this roller-coaster "landscape," especially the steep valleys and the canyons?

Josef Giger can hardly be blamed for not having foreseen all the hardships of the coming years. For his part, he not only succeeded in building a beautiful hotel with all the latest comforts of the time, but he also succeeded in filling and managing it with distinction, right from the beginning. That was quite a feat even in the heady days before World War I. In the Engadine, as well as in Switzerland as a whole, the number of guests actually started to level off in the years before the war—though, admittedly, at a very high level—but as more new hotels were constantly being opened, more and more hotels were now competing for the same number of guests.

Overnight stays, winter

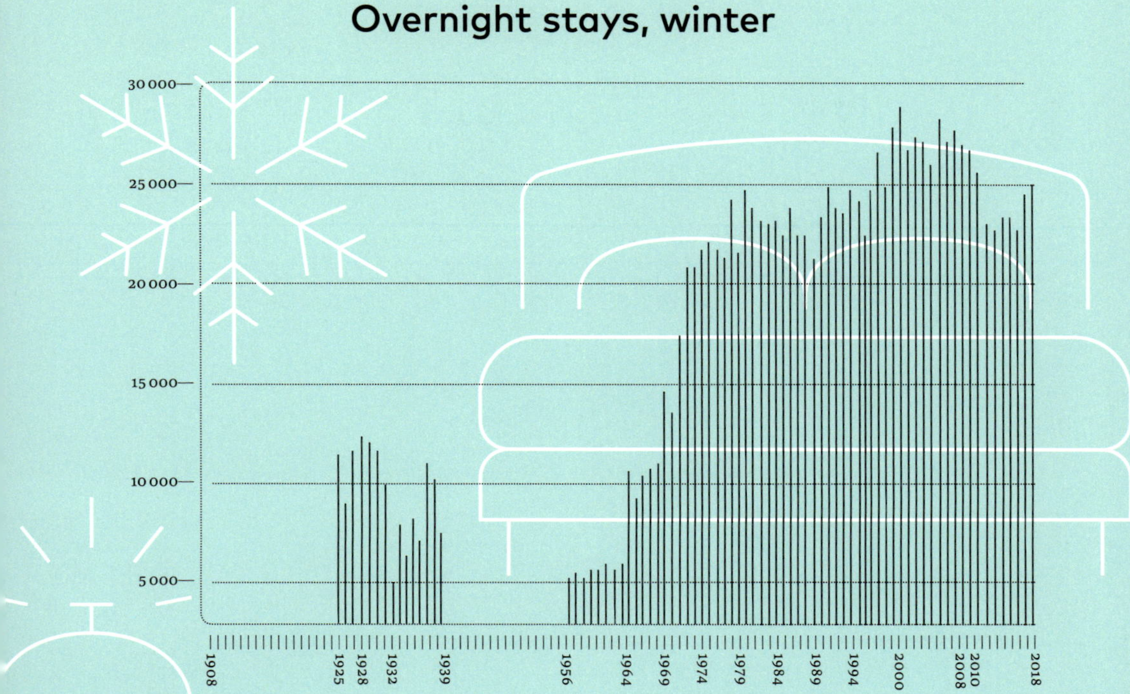

Overnight stays, summer

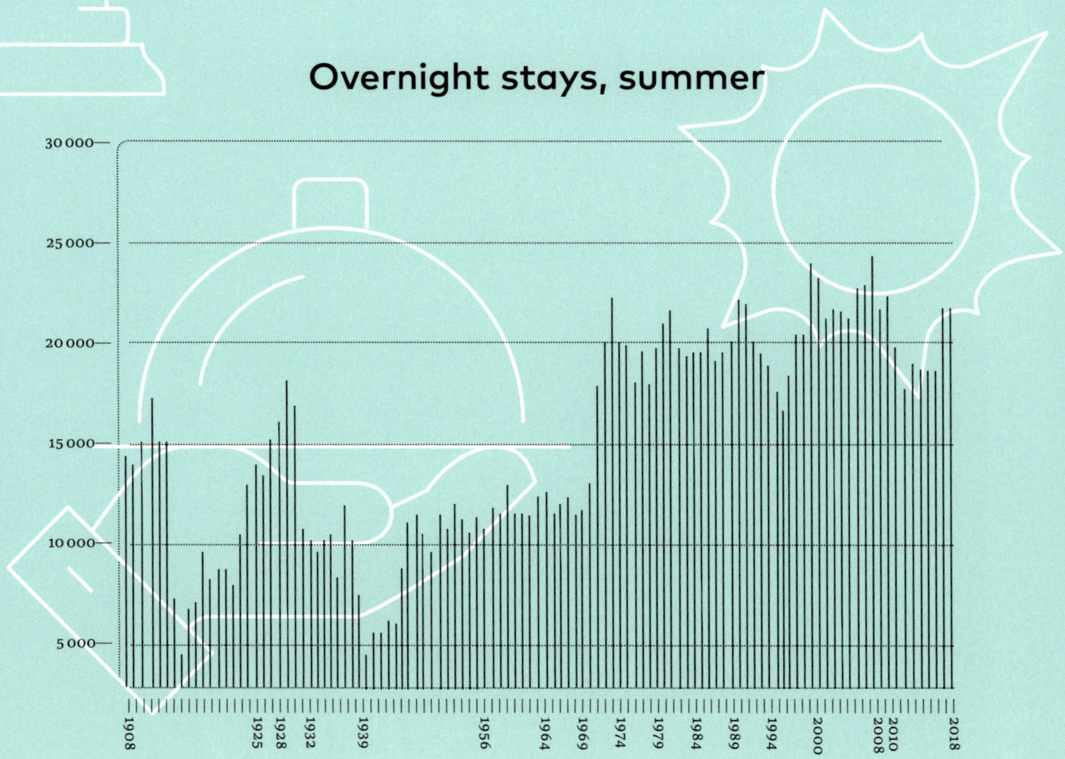

Levi's

← In the lounge, February 20, 2019

Fine and distinguished company

On June 15, Josef Giger stood at the main entrance of the Waldhaus in tails and top hat to welcome the first guests, a Baron Pechmann and his wife, nee Baroness Feilitzsch. They were not alone for long: in the three months of this first season, 620 more guests arrived. "Socially, we were extraordinarily fortunate," the first annual report says. "We had many prominent Italian aristocrats, also German nobility, a very satisfactory number of Britons and Americans—in short: fine and distinguished company." And if they did not have an aristocratic title ("Baroness von Nolcken, born Marschall of Bieberstein & servants, Berlin"), they were at least a "Rat," or Councilor: privy councilor, true privy councilor, district councilor, treasury councilor, commerce councilor, judicial councilor, provincial court councilor, Prussian royal district councilor, at times in combinations like the "Excellenz Geheimer Rat Professor Doktor," or with a title transferred to the grieving widow such as the Königliche Regierungsratswitwe and the widow of a large-scale landowner who was entered, without any irony, as Frau Grossgrundbesitzerswitwe.

There is some poetic justice in the fact that the entries in the 1908 guest list which we first notice today are not always the longest ones ("Son Excellence Mlle de Hahn, Demoiselle d'honneur de Ses Majestés les Impératrices de Russie, avec dame de compagnie"). We are struck by "Madame Henri Schliemann" from Athens (indeed, the widow of the rediscoverer of ancient Troy) or, a bit later, Professor & Mrs. Pringsheim from Munich, the in-laws of Thomas Mann. Many other names could probably tell a story, if we had more time to examine them. Professor Liebermann of Berlin, was that Max Liebermann, the great painter? (Actually, we now know the answer to that one: it was, more than once, his wife and daughter, but the great painter himself was apparently not along. Too bad. It would have been good for him.) Was "W.W. Asquith" actually "H.H. Asquith" and thus the man who in the same year became prime minister of Britain? And so on.

The fact that the annual report gave special prominence to the aristocrats who came is more than just a case of snobbery, ill becoming a republican Swiss. Well-known names clearly had an impact on business, as illustrated by the report for 1913:

"Despite the persistent rain in July and the largely unfavorable weather in August, we had a higher occupancy rate than we originally expected. (...) On June 7, Princess Loewenstein-Wertheim-Freudenberg arrived for a long stay, which attracted other guests to the Waldhaus. In fact, it turned out to be the busiest June since the Waldhaus had opened. (...) September also exceeded our most optimistic expectations. This may have had something to do with the prominent visit by Chancellor of the German Empire von Bethmann-Hollweg."

In terms of where the guests came from, the following percentage shares of total "guest-nights" in 1908 and 1911 characterize the early years:

Germany	44%
Italy	14%
France	10%
United Kingdom	9%
U.S.A.	8%
Austria-Hungary	7%
Switzerland	4%
Other	4%

It may be surprising to see that there were relatively few Britons. However, this was typical for Switzerland as a whole at that stage. Large numbers of visitors from overseas and from the Continent, especially from the rapidly industrializing German Empire, were already following in the footsteps of the British. Thus, the latter, who had been the true pioneers of early tourism in Switzerland, now began to find themselves in a minority in many places. (This was only the case in summer; British visitors unequivocally continued to dominate winter tourism for many years to come.) There were, of course, also differences from town to town and from hotel to hotel.

A specific Waldhaus specialty was the remarkably high share of Italian guests, particularly aristocrats: princes, dukes, marquis and counts with such distinguished names as Borromeo, Doria and Gonzaga, but also industrialists like Agnelli and Pirelli. In the opening season, Prince Marco and Princess Anna Maria Borghese with children and servants, a total of eight people staying from July 1 to September 9, accounted for close to 5 percent of all guest nights for the whole summer. Count and Countess Joseph Visconti di Modrone first came to the Waldhaus from August 4 to 28, 1910 (in rooms 51, 52, 53, 54 and 91, 92, 93, 94 and 130), with five children, governesses and two servants. Three-year-old Luchino, whose visits with and without family would repeat themselves into the 1950s, was also along. It is fair to assume that the portrayal of life in a grand hotel in his celebrated "Death in Venice" (1971) may contain a few memories of summers in Sils Maria as well.

Kneeling: Syed Waris Ameer Ali from India, guest in our first season 1908

Syed Waris Ameer Ali and Lady Eleanor
60 years later at Waldhaus entrance

In the midst of this abundance of titles, it is easy to overlook a more modest entry from 1908 for the "Right Hon. Ameer Ali, CIE, ICS" from India, who arrived with his wife and two sons. One of the sons, later Judge Syed Waris Ameer Ali, C.I.E., who was about 20 years old when the Waldhaus opened, returned almost every summer until 1928, except during the war years, first with his parents, then on his own and with his wife. Then, he stayed away for a time—having become chief justice of all of British India—but was back in 1957, and continued to come nearly every year until 1970, a visitor from our own past.

Hotel life in 1908

Few of these guests came alone. Many came with large families, with friends and retinue: with governesses and maids and valets and an occasional courier (a private travel guide). They needed bedrooms, sitting rooms, bathrooms, rooms for the children and for the servants—sometimes half a floor at a time. At full capacity, the hotel would host just under 200 "real" guests and as many as 50 personal servants, called "domestiques" in our best hotel German; in addition, of course, there were the hotel's own 115 employees (today there are some 150 or more). The guests' servants had their own dining room on the floor below the kitchen, the "courier" room. It eventually became (and still is) our staff cafeteria, but kept its old name for many years.

AVERAGE TURNOVER per guest and per night (per "guest-night," counting children and servants only half): in 1908, CHF 28.90; in 1911, CHF 34.80, without tips and the service charge. That was about equal to the monthly cash wages —again, not counting their share in the service charge— of a waiter or a maid. What would that be in today's money? Meaningful comparisons across such a long period of time are almost impossible. The multiplier might be 40 for construction costs, for instance, and 4 for the price of a bottle of mineral water.

And, those who came stayed for a long time. The ten-week stay of Prince Marco Borghese and his family may have been above average, but was not uncommon. The average stay amounted to more than three weeks, four times what it is today. Given that the hotel's average income per guest, per day, amounted to 30 francs or more, you can imagine the cost of such a vacation!

The built-in closets which still line some of our corridors (others have disappeared during remodeling) are a reminder of the mountains of luggage brought along for those long stays, often overflowing from the rooms into the corridors.

If people measured their stays in weeks and months rather than in days, that obviously had something to do with the long and complicated journey to reach the Engadine. They could travel by train to St. Moritz or, coming from Italy, to Chiavenna, but even the train ride took considerably longer than today. The final leg would be by postal coach or private horse-drawn carriage. Travelling time from St. Moritz to Sils was one hour, from Chiavenna to Sils, steeply uphill, all of seven hours. Incidentally, the Waldhaus never had stables and horses of its own, but used the services of one of the carters in the region, some of whom owned hundreds of horses.

The age of the automobile was still a long way off in our corner of the woods; cars were only allowed in Graubünden in 1925.

Josef Giger's letters mention a wide range of other projects intended to bring Sils closer to the big, wide world. A railroad from Chiavenna to Austria via the Engadine or a north–south train line over the Muretto Pass to Maloja and then underneath the Septimer to points north—projects which the builder of the Maloja Palace had dreamed of—were no longer being seriously considered, but an extension of the Albula line from St. Moritz to Sils and Maloja was still under discussion. A somewhat more unorthodox idea was to link the lakes with canals and locks so that guests could take a boat from St. Moritz to Maloja. None of these projects was ever realized.

If it was complicated for the guests to get here, we can imagine how difficult it also was to procure all the needed goods, food, wine and fuel, including the 500 or 1,000 pounds of ice needed daily. Little wonder that in the hotel's accounts the cost of supplies added up to considerably more than the total payroll (keeping in mind that the lion's share of the employees' compensation came from the service charge and did not enter the regular accounts).

Once the guests were here, their life was probably not too different from today. They went hiking, perhaps also mountain climbing, rented row boats on the lake, played tennis on the two hotel courts ... Golfers could take the motor boat to the golf course in Maloja, then have lunch

Five-horse post coach at the Sils Maria post office, 1909

at the Palace there and return to Sils; unfortunately, the links in Maloja are long gone, but the same motor boat kept running until 1984 and luckily has found a modern successor (with the active support of the village of Sils). In 1908, the boat ride from Sils to Maloja cost an impressive five francs; in view of inflation, today's 17 francs, by comparison, makes for a cheap pleasure, and if you are staying at the Waldhaus, it is free. Dear guests, you see how much better off you are than your predecessors of generations past!

Back at the hotel, as many as eight musicians under the direction of Maestro Romualdo Moro of the Covent Garden Opera in London provided entertainment, though that seems to have been limited to July and August, so that we could claim, splitting some hairs, that we currently sport just as many musicians if you average it out over the whole season! If there was dancing, it was probably in the lounge. Or was it in the "music room"? Today's bar served as a reading and billiards room, with the hotel library and a stuffed eagle, we might say it was the gentlemen's salon, although it was not referred to as such. A "bar américain" took up part of today's Sunny Corner. The Empire salon with its beautiful appointments which remain virtually unchanged today, was the "music room," although we are no longer sure where the name came from.

Perhaps, the guests themselves frequently made music there. Or did the hotel orchestra originally play there instead of in the great lounge? In any case, the Welte-Mignon piano (see p. 47) originally stood here.

The two dining rooms had somewhat different purposes. "Table d'hôte" was served in the main dining room: all the guests who ate there were served the same menu at the same time, although they were served at separate tables, by contrast with the early days of tourism when everyone was seated together at long communal tables. A gong rang punctually at noon and 7 p.m., each course in turn being served to all, like at a banquet. ("Latecomers will be served cold!" as a sign in another hotel somewhat ambiguously warned its guests.) The second room, the one which we now call the wedding room, was the "restaurant"—not in today's sense of the word, but the name indicated that it was reserved for guests who did not want to submit to the strict discipline of the table d'hôte (and paid extra for the privilege). More akin to all "pension" guests of today, they could come and go as they pleased within a certain time period and had a wider choice of dishes. It was only in 1931, in the Great Depression, that the distinction between "restaurant" and "dining room" disappeared.

We do not know very much about the social life at the Waldhaus in those early years, since those who could tell us are now partying somewhere else. One thing that must have made a difference was that many of the guests stayed for much longer and had more opportunities to get to know each other. We can also assume that many Waldhaus guests of that time led a far less stressful life than we do today (did they really? What about the likes of Josef Giger and Karl Koller?), so that they were probably here less because they wanted to rest and relax than because they wanted a change of scenery.

"The first coffee cook"

Claudia Duschletta-Müller

"In 1976, it was still possible to pick and choose where you wanted to do your apprenticeship, and so I went down in Waldhaus history as the first commercial apprentice. Strangely, I had the feeling that I knew more than the new couple of "junior managers" by the name of Felix and Maria Dietrich. My rationale was that I had been working there before they had, and I thought I knew the lay of the land. This led to heated discussions, particularly with Felix. Maria knew how to explain double-entry accounting and the logic behind it ... but Felix is just like I am: obstinate and stubborn. Our letters were composed on typewriters, and of course, Felix held each letter up to the light to see how many times I had used white-out. Even now, we laugh about such scenes. He lets me know when he passes through Zernez, and we meet up for a coffee.

Once when we did that, I gave him a photo of the Waldhaus's first coffee cook Anna Joos. I had written an article about her for a staff newspaper, which we produced in 1979. It was not as professionally done as today's Waldhaus News. It was simply loose A4 sheets on which I had collected various articles and then stapled them together. By coincidence, I had met Anna Joos when, during my apprenticeship, I had to have foot surgery at the hospital in the Münster Valley. She lived at the retirement home there, and when she heard that I was working at the Waldhaus, she started telling me stories. She worked at the hotel in the summers from 1908 to 1914. At age 23 she came to Sils from Taufers on the South Tyrolean end of the Münster Valley. She spent the war years back home, where she married Johann Albert Joos. I think he was a farmer. Unfortunately, I don't remember much from her stories as that was a long time ago. I do

CLAUDIA DUSCHLETTA (nee Müller) finished her commercial apprenticeship at the Waldhaus in 1976 and later returned from the Lucerne Hotel School for internships in the kitchen and in the dining room. For many years, she headed the tourism office of Zernez, where she and her husband had a farm. They have now turned the farm over to their son. For 26 summers she also managed the Cluozza Lodge in the Swiss National Park.

remember her description of the huge, steaming, monstrous coffee machine. Now, even the one that I remember hearing hissing myself, which was from 1946, has been in the Waldhaus Museum for some time. Anna Joos also talked about working conditions and the hotel's owners, but when I reread my 1979 text, I know why I didn't become a writer.

"I never again encountered such wonderful treatment of employees. This familial feeling of being at home also affected the guests. They never gave me the feeling that they had money and I did not. Very special guests."

I would happily return to the Waldhaus, it was a great time, and I felt very much at home there. Apparently, that is what I must have conveyed at the Hotel School in Lucerne, as everybody there ended up thinking that the hotel belonged to my parents."

Maybe it was Uncle Gustav

Josef Giger opened and managed the hotel just as he had built it: he personally saw to even the smallest detail.

His two unmarried daughters Fanny and Helen and his son Gustav were by his side, Gustav at the reception desk, Helen as housekeeper and Fanny in the "underworld" of pantries and kitchens and storerooms. Both Fanny and Helen got married in 1911, Fanny married Gebhard Lutz, a lawyer from the canton of St. Gallen, and Helen married Oskar Kienberger, who will soon take center stage in our history. Amalia (Mali), the oldest daughter, then took their place in Sils. Mali's husband Josef Wolflisberg had taken over the Europe in St. Petersburg after Josef Giger's guest appearance there. Wolflisberg was very successful and thoroughly enjoyed his position. Mali did not warm to Russia and soon started coming back to Switzerland with her two children for more and more extended stays, eventually remaining in Sils for good, while her husband only left Russia after the Revolution. He apparently stuck it out until 1919.

Despite being confined to a wheelchair, Amalia Giger, the mother, still took an active interest in the hotel business. On the mezzanine, where the family lived, there were several windows which looked down into the various public rooms and working areas. For instance, she could see into the pantry adjoining the kitchen from the family dining room. If she saw that something was amiss, she could just pick up the telephone and intervene.

Nevertheless, it was clearly Josef Giger who made the final decisions on all matters large and small. That went well as long as he had the strength and energy for it. Even when the hotel first opened, though,

The mighty "Europe" in St. Petersburg, Josef Giger's domain in winter 1900/01 and Josef Wolflisberg's (his son-in-law and Waldhaus co-investor) until the Revolution

he was no longer young and not in the best of health. And he was not the person to slow down and husband his strength. Within a few years, sadly, his eyesight and general state of health deteriorated to the point where he had to give up more and more of his management duties, finally spending the last eight to ten years of his life in seclusion, partly in Sils and partly at the Neuhof in Ragaz.

This meant that Gustav suddenly became a key figure. Josef Wolflisberg, whom Josef Giger would have been happy to have as his successor, did not want to give up his brilliant career in Russia. And Oskar Kienberger, who was happily and successfully established on the Rigi, had made it quite explicit upon his marriage to Helen Giger, as old letters reveal, that he was not planning a move to Sils.

Except for some schooling and travels away from home, such as in French-speaking Switzerland, in England, and even in Egypt, and an apparently rather rocky experiment as a hotel manager in Sicily, Gustav, who was now in his thirties, had never really managed to get out from under his father's shadow. He worked as his assistant and right-hand man and accompanied him wherever he went, but was never given much responsibility of his own. He experienced first-hand the contradiction that Josef Giger professed to build the Waldhaus "for his children," but did not let them or anyone else deviate in the slightest from his own exacting ideas,

"Everyone is trying to make economies; even we who have been spoiled by the hotel are limiting expenses. [...] Apple cider is the only drink served at lunch, and even Gustav, who always disparaged the cider, has now taken to drinking it; now that there is the war, it suddenly seems to agree with him after all."
Amalia Giger-Nigg: The War Year 1914. *See p. 105*)

gained in his many years as a hotel manager, of how to set up or run the hotel. This was certainly not conducive to preparing Gustav for managing it on his own, quite apart from the question of whether he was the kind of person for such a calling to begin with. Gustav was sociable and good-natured, preferring—unlike his stern father—to look at the bright side, always ready for a good joke, and with a certain predilection for what his father called "unsound visits to taverns."

At first, things did not go badly. The results and our guest books show that the hotel was run well and to the satisfaction of its very demanding guests. But then, World War I opened a radically new chapter. Gustav was quickly overwhelmed by its enormous challenges. The relatives who held a stake in the hotel were especially worried by what they saw as his imprudent and inept dealings with financial matters, with banks and the authorities. That could have disastrous consequences in these hard times. In a partnership like "Giger & Co," the partners' liability is not limited to their share of the company's capital, but extends to all of their personal assets. Anton Bon's heirs in particular, whose share was actually quite small, called for a reorganization of the company and its management. The founder of the Suvretta, the husband of Amalia Giger's younger sister Marie Bon-Nigg, had died in 1915, in the prime of life; his five sons, self-assured and well-established, had little patience with the problem-laden business and their luckless cousin in Sils. Threatening that otherwise they would force the hotel into liquidation, they managed to get Oskar Kienberger to personally take things in hand in Sils in 1918, in addition to making a substantial financial commitment. For that purpose, Oskar and Helen Kienberger gave up their position in Rigi Kaltbad (where the busy summers would have left no time for Sils). Instead, parallel to their new obligations at the Waldhaus, they took over management of the Palace in Lugano, as Lugano, by contrast, did not have much of a summer business at the time. It also happened to be a very highly paid job.

Gustav Giger was supposed to remain as co-manager in Sils, but for a variety of reasons that became more and more of a problem. Finally, after seven years, the Kienbergers took the plunge in 1925 and moved to Sils year-round to concentrate entirely on the Waldhaus.

This transition may have been essential for the future of the Waldhaus, but it was surely very painful for Gustav Giger, and there were bound to be tensions. But it says a lot about his character that, for all the following decades until his death, he loyally remained as "homme à tout faire" (the man for odd jobs) at the hotel he had once managed on his own, and, in his capacity as uncle and great-uncle, won the hearts of the third and fourth Waldhaus generations through his good cheer and ready jokes. Even for us from the fourth generation, who only knew him when we were little (he passed away in 1957), his reputation as a prankster was so well established that when we were confronted with some misdeed and the question of who had done it, we would try to get out of it by saying, "Maybe it was Uncle Gustav."

He kept his signing authority for the company for quite a few years. If he had some documents to sign and perhaps had spent too much time in town the night before, he sat at his desk and practiced signing until his lovely, elegant signature looked the way he thought it should.

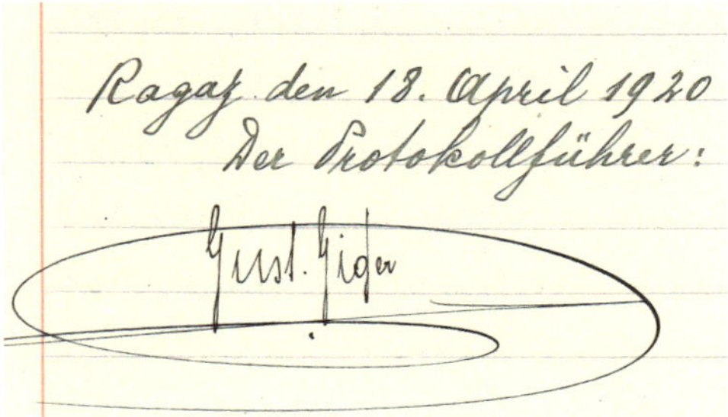

Gustav Giger's signature

"He was one of our best Brissago customers"

Christina and Maria Godly

CHRISTINA and MARIA GODLY ran the Marchetta restaurant and the Pensiun Andreola in the middle of Sils-Maria for most of their lives. In 1947, they took over the restaurant and the little store; they kept the general store open until 1969 and ran the much-loved restaurant until 2016. They were also responsible for the Pensiun Chastè, where they now live. "We still have a lot of things to do," says Christina Godly.

"To get to our restaurant, you had to go through the general store, where the cabinet with the cigarettes, the Rössli cheroots, the open tobacco, the Toscani and Brissagos was kept. At the time, people still bought such things! Sils had a number of Brissago smokers, but Gustav Giger was one of our best customers. Every day he would pick up the mail for the hotel and on his way back, he would stop by. But only when his supply of 'Brissago Originale' cigarillos was running low. You almost never saw him without a Brissago in his mouth. Before making a purchase, he would carefully examine each 'Ticino Virginia' cigar, pull out the straw, rubbing it between his fingers; he wanted to make sure that he only got the best. After buying them, he would sit down, order a glass of wine and crack jokes. I can't remember the jokes, but they were often about his own baldness. Or he would talk about his travels. He was a happy and deeply kind and friendly person. After a while he would tuck his briefcase under his arm and head back up the hill to the Waldhaus. Sometimes he carried it upside down and the Sils schoolchildren could earn a little money by picking up the letters that fell out."

← The cow shed (Kuhstall) on Alp Prasüra at Furtschellas, the summer pastures the Waldhaus leased in World War I for better access to milk products

World War!

That is what it says in red ink atop the August 1914 page of the "Recapitulation" where the hotel's earnings were recorded. 1911 had been a record year. 1912 and 1913 had also been quite satisfactory so that the young enterprise was able, for the first time, to declare dividends of 4 percent for fiscal 1912. Who could have predicted then that, with one lone exception in the late 1920s, it would take until 1971 before this would happen again?!

In any event, the outbreak of the war took the guests and owners of the Waldhaus completely by surprise, like everyone else. It was true that the 1914 season had begun rather slowly, but by July 25 the Waldhaus had more than 200 guests, despite the shots fired in Sarajevo on June 28. There was even a Prussian lieutenant general in active service ("zum Dienst"); there were "Mr and Mrs S. Fischer" of Berlin, the legendary publisher, or the industrialists, "Mr and Mrs Fritz Thyssen with daughter and tutor and maid" from Mühlheim on the Ruhr. There were Austrians, Hungarians, Russians, Britons, French, Belgians, Dutch, Americans and Italians, even a gentleman from Serbia—all still peacefully united just a few days before the war.

After Austria's ultimatum to Serbia, several families became worried and departed ahead of schedule. With the fatal chain reaction of nearly all the major powers declaring war on each other, and with Germany's invasion of Luxembourg and Belgium on August 2 and 3, there was no holding back. Starting August 1, the hotel saw the "flight from Egypt," as the annual report puts it. Four days later everyone was gone, the hotel empty and the season at an end.

Let's hear the story from someone who was at the Waldhaus at the time, in the very words of our great-grandmother Amalia Giger. She recorded her impressions of those days and the first months of the World War in longhand in four identical little black notebooks intended for her children Mali (Mally), Fanny, Gustav and Helene. It was obviously of great importance to her that future generations should know about this terrible upheaval. We gladly take her up on this and let her become our co-author in a lengthy excerpt from her notes.

> *On July 28, 1914, Austria declared war on Serbia. Everybody thought that this would soon be over and that the Austrians would win. But they hadn't reckoned with the other powers. Understandably, Switzerland in that situation decided to mobilize on July 31. The army had to report for duty on August 2, and all horses had to be presented. Our carter, Mr Meiser, had 120 horses to present, and he was only allowed to keep 4 of them. His coachmen and most of our employees had to report for military duty.*
>
> *In the first days after the declaration of war people lost their heads. Anyone who had an account at the banks, no matter how large or small, withdrew their savings, and this precipitous behavior brought the banks to the edge of ruin. In the aftermath, there was not enough currency in small denominations, which people desperately needed. The same madness applied to the purchase of food. People had the impression that we were all going to starve this winter already, in spite of all the provisions on hand.*
>
> *[At the Waldhaus] we already had a premonition of hard times coming in July, as the guests were noticeably scarcer than in earlier years, and we were quite worried. But by mid-July the outlook improved and Gustav cheerfully said: "So, Mama, you can stop worrying, by the 27th we will have a full house, and very fine guests at that." But, man proposes and God disposes.*

When on July 28, the Austrians declared war on Serbia, our Austrian guests departed immediately, and from that day on, the weeping and wailing at the hotel did not stop. When news came of Germany's declaration of war on July 31, and most of our male employees were called up, people took leave of their senses. Despite the loveliest weather, our guests did not go for their usual walks, but instead crowded around the lobby, the office and the post office in order to be on hand if telegrams were delivered. On Aug. 1 more than 200 cables were received at the Waldhaus alone. Only Gustav and Cecile were left at the office; the ongoing disruption by the guests made it difficult for them to work and they were hardly able to keep up with the bills for the many departures. If, with this huge crush, the trains had been able to carry them all, I think everybody would have left on the same day. Sadly, we watched 147 people leave over the next three days, while the 40 guests who remained were unable to exchange money or cash checks as the banks no longer accepted any foreign currencies. Many bills remained unpaid, and when the hotel closed there were 18,000 francs outstanding. We had to advance travel money to various guests. His Excellency Mr von Mumm had to borrow money to leave although he had a check for 10,000 German marks in his pocket. We didn't have enough coins and small bills at the cashier's office, although they were so badly needed. We wrote to the banks, to shops, etc. in vain. We only started receiving a few more notes after the Swiss National Bank issued 20-franc notes and, eventually, 10- and 5-franc notes as well.

Things were a mess at the train stations. Huge piles of luggage blocked the entrances, and it seems doubtful that all of the suitcases will reach their destinations. Our conductor Mr Lipp thinks this impossible as he says things are even worse in Basel, with dreadful confusion at the border.

Ah well, now we had said good-bye to most of our guests, and were left alone in the big hotel with dashed hopes, heavy hearts and empty tills. The key question, whether we should close or not with the 40 guests remaining, caused us many a sleepless night. We were very unsure, saying yes one moment and no the next. When we realized that even our remaining guests preferred to be less remote and closer to the train station, we decided to refer all to the Suvretta House, and most of them agreed. Only one family of good Dutch customers preferred to go to Pontresina instead. The die was cast, and the beautiful Waldhaus had to close its doors on August 5; only those who have been in the same situation can imagine how bitter our hours have been and how troubled our days. We do think that most of our guests were satisfied when they left, as they often praised the cleanliness, the service and particularly the food this year. That gives us hope that when normality returns, and with God's grace, the Waldhaus shall be full again; for the guests are promising that they will be back.

On August 2 we received an official order to inventory all food items within the next ½ hour, so that they would know how much could be requisitioned by the military. Coming on top of our many other misfortunes, this order upset us greatly. But we had to abide by it. An officer came the very next day to check whether our list was correct, which it was. In spite of the sad situation, you could not just sit there and whine and complain; there was much work to be done, we needed to make sure that the hotel was quickly cleaned up in order to avoid more labor expenses. Luckily, the clean-up went fast and Gustav had wisely put aside the money for salaries, so that we were able to pay them in full. Our employees, too, suffered greatly from the season ending at the height of summer, and the consequences will be felt throughout Switzerland this winter.

Carpet cleaning was left to the women as even the porters who had not been called up still left on Aug. 3 to be with their wives, abandoning their clean-up duties. All over, carpets were feverishly beaten, cleaned und brushed and the vacuum cleaner hardly got a rest. Mally helped from morning to night, and it was mainly thanks to her that all of our employees were able to leave after only a week.

We had already sent off the orchestra on Aug. 2, as nobody was in the mood for music anymore. The few employees who stayed on helped to beat all of the mattresses and set them out in the sun, as the weather was fantastic. We also had to try to cash in our surplus stocks, such as fish, meat, eggs and fruit, and the Suvretta House was a big help in that. They took almost 1000 francs worth of goods. We ate from the food that could not be sold for about 3 weeks so at least we did not have to purchase anything for a while, which we could only have done for cash.

Instead of the many guests and the full house we had dreamed of, August brought us one declaration of war after another. This wholesale killing in the 20th century makes a mockery of all peace movements and our entire civilization. One might as well tear down the Peace Palace in The Hague or turn it into a hospital for those wounded in the war. We have all been worried about Joseph in St. Petersburg, as we read about fighting between the Germans and Russians not far from the city. After 4 anxious weeks, we finally got a telegram which calmed our worries, as he wrote that he was in good spirits and business was going well. No letters are being delivered. Russians are not allowed to exchange their rubles in Switzerland and are having the greatest difficulties. From her return to Switzerland, Mally still has a 500 ruble note which she hadn't exchanged due to the low exchange rate. Our children on the Rigi [Helen and Oskar Kienberger] are in the same situation as we are. They have been just as disappointed as we were in their hopes for a good season. After war was declared, 200 guests left Kaltbad in 4 days. Oskar traveled to the border with about 40 Austrians to help them with their luggage and in any other way he could.

Although I have always stood up to life's storms, I nearly lost the will to live in the first few days after war broke out. I was not in fear for my own sake; I was plagued by a different kind of anguish. If the spring runs dry, where can you find water to put out the fire? Thank goodness, dear Papa is taking everything in stride and says, he expected all along that a world war would soon break out and now we just had to deal with it. The fighting has spread to every corner and although it is now the end of August, there is still no end in sight. You cannot rely on the news. Today they say that one of the warring parties has won, and tomorrow they say they didn't. Today is Sept. 9 and after all the news reports, I am worried that the war is taking on unimagined dimensions. The Balkan states and even the Moslems are starting to get involved, and hardly in the name of peace. One has to stand idly by while the best forces of humanity are murdered. Although the bravery of all concerned is admirable, one should also think of the countless parents, widows and orphans whom the war has robbed of their loved ones and providers. Help from above is needed if this carnage is to end. Those who are fighting will not surrender, they want victory or death.

At Maloja, 1000 men are guarding the border to Italy, there also are troops on the Bernina, in St. Moritz, in Silvaplana, etc. The men have been well-received in the region, and at least in the larger towns proper accommodations have been found. Many are able to sleep on mattresses with blankets and pillows in the public rooms of the hotels, sheltered from the wind and weather. On Sept. 7 a military exercise with 700 men took place in Sils on the meadows behind the Silserhof towards the Hôtel Margna. We could watch the entire proceedings from the terrace at No. 58 at the Waldhaus, and we could also hear the music splendidly. I really enjoyed this, as I had long wanted to see a large military exercise. I was also interested in the many pack animals, loaded with picks and shovels. On Sept. 8, General Wille [the Swiss commander-in-chief] visited the Engadine troops. Helen and Hansi [Mally Wolflisberg's children] wanted to be there to salute, with their donkey cart, as his car drove by in Baselgia, but they arrived a few minutes late.

Today on Sept.10, Mally received the first letter from Joseph since the declaration of war. He was able to give it to a Swiss who had been called up; otherwise, no letters get through from Russia and for the past few days cables have no longer been possible either. Thank goodness, he is still in good spirits and business isn't too bad.

Today is Sept. 20, and it's the Swiss Federal Day of Prayers. The bright sunshine of this day adds to my melancholy. The European War is being waged with a savagery that I didn't think possible in our much-praised age of progress. Our civilization has once again broken down completely and in its modern form has proved to be no stronger than the civilization of the ancients. Willfully or not, alliances and agreements have been ignored or trampled into the ground, peaceful countries, cities and villages have been attacked and destroyed and thousands of inhabitants have surrendered to misery. Unspeakable pain has descended on much of Europe.

The economic consequences are hitting us hard and will only become more pressing over time, but in spite of all of this, we should still be grateful. We have much that others have to do without, we still retain much that our neighbors painfully miss, particularly peace and liberty and order in our own country and above all, the life of our soldiers.

The outbreak of war reveals for all the world to see the utter worthlessness of many things that modern man was so proud of and which he revered as a special achievement of our times. Even those ever inclined to take things lightly need to accept this truth. We also need to recognize and admit our own personal culpability. It is not hard to say, "You have sinned." It is much harder to say, "We have sinned," but the hardest is the personal confession, "I have sinned." Let's hope that many learn this fact in these days of judgement, as that will lay the foundation for a "Day of Prayers" that brings us closer to God.

It has now been seven weeks since I wrote the last lines in this notebook. The battlefields continue to expand and the military hospitals fill up at an incredible pace. How will this terrible world war ever end? Doctor Bernhard [Dr. Oscar B. from St. Moritz], who was called to head a German military hospital, wrote his family in St.

Moritz that in his many years of practice he had never experienced or seen anything as horrific as what he had seen and experienced there. He only wished that those responsible for this war would have to spend 24 hours listening to the moaning and the sighs of the poor soldiers and see their tears and despair. Then they would surely think twice before going to war again.

Amalia Giger-Nigg, Das Kriegsjahr 1914

We knew about the little black notebook, but we were unable to read the old German longhand. That Amalia Giger's voice can now be heard is thanks to the archivist Markus Kaiser of the St. Gallen State Archives, who found Fanny Lutz's copy of the notebook when evaluating the Lutz family papers and got in contact with us.

So, the world was at war. Sils was far away from the battlefields, the mountains continued to be as beautiful as ever and the weather, in August and September 1914, was more glorious than it had been for many years, but in the Waldhaus books, the sun disappeared for a long time. A brief statistic illustrates the situation:

Waldhaus guests	Swiss	Foreigners
1911	38	692
1915	62	22
1916	95	74
1917	151	72
1918	226	95
1919	142	146
1920	97	184

As could be expected, a majority of our foreign visitors stayed away, and the Waldhaus and other hotels like it had not had very many Swiss guests in the years before World War I. Their numbers significantly increased now, e.g. captains of industry such as Geigy, Brown (-Boveri) and Hoffmann-La Roche and their families, but this could nowhere near compensate for the loss of foreign guests. Someone has calculated that—in Switzerland as a whole—each and every Swiss would have had to spend 18 days a year in a hotel to do that—at a time when most Swiss did not really have any vacations as we know them, let alone the money to stay at an expensive hotel!

Nevertheless, some foreigners—even American families—continued to come, an indication that the borders were not as hermetically sealed as they would be later in 1939–45. But the unparalleled freedom to travel of the "Belle Epoque" had definitely come to an end.

Not only did the guests become scarce, it was also very difficult to feed those few who did come, and to wait on them. The employees from abroad were gone, and many Swiss men were in the army, while their wives were at home holding down the fort. Imported coal became extremely scarce and expensive. Food rationing only started in 1917, and even then, it was not well prepared or enforced; for a long time, food supplies went to the highest bidder, causing prices to skyrocket. At the same time, the fact that hundreds of thousands of hotel beds waited for a very few guests was hardly conducive to raising hotel rates. The average income from each guest at the Waldhaus in 1918 was below that of 1908, while prices for food and fuel had practically doubled.

In the midst of these difficulties, someone came up with the surprising idea that "Giger & Co" should lease the summer pastures on Alp Prasüra from the village of Sils, probably with the intent of at least ensuring the availability of milk products.

Under the circumstances, it is remarkable that the family did not simply give up. The worst year was 1915, the first full year of the war. There were never more than 44 guests at one time; average occupancy was 28 guests for the entire season, which only lasted two months. Revenue was less than a tenth of the prewar years. By using up food stocks and with the family largely forgoing their own salaries, they miraculously managed to break even on an operative level. (Hats off to Uncle Gustav!) But, not one penny was earned to cover the interest on the mortgages and other loans, to say nothing of maintenance and amortizations. As good as the first years of operation had been, they had not yet been enough to decisively improve the hotel's financial situation which had been so problematic at the outset. The hotel still had to pay interest on mortgages of CHF 1.25 million, plus the loans from partners and other family members.

The bank reacted to the dire situation by raising the interest rate from 5 to 5.5 and finally to 6 percent, and, of course, the interest which could not be paid turned into ever more debts, on which yet more interest would be due. Over the next nine years, the Waldhaus found itself in the paradoxical position of seeing its earnings increase year after year and yet falling further and further behind. Except for 1922, each of these years brought higher operating results than the previous year. For example, after the "positive" or "negative" zero of 1915, there was an operational profit of CHF 20,000 in 1916. Alas, the growing surpluses were not enough to cover the annual interest due, causing the debt and with it the interest load to grow higher every year. By 1923, the annual interest due corresponded to about half of our entire revenue. Only the introduction of a winter season and the exceptionally good results of the years from 1924 on forward made it possible to escape this vicious cycle.

← Das Kapital: both hot and cold, like pastry chef Renato Pellegrinelli's Baked Alaska

Capital, revisited

Along with a reorganization at the top, these dire straits also prompted an overhaul of the hotel's corporate and financial structure, which took effect on January 1, 1918. The partnership, "Giger & Co," was turned into a joint stock company, which would have the long-run advantage that the partners no longer held unlimited liability for the company's debts, but "only" to the extent of their capital investment. Given the highly uncertain prospects of the hotel, this was anything but a mere theoretical distinction. In reality, the situation of the original partners did not really change right away, since the bank as the main creditor only consented to the reorganization on condition that the partners continue to personally guarantee the hotel's bank debt. This remained in force until 1930.

In the process of forming the joint stock company, the shares of the original partners were written down by 40 percent. Josef Giger's investment of CHF 355,000 was now valued at CHF 213,000. The money the partners and other relatives had lent to the company was also converted into shares (which meant it would no longer earn interest, much less ever be repaid). Lastly, Oskar Kienberger and to some extent the Bon heirs provided new capital by subscribing additional shares, funds which could be used to pay off some of the debts. The new family corporation thus had a share capital of CHF 500,000, with Josef Giger (CHF 213,000), Josef Wolflisberg (CHF 115,000) and Oskar Kienberger (CHF 89,000) as the main shareholders.

Thus, Oskar Kienberger not only had a new responsibility, the huge challenge of rescuing and running the beautiful, but very troubled hotel in Sils, he had also already made a substantial financial commitment to it. Keep in mind that we are not talking about today's monetary values, but about a time when each franc had so much more weight.

And that was just the beginning, even if none of the participants may have realized it. In the course of the following ten to twelve years, Oskar and Helen Kienberger quite literally ended up gradually buying the Waldhaus—or at least a major part of it—from the other partners. This had two reasons.

Josef Giger passed away in 1921, his wife Amalia three years later. With their deaths, their shares would theoretically have gone to their four children. However, they went hand in hand with large personal debts, and none of the children or their spouses really had the means to service those. The one exception was Oskar Kienberger, who had prospered on Mount Rigi and in Lugano and, by choice or necessity, now assumed the lion's share of both.

In 1918, the second largest investor after Josef Giger was still Josef Wolflisberg, although he, too, had been affected by the 40-percent write-down. Separated from Mali Wolflisberg-Giger for some time but apparently not yet divorced, the heretofore successful hotelier had lost much of his wealth, but none of his ambition, in the Russian Revolution. After the war, he first took on the Kaiserhof Hotel in Berlin. In the late 1920s he was involved in a big hotel project on the Dalmatian coast, which did not pan out. In 1930, he founded a factory for Swedish-style crispbread in Dietikon near Zurich, where he spent the rest of his life (he died at age 90 in 1963). For years he sent pleading and demanding letters to his (ex-) brother-in-law in Sils, who eventually bought up all of his Waldhaus shares at par value. Thus, Wolflisberg became the only Waldhaus founder to ever recoup at least a substantial part of his original investment. By the end of the 1920s, Oskar Kienberger's share in the Waldhaus family corporation amounted to CHF 324 000 = 65%.

For the hotel itself, these transactions were a zero-sum game. And yet, the fact that the Kienbergers were both able and willing to commit themselves in such a way was a double stroke of luck for the hotel. Just in the nick of time, the Waldhaus gained the successors to its founders it so badly wanted, a dream team of supremely gifted hoteliers. O.K. was a navigator who knew how to take full advantage of the late 1920s boom years, but also how to meet the almost diametrically opposed challenges of the exhausting crises which preceded and followed them. He was like a ski racer with the (rarely compatible) skills to be both a downhill and a slalom champion. It is with undisguised admiration that my father describes these qualities and accomplishments in the following chapters.

Swiss and discreet, my father says much less about the other central factor of that story, which turned out to be just as important and just as vital for the hotel: his parents' prodigious financial commitment. In hindsight, considering the ownership structure of 1918, it is clear that without their commitment, our family would soon have lost control of the hotel. Neither the other Giger heirs nor Josef Wolflisberg would have been able or willing to hold on to their shares for much longer. At the same time, Oskar Kienberger undoubtedly welcomed the fact that these transactions also made him the undisputed master of the hotel.

The other side of that coin soon became apparent. At the very moment when the shift in ownership came to a conclusion, a new, bitter and seemingly endless crisis began in 1930. Faced with it, Oskar and Helen Kienberger were now pretty much on their own as well. Earlier, it was "only" a question of repayment of shareholders who no longer could or would keep their shares. Now it was a matter of sheer survival. My grandparents met the new circumstances head-on, fearlessly and with great skill—both in human and entrepreneurial terms. Their last penny now went into the hotel. As had happened during the war, they virtually stopped drawing down their salaries (which were reduced to a minimum in the crisis anyway), the hotel eventually owed them more than CHF 100,000 in back pay and interest and new loans. OK even used his life insurance as collateral in order to free more funds. Finally, as part of yet another debt restructuring in 1936 (or was it 1940?), they agreed to convert nearly all their claims, plus an additional CHF 50,000 from other family members (mostly from Oskar's brother Josef), into new equity, with the old share capital having been written down by 90 percent yet again. The amounts involved for Oskar and Helen Kienberger were staggering: their "old" share, valued at CHF 324,000 in 1930, was now on the books with CHF 32,400, and their share was newly augmented by claims totaling CHF 123,000, converted into equity with no promise of repayment or interest.

That all of this was written down by a further 50 percent in 1943 sounds almost routine in comparison. For a total investment of somewhere around CHF 450,000, Helen and Oskar Kienberger now held Waldhaus shares officially valued at CHF 77,750 on the Waldhaus balance sheet (still two-thirds of the total share capital of CHF 117,000). It remained that way until after their deaths. She passed away in 1959 and he in 1965; in 1971(!) a modest dividend was declared for the first time. A rather depressing story, on the face of it. A wonderful story, if we look back and see what kind of future our ancestors secured for us and the Waldhaus.

Now let us turn back to more entertaining aspects of our Waldhaus history. In the next twelve chapters (pp. 122–205), it takes the form of a first-hand account by Rolf Kienberger (1917–94) from the third Waldhaus generation, written in 1983 and now accompanied and complemented by various "eye-witness reports," recorded by Andrin Willi.

Banks and hotels: the other side of the coin

Aldo Balzer

It hardly comes as a surprise that World War I, the New York stock market crash in 1929 and World War II also shaped the history of Graubünden's banks. Many of them, including the Graubündner Kantonalbank GKB founded in 1870, were active in tourism financing.

ALDO BALZER grew up in Chur, where after graduating from the cantonal school in 1948, he went to work at Bündner Privatbank. After stays in Geneva and England to improve his language skills, he joined Credit Suisse in Zurich, before Bündner Privatbank again recruited him, "under the pretext that there was good skiing in St. Moritz." From then on, he worked with the Waldhaus.

In 1933, Bank for Graubünden (not to be confused with the GKB) got into serious difficulties. Two years later, in an effort to save the bank, Bündner Privatbank was launched. "It assumed the sustainable mortgages, such as those of the Waldhaus," reports Aldo Balzer. To put it bluntly, he thinks it was squarely due to their exposure in tourism and hotel financing that so many banks in Graubünden, such as St. Moritzer Bank and Bank for Davos as well as Engadiner Bank, which closed in 1934, went bankrupt or were taken over by other banks. "The hotels were simply unable to make interest or amortization payments anymore, so they stopped. That was fatal," he added. It was a disaster for the banks. The hotels themselves somehow or other kept going and even slowly started to pay interest again when things improved. "In the case of the Waldhaus, the bank always stood behind it, it was considered a good hotel and the mortgage was not considered at risk," he remembers. In 1962, Bündner Privatbank was taken over by Union Bank of Switzerland, today's UBS AG. Aldo Balzer continued to be in charge of the "Waldhaus" account at the bank. "During these years, too, the bank thought highly of the owner family's abilities; and in my own case, the personal contact was important for that assessment," Balzer emphasizes. It seems to have been appreciated by both sides. "When I retired, Rolf and Rita Kienberger invited me to the Waldhaus. My wife and I spent the night in one of the best rooms at the top. I have never forgotten that."

UBS AG and the Waldhaus continue a close relationship.

← Loggias, the fifth floor, the winter season: three legacies of O. K.

Oskar Kienberger-Giger (1879–1965)

Oskar Kienberger first saw the light of day at the Quellenhof in Ragaz. His parents, Josef and Sophie Kienberger-Singer, had managed this famous spa hotel since its opening in 1870. Oskar grew up as the fourth of six siblings in the atmosphere of this special place where the great and famous of his day alighted. When his father Josef Kienberger died, he left each of his three sons a gold watch that he had received as a gift from a king. Already in his childhood, Oskar thus came to know the joys and sorrows and the challenges of running a large hotel.

Not only the dogs danced to his tune. Oskar Kienberger at the front door with Barry, the St. Bernard of the Villa Spitzer caretakers, about 1935

Oskar's own aim was to become an engineer. To prepare for it, he attended the technical section of the cantonal grammar school in St. Gallen. At age 18, he abruptly had to leave school and take over the lease of what was then Switzerland's largest hotel, the Grand Hotel Gurnigel in Gurnigel Bad, in the foothills of the Bernese Alps. Oskar's mother had died in 1897, upon which his father left the Quellenhof to take on the hotel in Gurnigel Bad. But then, his father died quite unexpectedly as well, before the lease had run out.

Where Oskar Kienberger, at 19, discovered what he was good at: Grand Hotel Gurnigel Bad

Oskar's older brother Josef had succeeded their father (for whom he was named) and assumed management of the Quellenhof in Ragaz. Faced with this quandary, the siblings asked Oskar to take over in Gurnigel Bad, with his brothers' help from a distance, until the lease came to an end. In spite of his youth and inexperience, Oskar apparently rose to the colossal challenge to the satisfaction of all involved.

The unplanned intermezzo inspired the young man to change his plans for the future, and he decided on a hotel career. He returned to school, graduating from the Ecole supérieure de commerce in Neuchatel with a solid knowledge of French and of basic business principles. Next came a three-and-a-half-year stay in the UK, where he became proficient in English and turned into a lifelong Anglophile. At the posh Claridge's Hotel in London, moving from department to department as an intern, he was initiated into the secrets of the hotel business from the ground up. We know, for example, that for a time he accompanied the head chef to the market at 4 every morning to personally select meat, fish, vegetables and fruit for the hotel (he would be an expert on this subject for the rest of his life).

Further stations in his hotel career were the Grand Hotel in Naples, Shepheard's in Cairo and the Métropole in Cannes. For a couple of sum-

Helen Kienberger-Giger (1882–1959)

In Lugano, around 1920, with Rolf and Gertrud, Helen jr. and Oskar jr.

mer seasons, he served as Chef de Reception at the Du Lac in St. Moritz Bad under his future father-in-law, Josef Giger.

His first independent position was that of managing the Engadinerhof Hotel in St. Moritz-Bad (a hotel which would later be combined with the former Metropol Hotel into the nucleus of the present-day Laudinella). In 1909, he was chosen as general manager of the Grand Hotel Rigi-Kaltbad. This highly diverse and lively property, situated all by itself high above Lake Lucerne, was a perfect match for the 30-year-old hotelier's wishes and disposition, allowing him to make full use of his natural gifts and his experience gained at home and abroad. He felt that he had thoroughly arrived.

On May 28, 1911, he announced to his siblings his engagement to Helene Giger, the youngest daughter of his erstwhile mentor Josef Giger. He wrote: "(That is why) I went my own way, to find my own place in the sun. I did find it in Kaltbad, as you know. I am my own master in an independent and enjoyable job with a secure income, plenty to do in summer and winter, and a few weeks off in-between, in spring and in the fall, a very tolerable fate!"

Oskar and Helene married in November 1911. She not only became a truly caring and understanding spouse, but they also complemented each other in an ideal way at work; hard-working, circumspect and kind, she was a true "lady of the manor" in the hotel. Even during World War I, the exemplary hotelier couple managed to keep the Grand Hotel on Rigi Kaltbad running with decent results.

Things at the Waldhaus in Sils were another story altogether. Its remote location and financial burdens put the hotel in a very different situation than that of Kaltbad in the years after 1914 ("Uncle Gustav," "World War" and "Capital revisited," p. 98 ff.). Gustav Giger, Josef's only son, achieved creditable results in relation to the modest number of guest nights. But little was left for the interest on the capital and the debts grew and grew. In 1918, the partnership was reorganized as a stock company. As a condition for their continued support, the partners demanded that O.K. participate financially in the stock company and also that he take over the hotel's management. With a heavy heart, Oskar Kienberger decided to leave Rigi Kaltbad and take charge of the troubled enterprise in Sils-Maria. At first, he shared the management with his brother-in-law, Gustav Giger. This enabled him to simultaneously assume the position of general manager of the Palace Hotel in Lugano. At that time, the Palace was part of the prestigious Bucher-Durrer group, and under Oskar and Helene Kienberger's guidance it experienced an encouraging upturn in the first years following World War I.

Palace Lugano. After falling into ruin for many years, it has now become LAC, a grand cultural center (Photo: H. Rüedi, Lugano)

Curling, about 1926. With Oskar Kienberger front and center, Gustav Giger (w. peaked cap) in left field

During the summer months, which were a quiet time for Lugano, O.K. left his wife and an experienced reception manager in charge of the Palace, while he went up to the Waldhaus in Sils. There it soon became clear that in spite of a strong increase in the number of summer visitors, the mountain of debts would remain intractable with just a single season per year. As other places, especially St. Moritz, were prospering ever more in winter, the family decided to open the Waldhaus in winter for the first time in 1924/25. The very first winter season was a success and generated enough of a surplus to cover the CHF 100,000 it had taken to winterize the hotel.

With the introduction of the winter season at the Waldhaus, Oskar Kienberger decided to once again place the needs of the family business ahead of his own interests and preferences. He gave up his cherished position in Lugano in 1925, in order to devote himself completely to the Waldhaus. This proved to be the right decision. By 1931, he had not only succeeded in restoring the hotel's financial health, but had also been able to carry out an impressive list of additions and technical improvements.

His good fortune did not last long. By the end of 1931, the Great Depression was in full swing. As a 15-year-old high school student I spent that Christmas vacation at home. Instead of the 250 who had been expected for New Year's Eve, the Waldhaus hosted all of 46 guests. The mood at the ball in the bar on New Year's Eve was so gloomy that I don't think I have ever had such a crushing experience since. O.K. was a realist and quickly understood that now the seven lean years had come—or the 15 lean years, as it turned out. With the same skill and determination with which he had guided the Waldhaus to prosperity, he now trimmed expenses to a minimum and streamlined operations. The devaluation of the Swiss franc in the fall of 1936 finally brought some relief, but World War II pushed the Waldhaus to the brink of ruin again.

In the 1930s: "Le rendez-vous de l'élite internationale." A proud hotel even in difficult times

After 1939, the winter season had to be discontinued and summer operations adjusted to a minimal occupancy rate. O.K. and the family set up their winter quarters in a few very modest rooms above the garage, so that the hotel's water and heating systems could be emptied and closed down. At the beginning and end of the summer season, when the number of guests was in the single digits, which could last for 14 days or more, they put two large guest rooms on the bel etage into service as a dining room and a lounge. Gertrud, my younger sister, an accomplished and imaginative cook, attended to the kitchen. For the "high season" Oskar Kienberger borrowed the executive chef of the Three Kings Hotel in Basel from his nephew, Fredy, and a large wood-burning stove helped keep the great lounge warm without having to turn on the central heating. It was at this time that an admiring foreign diplomat told my father, "Monsieur Kienberger, vous n'êtes pas un hôtelier, vous êtes un acrobate."

Having seen first-hand in 1918 what havoc four years of war had played with the finances of the Waldhaus, O.K. was determined to spare himself and those who came after him a similar fate at the end of World War II. Taking advantage of measures in support of the hotel industry instituted by the federal government and negotiating with great skill

"I was at the Waldhaus for the first time with my parents and sister in 1933. An impressive hotel. The men came to dinner in tuxedos and the women were equally well dressed. The next time we came, only about half the men wore tuxedos. In the previous year, 1933, Hitler had come to power. In any case, I noticed that something had changed," PETER HEFTI (1922–2012) told Andrin Willi in 2008. Peter Hefti's children and grandchildren, and the children and grandchildren of his sister, are still Waldhaus regulars. In the early days, Peter Hefti's maternal grandfather came along as well, Dr. Robert Haab, a former Swiss Federal Councilor and two-time President.

with authorities, banks and federal agencies, he arranged a debt write-down. We owe it to this arrangement and to my father's circumspect business practices that the Waldhaus remained in the family at all, and that we were able to resume relatively normal operations immediately after the war.

My father's interests were in no way limited to the hotel and its standing. He was very well-read, loved music and the theater and could brilliantly converse with his guests on practically any topic. When we children wanted to have our own way, we would choose a moment when he was engrossed in a book. He would only half listen to what we wanted and would agree to anything if we just let him return to his book. His main virtue, though, was that he never, ever let even the most difficult of situations get the best of him.

"Oskar Kienberger must have had two sets of ears"

Rose-Marie Hunziker

"I came to the Waldhaus for the first time in 1934, when I was six. Here's the evidence, showing Rolf Kienberger with a rucksack, and me sticking out of it. Indescribable, everything that I have experienced up there over the following years. I spent my summer vacations at the Waldhaus, and Rolf would come to visit us in St. Gallen. Rolf was always in good cheer, even when the hotel didn't have much money. And Gertrud Kienberger was like an older sister to me, she was incredibly kind to me throughout her life and always offered her help. Rolf tried to teach me how to swim in cold Lake Sils. I was a 'scaredy cat.' He simply put me on his back and swam far out into the lake—but I survived ...

The three of us built elf houses out of rocks and moss and with pine cones, Lego didn't exist. There was no elaborate children's playground then, there were a few rings and you could turn somersaults. We could have run into Anne Frank in the woods, as she spent her summer vacations of 1935 and 1936 at the Villa Spitzer (Villa Laret) behind the hotel. Famous guests stayed at the Waldhaus and their eccentricities and more were discussed at the family table. We children knew that it was taboo to talk about such things outside of the family. Once a princess was staying there. I imagined a fairy princess and was bitterly disappointed when I saw her: heavy-set and old, dressed in black with a large pearl necklace. That was not how a princess was supposed to look. Oh well. We children didn't spend much time in the areas where the guests were; we found it much more exciting behind the scenes. I always enjoyed

After high school, ROSE-MARIE HUNZIKER, whose aunt Anny Reich worked at the Waldhaus for many decades (see pp. 193, 234), would have liked to become a nurse and work for Albert Schweitzer in Africa. Her father found it easier to accept that she went to the translators' school in Geneva. With her translator's diploma and first-in-class in international law ("I finally excelled at something"), she became a radio newscaster and announcer, first in St. Gallen and then in Zurich. Following a break, while her husband Alfred Hunziker (1928–2018) built up one of Switzerland's earliest group practices for doctors, she worked at the Institute for the Preservation of Historical Monuments at the ETH (1978–1988), where she translated specialist literature into English. Time and again, Urs Kienberger would visit. "And so we got to know the next generation and kept our close ties with the Waldhaus," she says.

"I came to the Waldhaus for the first time in 1934. Here's the evidence: Rolf Kienberger, with me peering out of his backpack." (Rose-Marie Hunziker, nee Engeler)

doing laundry and spent a lot of time in the hotel laundry. Once I was in the elevator with the pianist Dinu Lipatti, it must have been about 1945. Incredible.

At school we learned about Thomas Mann and Marc Chagall. At the Waldhaus they sat right in front of my nose in the great lounge. I was too shy to talk to them; things were more strictly divided than they are nowadays. We children and the family used the staff entrance. Everything was different than it was at home. In the family's private dining room on the mezzanine (they also lived separately from the staff), there was a dumbwaiter in which the food was magically transported to us. There was no trace of a kitchen. At home we had to help out a lot with household chores, but we never had to do anything at the Waldhaus. Just mind our table manners. I was fascinated by the lovely bathroom next to the family's dining room. It had a high seat, and it was sometimes the salvation for us children, as we could take the porridge that we had for breakfast out of our pocket and flush it down the toilet. I don't like porridge.

In the evening we sometimes scurried away; we sat down very quietly in our pajamas behind the large round windows and looked down into the big dining room. I enjoyed doing that. The women wore black dresses, the men wore big ties. It was like being in a church and sitting in the gallery, observing who was coming in. At that time all the guests were elegantly dressed in black, as if they were going to a concert. It is true that the hotel was always full of music and musicians.

"What I enjoyed were all the toys they let me play with. There was a dollhouse, fully furnished from cellar to attic. It was full of old dolls that lived there."

Strains of music from the hotel orchestra which played outdoors on the terrace for afternoon tea,

Gertrud Kienberger (1919–1995). "Gertrud was like an older sister to me" (Rose-Marie Hunziker)

sometimes woke me up from my afternoon nap. We didn't have anything like that in St. Gallen. It is one of my loveliest memories. Also, the strong scent of patchouli, wafting towards me on the mezzanine. Oskar Kienberger on the violin and his wife Helen on the piano played classical music there, often for an hour a day. Oskar Kienberger was very musical. He knew all of the operas and operettas, and everything that the musicians played in the afternoon. He had something like two sets of ears. For me, though, he was primarily the man who ran the business. He was shorter than his wife, who added a softer touch to their music-making and in many other things.

And then there was the fun-loving Uncle Gustav, Helen Kienberger's brother. He was a real cut-up. He often played with us, kept teasing us, he was always in a good mood. Sometimes he went down to the village to fetch the mail and to stop off for a drink. Afterwards he came back and was in an even better mood. We liked him so much.

We always did the Christmas shopping for Helen Kienberger in certain St. Gallen stores. Sometimes they had to send things back as they were the wrong size.

"Gertrud Kienberger held a very important position in the 'Economat.' A kind of in-house grocery store. There she was responsible for ensuring that the food went to the guests and the kitchen rather than to the employees."

How Helen Kienberger had to work during the war! They lived in the garage apartment, under the simplest conditions, she did the cooking. Her great advantage (amidst war-time restrictions) was that at least she had provisions. Even when there were no guests at the hotel, she was always elegantly dressed, always in black. They heated with a small round iron stove. It was quiet. In the evenings they played cards, rummy, canasta with Uncle Gustav and the local priest. What else could they have done? Everything in town was closed. I always found the Kienbergers to be somewhat detached from the village. Was it because they were Catholics in a protestant town? Or simply because they led a very different life from the villagers?"

A garage report from a child's point of view

Walter Natsch

Protagonist:
DR. WALTER NATSCH,
Herrliberg

"Have you ever taken a good look at the squat garage building across from the hotel? It was built after the men in Graubünden (only they were eligible to vote) abolished the cantonal ban on automobiles on June 21, 1925." As a result, guests started to arrive in Sils by car, although for most of them "driving" meant being driven by their chauffeurs. "That an ordinary person could handle his own car was unthinkable," says Walter Natsch archly. With the garage building, the chauffeurs had four small rooms and their cars had four stalls and a stall for maintenance.

Then, the Second World War broke out. The garage and much else stayed empty at the Waldhaus. Walter Paul Natsch, born in 1888, the former head of the Swiss-German school in Lugano who had taught Oskar and Helen Kienberger's children there, must have known this. The Kienbergers had turned the chauffeur rooms into a small winter apartment for their own use, since the winter season had been suspended since 1939, and the empty hotel wasn't heated. They did not need the garage apartment in the summer, and Oskar Kienberger agreed to let it to the Natsch family with their children Walter, Peter and Ruedi for their summer vacations. "And so we may not have become real Waldhaus guests, but we, especially we children, did become hotel bystanders, receiving countless memorable impressions," says Walter alias Walterli

Cars and drivers in front of the Waldhaus

Natsch, who incidentally ended up becoming a "real" Waldhaus guest at 75 years of age. "At the time we were the only children," he says, people didn't take their children along on vacation. There were teenagers who were meant to be introduced to high society.

"We petit-bourgeois children were fascinated by the last vestiges of the belle époque," he said. There were the elegant coaches, delicate, two-horse landaus, which drove past the garage to the Fex Valley, and the waiters who polished the silverware until it shone and put the white tablecloths on the tables. Expensively dressed guests: overwhelming and unforgettable impressions for a twelve-year-old boy. "We hardly ever ate at the hotel. More often we cooked on the hotplate in the garage apartment. As self-catering guests, we bought food from Zuan in the village, and if we needed something special we were also able to buy it from Mrs Rageth in the hotel breakfast kitchen," he says, and his memories appear as vivid as if everything had happened only yesterday. Yet, the war years were anything but easy. That applied to the hotel as well, where Walter Natsch remembers that the season began with a mere nine guests. "In the summer of 1944, the dining room made anything but a grand impression," he says. "The few guests were served in the Arvenstube."

"I was impressed by the young upper-class ladies. In their short, snow-white skirts, they learned to play tennis under the instructor's watchful eye, or practiced it with a boyfriend. As ball boy, I gathered up the balls barefoot and brought them to the players who rewarded me with an enchanting red-lipped smile. Red lips, much to the displeasure of middle-class families like ours. I also got paid a franc per game. The first money I earned myself."

At the time, Swiss army personnel were often stationed at the Waldhaus. Officers occupied guest rooms, while soldiers, e. g. an infantry company, slept on straw sacks in the "couriers" dining room a floor below the kitchen, which had been turned into makeshift soldiers' quarters. "The access was strictly guarded," remembers Walter Natsch. An armed guard stood in the middle of the corridor from the great lounge to the kitchen. He carried not just a carbine but what the children called a "toad gun," a loaded submachine gun with camouflage paint, which the soldier carried at the ready across his chest, and greatly impressed (not only) the children.

Even so, Switzerland's national holiday on August 1 was duly celebrated. "To me, the ball seemed the height of elegance. All that we saw, of course, were the guests arriving from other hotels. We would never have thought of sneaking into the Waldhaus to 'spy.' We stood with open mouths on the side of the road as we children had never seen anything like it. The women alighted from the coaches and taxis on the Fex Road in their long dresses, which they daintily lifted to elegantly climb the stone steps to the hotel entrance. My father was appalled, finding it shameless and un-Swiss how the guests showed off their wealth on our country's birthday," says Walter Natsch.

His grandmother, too, turned up her nose, but more because of the hotel's garbage cart parked in the road right in front of the cellar door, day in and day out. It was about the first thing you saw when you approached the Waldhaus. "Such a filthy cart does not belong in front of such a hotel," she said and went on about this "disgrace." The unsightly wooden cart with large spoked wheels and a drawbar was periodically picked up by a horse—and in later years by a jeep—and emptied at a landfill near Lake Silvaplana. Now *that* was a disgrace, at least by the standards of later generations.

The summer vacations flew by. In 1946, the Natsch family spent a long vacation above the Waldhaus garage apartment for the last time. "Gradually it was used for its original purpose again. But now the guests themselves were at the wheel. No more fancy chauffeurs, and so the hotel hired an attendant who also took care of the cars. We simply called him Franz. He was in charge of washing the cars, making small repairs and, above all, filling them up. The garage had a single gasoline pump with two elongated gauge glasses and an underground tank. As requested, Franz started pumping by hand until one gauge was full, then flipped a lever and the contents flowed through a hose into the car's fuel tank.

"The pump is long gone, but the Waldhaus still fascinates me. We were able to experience a world different from St. Gallen's dreadful petit-bourgeois life, and we looked forward to our next summer vacation, which always lasted pretty exactly five weeks. City children were all believed to be in bad health, and breathing in the fresh mountain air was only held to have an effect if a child stayed for at least four weeks. We were very happy with the Waldhaus then, and still are today."

First additions and renovations

The years take their toll on the buildings and furnishings, technology marches on and guests' demands grow constantly. The longevity of a hotel depends to a large extent on its success in keeping its premises, its technical equipment and its furnishings up to date. The crux of

New times bring new needs. Also see "How to square a bathroom," p. 269.
Photo: Ralph Feiner

this matter lies in how to finance the needed renovations. There are different possibilities. One could sell the property to a financially potent hotel group or other investors who could afford to inject millions without needing immediate returns. One could build and sell condominiums and use the proceeds to finance renovations. In either case the hotel's owners lose some or all of their independence. And that is exactly what we have wanted to avoid at all costs. Defying the competition, we decided to renovate step-by-step, largely relying on the hotel's own earnings to do so. That even small steps can carry you far if you persevere long enough is illustrated by what we have been able to achieve. And, for years our hotel has had an occupancy rate of 70–75 percent, compared with a nationwide average of 40–50 percent in our industry.

The policy we have chosen demands clear priorities. Little steps get you somewhere only if you know where you are going. Crucially, you always have to know just how far out on a limb you dare to go financially. The 75-year history of our hotel (as Rolf Kienberger wrote in 1983) repeatedly brought lean periods during which we could hardly afford to hammer in a nail. And the times when we do have the means to invest unfortunately often coincide with the times when construction costs are at their highest.

When it first opened, the Waldhaus had almost 40 private bathrooms. In the years between the Wars, the other guest rooms got running water and gradually more bathrooms were added. Apart from that, the first additions and renovations were mainly triggered by two developments: the admission of the automobile to the canton of Graubünden and a fire.

"My husband was a carpenter; in those days he was a journeyman at a larger workshop. The Kienbergers needed to repair the shutters. Mr Kienberger discussed with my husband's boss what could be done. 'At the moment, we have no money for putting up a scaffold, but we really need to have them fixed.' And the boss said, 'One of my men is a mountain climber, and he is left-handed to boot and can work with both hands.' They asked my husband whether he would do the work without scaffolding and he said, 'Yes, I can do it.' He then spent many weeks up there, working on one set of shutters after the other. He straddled the window sill and worked on one side, then turned around and was able to work outside on the other. Rolf Kienberger never forgot that." MARCELLA MAIER (1920–2018), honorary citizen of St. Moritz, 2008 in a conversation with Andrin Willi.

The automobile

The people of Graubünden are not given to rash innovations, and for a long time they fought tooth and nail and even with rocks against the newfangled vehicles which polluted the clean mountain air with their fumes and the dust they stirred up, and pierced the stillness of the Alpine valleys with their clattering noise. After the automobile ban was introduced in 1900, it took nine cantonal referendums until cars were officially permitted in Graubünden in the summer of 1925.

At the end of October, 1925, my parents and their four children moved from Lugano to the Engadine, in order to assume full responsibility for running the family business. At the St. Moritz train station, we were met by a smart horse-drawn sleigh which carried us to our new home in Sils, bells on the harness tinkling brightly. At the time, automobile traffic here in the mountains remained limited to the summer half of the year, and even the post buses were at first still replaced in winter by romantic sleighs drawn by five horses.

The first two "garages" we had when motorists started arriving were romantic as well, made of wood and corrugated iron. Soon a third shed was added, and then two stately garage buildings. One of them incorporated steel girders from the former Grand Hotel in St. Moritz, which my father acquired for a bargain following its demise in a great fire. A garage attendant would direct guests to the right "boxes," supply their cars with gasoline and oil and polish them to a high gloss. Today, it is not only guests, but also our staff who arrive by car. The number of cars that need parking on our premises surpassed the one-hundred mark

The first winter post bus between St. Moritz and Maloja

By then, cars were almost commonplace: Rolf and Rita Kienberger set out on their honey-moon in a Fiat Topolino, 1951 (sister Helen got out first)

some time ago, and parking space became ever more of a problem. Having opened an underground garage for 60 cars in December, 1982 (my father proudly wrote in 1983), we can now easily accommodate as many as 150 cars, 80 of them indoors.

"Today we would call the horse Amazon"

Martin (Tino) Conrad

"When I was a boy, I used to drive a horse carriage during school vacation. That was in the 1950s. In winter, the roads were covered with snow, and so the guests could take a horse-drawn sleigh all the way from St. Moritz to the Sonne Hotel in the Val Fex. A day-trip. 50 francs for a two-horse sleigh and 35 with one horse. Plus, a tip of 5 francs, of course. I had two medium-sized Norwegian fjord horses. Although they took small steps, they were the fastest. For the guests we had blankets ready and under them 1-meter-long (3 feet) hot-water bottles made from copper. We lined up in front of the hotels to receive the guests who wanted to go have lunch at the Sonne Hotel, and then returned them to St. Moritz in the afternoon.

MARTIN (TINO) CONRAD grew up in the coach and transportation business. His grandfather (Martin) moved from Andeer to the Upper Engadine in 1904 and built a home on Via Somplaz in St. Moritz. His father, Martin II, continued the business during the difficult interwar years, but the World Wars took their toll, with the army requisitioning the horses. "I was apprenticed as a car mechanic at the Kulm Garage in St. Moritz," said Tino, who experienced the change from horses to automobiles first hand. For the record, his first car in the 1960s was a spiffy Alfa Giulietta. "Used," he adds.

My grandfather moved from Chur to St. Moritz in the early 1900s, when many hotels were being built, and started a carriage and transportation business. Everything was delivered by horse. We had as many as 350, which were kept in stables in Samedan, St. Moritz and Maloja. I know this from my aunts. After the Maloja Palace hotel went bankrupt, my grandfather was able to buy a lot of land in Maloja; he also had to take the Schweizerhaus inn and the Belvedere tower with the moulins. Hotels and such weren't worth much at the time, and my grandfather was more interested in the land. Livestock were always falling in the glacial potholes, animals looking for water. My father was annoyed and would have preferred to fill in all the 'moulins.' He was saved from having to do so by the Swiss Association for Conservation, a charity, raising funds through the sale of chocolate coins to buy the land in Maloja. For our family, every franc in our pockets was a good franc, everyone had to work hard just to get by. Hotels had stables but no horses. The coach companies had the animals. We were the coachmen for Badrutt's Palace. We also brought the mail from the train station to the St. Moritz post office, which used to be located in the middle of St. Moritz Dorf. Since so much of the mail was mail-order packages from Jelmoli, we christened our postal horse Jelmoli. Nowadays, we would call the horse Amazon ...

"In winter we cut ice blocks from the lake in St. Moritz. Huge blocks were cut out and we loaded them up and took them to the Palace, which had a large ice cellar with ice in it to last until the next winter came around. At the time the hotels were heated with coal. We delivered that as well. Graubünden held six votes for or, rather, against automobiles. Coachmen, saddlers, blacksmiths, they were of course all against the polluting vehicles, but they were unable to stop progress. The need for horses did not disappear right away. At some point, however, the roads began to be plowed down to the bare ground for the postal buses, and so we were no longer able to take guests to Sils with sleighs in the winter, and I stopped going past the Waldhaus. My father was forced to gradually sell off his horses. He turned to farming, but that didn't have any future either. The last horse left our stables in 1962, and my father started his taxi business. He got his taxi license in Zurich, as Graubünden did not even have a department of motor vehicles yet. My father had to adjust, had to think ahead, and when I returned from Canada at age 21, we slowly started with the trucking business. It was tough. But we had almost no competitors. Our original three trucks have grown to thirty, and the fourth generation is now in charge."

"After the war, my father had no money, nothing. Whenever a yellow envelope arrived with a few francs, the blacksmith would stop by. He wanted his share, too."

Hotel Phoenix

On March 11, 1927, a sunny day heralding the spring to come, I sat in school. My relationship with our teacher, Mr. Gotsch, had been somewhat strained for the past few days. In geography class he had explained to us that water always flowed downwards. That did not square with what I had learned at home. I pointed to the rising main of the heating system and protested: *Ma co l'ova vo tuottüna insü*, but here the water is clearly going up! A ringing box on the ear was the schoolmaster's reply ... and that March 11 was to cruelly teach me who was right. Shortly after 9 a.m. all the church bells started ringing in alarm from the neighboring church tower. The teacher was called to the door by his wife; he reappeared shortly with a fire helmet on his head and dismissed the class. When we stepped out into the school yard, we were shocked to see the Waldhaus in flames with thick black smoke rising from the south side of the building.

The night before, a fitter had used a blowtorch to do some repair work in a bathroom on the second-highest floor. It must have ignited the insulation material inside the wall. That fire smoldered, undetected, inside the wall and worked its way up to the top, where it broke out into the open by setting the hardwood paneling of a staff bedroom on fire. My father had just said good-bye to the last winter guest, as it was the very day on which the Waldhaus was closing its doors after a busy season. This guest told my father that upon leaving his room and stepping into the corridor, he had smelled something burning. At about the same

time, a post bus chauffeur called from Champfér to say that he could see a large column of smoke rising from the Waldhaus.

The in-house fire brigade went into action and in a surprisingly short time was relieved by the Sils fire department led by the other school teacher, Stefan Hartmann. Reinforcements from the neighboring towns rolled in by bus and horse-drawn sleighs, with as many as 150 firemen and eight fire hoses in action by noon. Although a stiff westerly wind had come up at about 11 o'clock, fanning the fire, the combined and selfless efforts of the men under the fire chief's clear-headed direction succeeded in getting the situation under control and extinguishing the fire. The skeptical pupil could now see that his teacher's theory was correct. The water used to douse the fire flowed downwards with a vengeance, in torrents: down the stairs and the elevator shafts, working its way through floors and ceilings from floor to floor, causing indescribable havoc. The south wing of the hotel was gutted down to the third floor, and the roof and the top of the tower had caved in.

With the last guest's departure, hotelier Oskar Kienberger may have been looking forward to a quiet off-season, with time for his family, for

Reconstruction (view from southwest)

reading his beloved books, vacationing and relaxing. Instead, what was probably the most hectic time of his life began. The rubble had not yet been cleared away when he made up his mind. In the first place, the hotel absolutely had to be ready for business again in time for the summer season. We could not afford to give up the income from a season, nor did he want to see the guests he had won over with so much effort move to other hotels. Secondly, he wanted to seize the opportunity and plan something new. Exposed to the sun and offering exceptional views, the top floor of the destroyed tower had only been used for staff quarters. Now, they could and should be converted into guest rooms, while the employees could move into what had been guest rooms underneath the dining rooms. It was also a chance to continue the modernization of the hotel, which had barely started, and to add more private bathrooms.

With extraordinary energy and creative power, the two Ks—Oskar Kienberger, the seasoned hotelier, and his old friend and advisor Karl Koller, the skilled and experienced architect—set to work. They started drawing up plans at once, while negotiating with insurance companies, authorities, banks and family shareholders. By March 25, fourteen days after the fire, the plans were ready, and the town council approved them in record time. Immediately after the fire, they had the burned wing covered with an emergency roof to avoid further damage. The new top would now sport eight handsome guest rooms, most of them with their own bath and their own balcony. On the lower floors, too, the many rooms damaged by fire and water were freshened up and a number of new bathrooms added.

On June 8, 1927, less than three months after the fire, Oskar Kienberger gave orders to hoist the flag to signal the re-opening and welcomed the first summer guests. I can see why my father would often and proudly recall that extraordinary spring of 1927 and all that was accomplished. My mother, Helene Kienberger, did so with a little less enthusiasm. It fell to her to make sure that the arriving guests would find their rooms and the corridors and public rooms in impeccable condition. My mother was the very model of a housekeeper and hotelier's wife; I believe that her staff would have done anything for her. She had been through many a difficult start of a new season at the hotel, but what she had to face in the spring of 1927 was an almost impossible task. No sooner had her staff finished cleaning a room, a stretch of hallway or a flight of stairs, than some workmen would return for a last-minute job and mess it up again.

In the end all the efforts and exertions of my parents and their hard-working crew were rewarded by a splendid summer season.

When all was said and done, the rebuilding and remodeling of that spring cost the then stately sum of CHF 220,000, with insurance covering CHF 61,000 for the building and CHF 25,000 for the interiors.

← Miniature golf from 1952/53: Rolf Kienberger's initiative in penniless times, paid out of his own pocket

The third generation

After completing my schooling in the bilingual city of Fribourg in 1937, I had a heart-to-heart talk with my father. I was toying with the idea of going to university. Oskar, my older brother, was in a banking apprenticeship in Geneva and saw his future in that field. My sister Helen had just finished her training as a nurse, and my younger sister, Gertrud, was furthering her language skills in French-speaking Switzerland and England. There wasn't really any money for university ...

Succession in the family business—it's a dare! At the Suvretta, about 1935, Rolf Kienberger (right) and his father Oskar (left), with Hans Bon (1882–1950), legendary helmsman of the Suvretta, and (center left) Anton or Fritz Bon

"I decided then and there: this would be my life's work!" Rolf Kienberger (1917–1994) takes charge.

but there was the Waldhaus, in which two generations of our family had invested all their money and their hard work with dogged determination. I had spent part of my long summer vacations in the kitchen and dining rooms of the Waldhaus, getting an inside view of the hotel's workings, just in case ... My father promised that, in spite of all financial constraints, he would somehow find a way to pay for my university studies. But he also wanted me to know what he thought about the future of our Waldhaus. He was convinced that, in more favorable circumstances, this hotel, so well designed and marvelously situated, could be made to prosper again. Yet, the chance of this happening would be very small if the task were left to hired managers. I decided then and there: this would be my life's work!

All marked by the Waldhaus, weren't they? Rolf Kienberger and his siblings Helen, Gertrud and Oskar, around 1960

Like almost every Swiss male, I was called up for basic military training at the age of 20. The year was 1937. The rough, but carefree life in the mountain troops agreed with me, and I was recruited for the non-commissioned officers' school, followed right away by the one for commissioned officers. By the middle of July, 1939, I had a lieutenant's commission in my pocket and was eager to begin my civilian career, hoping to see a bit of the world in the process. At first, though, I simply moved across town in Lucerne, from the army barracks to the Schweizerhof Hotel, steeped in tradition, where I was hired as a secretary for the summer. The previous winter, I had already spent some time between

The fourth Waldhaus generation, Oct. 1960: top Maria and Urs, below Jürg and Claudia

stints in the army, as an inventory supervisor at the Engadine Kulm in St. Moritz.

I had a contract for the position of assistant manager at Brown's Hotel in London for October 1, 1939, and had already lined up positions in Paris and Berlin after that. But then World War II broke out, and instead of cosmopolitan London, I ended up in the remote and uninhabited Val Chamuera, a side valley of the Engadine, patrolling the mountains on the Swiss-Italian border with my army unit. What followed were long stretches of military service and, between them, jobs at hotels such as the Park Hotel in Lugano, the Suvretta in St. Moritz, the Bristol in Lugano, the Waldhaus in Vulpera, the Flüela in Davos and the Park Hotel Waldhaus in Flims, as well as our own Waldhaus in Sils. I attended courses to further my professional qualifications, and in the army, I used every free minute to expand my foreign language skills.

As much as I regretted the war preventing my stays abroad to which I had so much looked forward, I have to admit that military service taught me many things which came in useful in my later professional life.

In 1946, I was appointed general manager of the Park Hotel in Lugano. My father patted me on the back and told me that he certainly appreciated my gathering my first experiences at somebody else's expense. Looking back, I think I can modestly say that I not only brought them expenses, but also quite a handsome profit. Starting in summer 1950, I joined my father in running the Waldhaus, anticipating the arrangement I have today with my son-in-law, Felix Dietrich.

At the time, the Waldhaus was only open in summer. In the winter, from 1950 to 1953, I managed the Seehof Hotel in Davos and from 1953 to 1963, the Chantarella Hotel high above St. Moritz.

In 1951, I married Rita Müller from St. Gallen. My mother not only welcomed her with open arms but also lovingly and thoroughly introduced her to the varied responsibilities of a hotelier's wife and partner. She taught Rita the exacting art of balancing her time between business and family. My success in the hotels I have run owe much to Rita's calm and steady contributions.

In addition to my wife, my sister Gertrud was an important and valuable member of our team. Like me, she gathered experiences in other hotels and then returned to the Waldhaus, where for decades she was in charge of purchasing and managing supplies, keeping track of bills and supervising the pantry, the breakfast kitchen, the storerooms and the wine cellar. My brother Oskar Jr. was an accountant and HR manager at the Du Théâtre Restaurant in Berne, but in summer he would usually take a few weeks off and come to Sils, where he was a great help to us, never more so than during the hard and complicated times when food was rationed. Our other sister, Helen, the nurse, also returned

Rolf and Rita (Rita Kienberger, 1926–2006)

home regularly for shorter or longer stays, particularly to care for our parents in their old age. She would also look after sick guests and staff, and relieve my mother and later my wife from some of their many responsibilities.

"You can't copy the Kienberger style"

Annalisa Cavelti

"Toni had known Rolf Kienberger since 1944, they had worked together in Lugano. I was at the Waldhaus for the first time in 1953, shortly after we got engaged. Rolf's parents Oskar and Helen Kienberger made a lasting impression on me then. Rolf's mom was a true Lady as a hotelier, and his dad was a role model for me. We sat together in the privé, a wood paneled room with a table in the middle. Lovely chairs were in the corners of the room, Rolf's mom always sat in the same chair. Gertrud was also there of course. Rolf and Toni lovingly called her "Tübli," little dove, as she could quickly fly off the handle. She was very capable, stayed on top of things. Sometimes temperamental, but always correct. When we got together, we had tea or sherry and we talked, those were the best times. Rolf and Rita were noble, authentic and honest. True friends.

ANNALISA CAVELTI and her late husband Toni (1920–2012) were close friends of Rolf and Rita Kienberger and the entire Dietrich-Kienberger family for a long time. Until 1959, they ran the same hotel in St. Moritz, the Du Lac, that Josef Giger had managed in his time. In 1960, Annalisa Cavelti and her husband opened the Cristal Hotel in St. Moritz. Later, until 1986, they ran the Cresta Palace in Celerina.

Yes, we were competitors, but our friendship was more important. Of course, now and then we also talked about hotel problems, but we had more to talk about than professional matters. I think that our husbands, who also went on mountain hikes together, knew better how to relax than we wives.

I looked at other hotels discretely, but with open eyes. I often found something to copy. You can always learn something new. Rolf and Rita did many things differently than Toni and I, but the Kienberger style can't be copied. I can't even describe it, Rolf probably adapted it from his father. I still feel like part of the family and have strong ties to the Waldhaus. It is a place of friendship, in which I never feel alone. I love to sit in the lounge, where I have so many people sitting around me. The lounge is just the opposite of the privé—yes—but both are part of me, as I was thrown into the great hotels of the world as a young woman. I love large hotels, and I love small sitting rooms. The main thing is to feel safe and cared-for there."

The Du Lac Hotel (on the right) in St. Moritz Bad. Opened in 1875 and torn down in 1974. Now there are plans to build a care center there. Will we spend our final years where our ancestors were once in charge?

helvetia
17367
ROSSIGNOL
16873

← Engadine Ski Marathon, a boon for our winter season since 1969

Reintroduction of the winter season

In the first years after the war, the Waldhaus was closed in winter. Our operations were limited to three or three and a half months in summer, with annual revenues of CHF 270,000 to 390,000. Thanks to a relatively limited bank debt, and by carefully husbanding our resources, we managed to meet our ongoing obligations. There was no question of resuming our renovation program, which had come to a standstill in 1931. For the hotel, it was too much to fail, but too little to survive in the long run.

Faced with this situation, I vigorously pressed for the reintroduction of the winter season. My father, who 30 years earlier had successfully chanced precisely that, now no longer believed in it and vetoed the idea. I had to admit that skiing had changed and that a winter resort now needed cable cars and ski lifts to succeed. But as we were only seven miles from St. Moritz, I suggested offering our guests a courtesy bus to the St. Moritz lifts. In 1953, a T-bar had been built in Sils, which would at least partly satisfy beginning and intermediate skiers.

In the winter of 1955/56, we took the big step and opened the Waldhaus for the winter. Result: 2,464 guest-nights, revenues of CHF 113,000 and a net operating loss of CHF 10,000. I should add that we had the bad luck of opening in one of the harshest winters of the post-war years. The thermometer repeatedly dropped below -30°C (-22°F), and fearsome winds made our life miserable. In front of the Chantarella Hotel, one of the sunniest spots in the Engadine, we measured -18°C (0°F) at noon in the sun. The ice on Lake Silvaplana was 50 inches thick; you could have built a house on it.

Considering these adversities and the fact that it was our first winter season in 17 years, and in view of the future, I saw the CHF 10,000 loss as an acceptable result. My father did not agree, and so we settled on a compromise: to keep the Waldhaus open only three to four weeks over Christmas and New Year's. This proved successful. From 1956 to 1963, these miniature seasons brought us between 2,600 and 3,200 guest-nights each and revenues of between CHF 142,000 and 200,000. With these results and our summer business, we were at least able to start some renovations at the hotel. We had taken a first step towards a better future!

The construction of the Corvatsch cable car finally provided us with a ski area closer to our hotel, i. e. at a distance of only 3 or 4 miles. Unfortunately, there were some construction delays, so that the opening of the first section had to be postponed from Christmas of 1962 to March 23, 1963.

On May 17, 1963, the Waldhaus board of directors—our family council—gathered for one of the more dramatic meetings I had experienced since taking my seat on this body twelve years earlier. I called on my fellow directors to open the Waldhaus for a full winter season from 1963/64. I pointed out the enormous need for renovating and improving our facilities which in my opinion could only be tackled if we had longer seasons and correspondingly higher revenues. The other members were divided; my 84-year-old father clearly had no truck with the idea. My motto, "Chi non risica, non rosica" (nothing ventured, nothing gained), was patently not his.

Timeless: the Waldhaus in winter

March 11, 1973. The venerable Waldhaus and the young Engadine Ski Marathon—meant for each other from the start

After a brief silence, he looked straight at me and said he would agree, if Rita and I gave up our position at the Chantarella and managed the Waldhaus year-round. It did not take me long to reach a clear answer: I accepted my father's challenge.

As expected, the first full winter season in 1963/64 brought peaks of high occupancy over the Christmas holidays, Mardi Gras and Easter, but extended very lean periods as well. For two weeks in January the number of guests sank to single digits. This, with a payroll of 56, plus a 3-piece orchestra! We were encouraged, though, by the fact that the very same guests were back in January, 1965, and even brought along friends. The winter of 1963/64 resulted in 8,598 guest nights and revenues of CHF 488,965.

The best part for me was that my old father had lived to see this success.

The unexpected popularity of cross-country skiing, the opening of the Furtschellas ski area in February 1972, and the construction of our indoor pool in the larch forest are among the factors which have now helped our winter season to grow even beyond my own most optimistic expectations.

"We would have hugged him if we could"

Michael Matantos

MICHAEL MATANTOS comes from a Greek shipowner family. He grew up in England. In 1956, at eight years old, he came to the Waldhaus for the first time. He returned in 1961: "A very different experience, but very pleasant, just different." 60 years after his first visit he saw in a train magazine that the Waldhaus still existed, and so he returned in 2017 and has come back every year since. By train.

"That winter holiday, which began on December 23, 1956, we were six: Daddy, Mummy, our governess Anna, our English nanny who had been with us since I was six-months old, my sister Sophie, and myself. Despite my eight years of age I was no stranger to Victoria Station. Or, more exactly, to platform 8. Platform 8 was a very gentlemanly platform, the London home of Britain's smartest train, the 'Golden Arrow,' an exclusive Pullman train bound for Folkestone, and thence to the Continent. On that day, I was treated to the sight of the tail end of the 'Golden Arrow' drawing out at 1 p.m. sharp, without us. But we had not missed our train, we were heading for its down-market neighbor on platform 7, the 'Relief Golden Arrow.' Fortunately our own train was all-Pullman as well. It would be leaving Victoria ten minutes later. Our Pullmans turned out to be elderly stock of an earlier age, comfortable and luxurious of course, but their late-Edwardian décor suggested they had probably been built before the first war and were now reserve stock for use in peak periods.

The soup was served immediately after departure, followed by roast turkey, stuffing, sausage and Brussels sprouts, gravy and bread sauce, Christmas pudding and brandy butter. Just before the train arrived at Folkestone, it stopped for a good ten minutes, during which I became convinced we would miss our ship, the S.S. Invicta, well-known to us from countless cross-Channel trips. Presently the train awoke from its slumbers, and slowly reversed into the port station. As Pullman travelers we were allowed on the Palm Court Deck, with green wickerwork arm chairs and panoramic windows. Just before 6 p.m. we sat in another train in Calais, the Engadine Express, which according to our tickets would bring us to

Coire overnight. Without any breakfast, as there was no restaurant car after Chaumont.

In *Coire*, absolute silence. Was this *Chur* really *Coire*? We only had the word of the *conducteur*, now drawing out of the station in his empty sleeping car, that we were in the right place. Here we were in the dark, freezing fog where we stood for about 10 minutes, the longest 10 minutes I had ever spent in my young life, by the end of which we were all frozen to the bone. Eventually, with no warning, powerful platform lights were switched on, loudspeakers crackled into life with an incomprehensible announcement. Moments later, a surprisingly massive Rhaetian Railway electric locomotive emerged out of the gloom.

We settled down in the blessedly warm train, a kind of miniature Pullman, and I fell asleep shortly after 8 a.m. as it made its journey up the mountains, the engine whistling mournfully. After a while I awoke, because no closed eyelids could keep out the light that suddenly suffused our carriage. I had never seen snow before, not counting the annual visit to Father Christmas at Selfridge's in London's Oxford Street where artificial snow was very much in evidence. By about 10.30 a.m., we alighted at Saint-Moritz, in brilliant sunshine, in freezing cold, and to spectacular views. There was no recognizable platform, no path, indeed, no road either: everything had been obliterated by a thick crisp layer of snow. We walked—somehow—to two cars sent by our hotel. How would they get us there on the snow if we could hardly walk on it with our town shoes? Simple, with chains fitted to their tires! Past thick forests on the one side of the road and a huge, level white expanse on the other, they brought us to what was to be our home for the next two and a half weeks, the Waldhaus.

The short winter seasons from 1955 to 1963, limited to three weeks over Christmas/New Year, have left but a few traces in our family's collective memory. Generations III and IV never even experienced them; we moved to the Chantarella in St. Moritz every winter. For that reason, we were very pleased when a guest from England wrote that he had wonderful and vivid memories from two childhood trips to the Waldhaus precisely at that time. He later wrote them down and sent us a detailed account.

Half castle, half commodious hotel, it was steeped in the Belle Epoque and remained frozen in time. Old fashioned, but warm, welcoming, beautifully clean and heavily staffed. We were welcomed by an elderly gentleman with a musical lilt in his voice, who proved to be the Principal of the Hotel, Mr. Oskar Kienberger. My sister and I thought him just about the nicest old person we had met and never failed to show him our affection throughout our stay which he always reciprocated. We would have hugged him if we could.

My parents had booked a suite with bedrooms leading off a very light and commodious sitting room. The two Governesses were housed elsewhere in the hotel, and this would be the first time my sister and I were separated from our beloved English Nanny, and would live in such close proximity to our parents.

Swiss resort hotels at the time only accepted guests on a *pension complète* basis, and it quickly became clear that we would not go hungry at the Waldhaus. Coming from an Anglo-Greek background, the eating experience at Sils Maria was a revelation, and a very pleasant one. There was veal in various forms—we'd never had veal before—including schnitzel, Zurich geschnetzeltes; pasta bolognaise, but not as made in Greece (simply, tomato sauce combined with fried minced meat), but a rich stew of meat, chicken livers, bacon and mushrooms, topped with Sbrinz not Parmesan; vols-au-vent with chicken, mushrooms and bacon *lardons* in a cream sauce; roast chicken Maryland with bacon, corn fritters and fried bananas; hot ham with Madeira sauce and spinach; and so many other—for me—new dishes I sadly can no longer remember. The main course would always come in covered silver dishes, which the waiter would then leave on a hotplate, containing a second helping. Thirdly, the salads: not lettuce *vinaigrette* as we'd always been used to in England, or tomato, goat's cheese and cucumber as we had in Greece, but a wonderful mixed winter affair with creamed celeriac, parboiled green beans, parboiled shredded carrot, cucumber and parboiled beetroot, ice cold and all arranged in a little pile. Last but not least, breakfast. The bread: neither sliced from a packet, as in England, nor *baguettes* as in France, but freshly baked, crisp round rolls, with unsalted creamy butter—far, far better than anything in England at the time, and, to spread on this, either Swiss honey or Swiss black cherry jam.

Nowadays, hotel guests keep to themselves. Quite often, they seem to prefer the company of their mobile phone to that of their companions, not to mention that of other guests. But those were different times, and the Waldhaus was different again. Guests talked to each other around drinks, children played with unknown children whatever their nationality. On Christmas Eve, a local choir sang carols round a huge Christmas Tree in the Drawing Room, so many of the tunes being the same as the English ones, even though the words were in Romansh or German. The adults did not come down in black tie and long dresses (which would have been the case in England), but in sports clothes. The community of Waldhaus guests, wherever they were from, was united by the festive spirit in a home from home, and I went to bed having had a memorable evening."

WALDHAUS

Guests

Waldhaus guests can be characterized by their loyalty and —literally—their phenomenal staying power. I estimate that some 80 percent of our patrons are regulars. Just recently, one of them celebrated his one thousandth day at the Waldhaus, and he does not even hold the record. There are families who have been coming here for five generations.

Austrian diplomat Max Baron von Löwenthal, simply known as "the baron" here at the hotel, who was born in the year the Waldhaus opened and died in 1995, made it to 2,247 Waldhaus nights.

Bruno Bandini, a masterful Italian head waiter who was with us for many years, once told me that he often felt like a lion tamer with the guests. I have never had that feeling. The guest may be king, but it is a constitutional monarchy. It is the hotelier's job to lay down the articles of that constitution and to see that they are followed, as unobtrusively and diplomatically as possible.

On a peaceful Christmas morning a guest burst into the manager's office, beside himself with anger. What had happened? On the previous night several younger guests had made fun of his daughter's extravagant dress! My father calmly let the angry gentleman let off steam; then he started softly humming "Silent Night." The effect was amazing, and the guest soon calmed down.

One of our prominent guests was Gottlieb Duttweiler, the maverick businessman and politician who founded Switzerland's big Migros enterprise. Mr. Duttweiler had made headlines when, in a fit of anger, he had smashed a window in the Swiss parliament building after his fellow members of parliament voted down a measure he had pro-

Our guests always towered above the rest: at the main entrance, about 1950. From left: siblings Rolf, Oskar and Helen Kienberger, parents Helen and Oskar Kienberger senior and John Steele, a friend from the UK

posed. The tall, broad-shouldered man was scheduled to arrive at the Waldhaus in his tiny Fiat Topolino for a well-earned vacation. An hour before his arrival, my mother was horrified to discover a cracked window pane in the room set aside for him and his spouse! To make matters worse, our carpenter was out sailing on the lake; but somehow, he was found and managed to fix the window in the nick of time, minutes before Mr. Duttweiler's arrival.

One morning a usually quiet and pleasant guest called to tell me that his marriage of almost 25 years was about to break up, and that it was all my fault. When I asked him what he meant, he told me that the green wallpaper in their room made him and his wife so nervous that the two of them, who had always gotten along so well, now did nothing but argue. I should point out that the husband, who was now so distraught, had come all the way from the Netherlands, a month earlier, just to select the room in person. I now proposed an immediate change of rooms in order to restore the peace. He chose a room where the wallpaper was blue, and said with relief that blue had a soothing effect. We were about to leave that room when he turned to ask me in which direction I slept. It surprised him when I answered that I would sleep like a marmot, no matter in which direction. He explained that one's head must always point west and the feet east. The beds in the blue room were facing north-south; sleeping there was out of the question. I had the beds turned by 90 degrees, and the situation and a marriage were saved.

"If they stay for five days, they usually come back"

Walter Nana

"The other day, three generations of regular guests were sitting at a table in our dining room. In which hotel can you still find something like that? It is good to see that young family members continue to come, not just with their parents. That is how the Waldhaus lives, fascinating one generation after another. The interactions between us and our guests haven't changed all that much in my thirty years of work. My predecessor Roberto Schilirò worked with file cards on which guests' preferences were noted. For example, a carafe of ice water, carbonated mineral water, Bordeaux, mixed salad, etc. Today we receive an info mail. Typically it says: gluten-free, vegan, vegetarian or lactose-intolerant.

WALTER NANA began at the Waldhaus as a busboy in 1985. He worked in room service, in the Arvenstube, in the dining room. After eight years, he was the third maître d' and after another three years, he was number one in the dining room. Today 27 waiters work there, serving up to 300 guests. Away from the hotel, you can usually find him on his bike, on skis or on his motorcycle. He knows nature like no other; whenever possible he pursues sports.

Hours have also changed, guests tend to come later. Nowadays guests have breakfast at 10.30, dinner has moved to a later time as well. This makes staff planning more challenging. Guests appreciate the fact that there is no special dress code. As far as I remember, there never has been, but I doubt that thirty years ago, a guest would have dared enter the dining room with bare feet. Sometimes that happens now, which seems surprising, as the guests, for their part, have generally become more demanding.

"Many guests reveal that they would rather come here than bequeath their money to their heirs."

Especially the Swiss. They know that taking a vacation in their own country has its price, and so they demand impeccable service and quality in all respects. Guests want the best for their money. I shouldn't generalize, but these French, recently ... every day they looked for something wrong with each dish and questioned everything. Why this combination? The entrecôte not grilled long enough, the veal fricassee cooked too long. Too small a portion, too much sauce, they complained about every dish. They brought us to the brink of despair. As an Italian, I don't like to say this, but Italians are not always easy to deal with, either. Macchiato, Caffè con la schiuma, Ristretto, this dish with that one, the other dish with this one, here in Switzerland they are somewhat restrained but in their own country that can be very stressful for a waiter. I like the Germans best. They try hard to speak Italian with us, are satisfied and happy when we do our job well and show their appreciation, which the Swiss and Italians do less often. Some Germans address us by name; the Swiss speak Swiss-German and the Italians never think of speaking anything but their native language. Obviously, exceptions make the rule.

"We once had a guest who always came for three months. He always sat at the same table, slept in the same room, had breakfast every morning at seven sharp and had a veal steak for dinner every evening."

Unfortunately, you can find impossible guests everywhere, but as maître d', I don't like to talk about that. We act discreetly and professionally. Many people are stressed out, and I see our job as building them up, without them noticing. Four days at the Waldhaus have an incredibly calming effect, and those who stay for five days usually come back next year. If we recognize them, welcome them by name, then all is right with the world. Many guests have returned for years and years. It pains me if they tell me on the very last day of their stay that next year they would like a different table. They should have told me that on their first evening here, after all we do our utmost to find the right table for each guest. I myself prefer a certain inconspicuous table in the background. There you sit with your back to the wall, you are almost invisible and can observe the whole dining room. Everybody, though, wants a table by the window. Even when they are alone, they prefer a table for eight at the window. There are guests who always want one and the same table, those who want table number so-and-so. Only that one. Certainly not the one just next to it.

Visitors eccentric enough to manage to astonish the other guests are becoming more and more of a rarity. Too bad. I like to see guests dress in their own style, such as that lady who is an Italian, lives in Paris, stays here for three months and wears clothes exclusively from the 1930s. She knows all of us, only drinks water. Most Waldhaus guests are fantastic, though, and so my most difficult job is not to make them happy, but to manage staff. I have to be constantly on the job, always take care, keep my eyes open.

> "There was a time when you made someone happy by giving him a nice table and then next to it a guest lit up a cigar. Luckily, you can no longer smoke in the dining room."

When everything is running well, the guests forget my primary job, and we can talk to each other on a different plane, not only about the food. I tell them which lake is best for swimming at the moment, which cycling tour is appropriate for them, which slopes are good, where there is the most snow, etc. By the way, when I'm off duty and am not wearing my tuxedo and I sit next to a Waldhaus guest in the cable car, few recognize me. A very pleasant feeling."

1986: the modernized Waldhaus chapel, a long-time dream of Rolf Kienberger's come true (designed by Ferdinand Pfammatter, altar and artwork by Willi Buck)

Monsieur Petrov's legacy

In the 1960s, we counted a Russian emigre among our most loyal winter guests, Madame Olga Petrov of Paris. She usually came by herself, but after her death her husband started to come regularly, always wanting the room in which she used to stay. Inspired by his stays in the Engadine, he asked whether he and his wife could have their final resting place in Sils. Our village priest agreed to the placing of an urn in the wall of the Catholic church. At Mr. Petrov's request, I arranged for an appropriate niche to be chiseled out. Upon his next visit in July 1973, he inspected the niche at the church and felt that it might be a little too small for the intended urn. Upon his departure, he reserved his room for September 13, and also asked me to have a mason come to the church on the morning of September 14, so that the niche could be enlarged. Pierre Petrov returned to the Waldhaus as planned, and told me on the following evening with visible relief that the mason had done his job well and the niche was now the right size.

On the morning of September 15, he called down from his room to tell me that he had had a very bad night and felt wretched. The doctor was called and diagnosed heart failure. He asked me to come to his room—for what turned out to be a final farewell to our dying guest.

In his will, Pierre Petrov provided that for four years, two of his friends and their families should spend a week at the Waldhaus every year, at the expense of his estate. They fulfilled his dying wish and continue to be among our regular guests.

Antoinette

Every once in a while, a guest will be in an uproar and report the supposed theft of his wallet, his wife's jewelry box or other valuables. Often, the guests know exactly who the likely culprit is; although it usually turns out that the missing items have simply been mislaid.

The "provisional" Waldhaus chapel of 1908 (Photo: Guido Schmidt, 1983)

Over the years, my wife has shown such a knack for tracking down missing objects that we have christened her "Antoinette," in honor of St. Anthony who is a great help in such cases.

Once a distinguished French guest had me called. He was shocked to find that while he had been swimming all of his wife's jewelry had disappeared from their room. Antoinette was called and accompanied the guests to the scene of the crime. The husband told her that whenever he left the room, he would put his wife's jewelry in the breast pocket of one of his suits in the closet, and that is what he had done this time. After checking all of the clothes, she discovered that the jewelry had simply slipped through a hole in the breast pocket and was lodged between the material and the lining of the coat. The criminal turned out to have been an accident.

Another time, a grandmother, on vacation with three of her granddaughters, noticed that her well-stocked wallet was missing. While Antoinette was discussing the case with the lady, one of the granddaughters wanted to show her the little mouse in a cage that she had brought along from home. As she picked up the cage from the table, grandmother's wallet appeared from underneath it!

My wife could tell dozens of similar stories; they would make an amusing collection.

"Hotel life? Don't ask a hotelier!"

Urs Kienberger

"People see us hoteliers as paragons of discretion, as we tactfully refrain from speaking about what goes on within our walls. Some praise and admire us for that, others find it annoying and affected. What very few people realize is that often the reason why we say so little has little to do with discretion. Often, we simply are not in the know. Much of what goes on under the roofs of our hotels day after day, the banal and the mysterious, the magical and the ugly, we simply do not see or understand. And that's a good thing. It would truly be a poor hotel, where what people experienced and noticed was strictly limited to what the hoteliers themselves are able to understand and imagine.

Thus, if you really want to know what is going on at the Waldhaus, don't ask the hotelier, who probably has no idea. Ask, for example, an author. Or nineteen of them (and then another one, who doesn't write but still has something to say)!

Will you then have your answer? Yes and no. Those who read all the stories in this anthology will be delighted by some and annoyed by others—funnily enough, not everyone by the same ones. You will quickly notice that it is not a very focused and carefully curated collection, but frankly heterogeneous. And that is a pretty good match for the Waldhaus itself. The inscrutable gentleman across the hall, the noisy family at the next table in the lounge, the old couple who dance every night in the bar as if the Titanic was still afloat: every one of them expects and sees something different in the Waldhaus than you or we do, and their presence in turn contributes to what this hotel is and means to you and to us. The hotel is a production that invites you to actively help shape and change it with your own thoughts and (inter)actions; we do not claim the sole right to tell you how to see and define it, nor do we grant that prerogative to anyone else."

Urs Kienberger. Excerpts from the preface to *Wie gross ist die Welt und wie still ist es hier* (weissbooks, 2014), a Waldhaus anthology by 19 writers and a photographer.

"Under the radar"

(An employee's tale)

"I got to know a very pretty young lady from Germany. She was younger than I, and her father wasn't supposed to know anything about us. 'Guests socializing with the staff,' etc. But there you are. It wasn't my fault; it was she who invited me in. When we were in her room, there was a knock at the door, and her father came in. I disappeared into the closet. Unfortunately, he saw my shoes standing there and opened the closet. I said, 'Buona sera!,' and left in a hurry. I think she got into trouble then."

Personally told to us by ... Well, does it matter?

← The indoor pool from 1970: at the time, a big risk, to this day, a big asset

Maintenance and improvements, 1955 to 1983

To list all the work carried out during these years would go beyond the scope of this book. I will just discuss some of the more momentous projects here.

The swimming pool (1969/70)

In the course of the 1960s, the number of winter guests grew while the summer season tended to stagnate. It became apparent that our old hotel needed something to give it fresh momentum and make it more attractive again. Considering the relatively isolated location of our hotel, I thought the answer might be to build an indoor pool. Otto Glaus, a first-rate architect from Zurich, drew up a preliminary project. Unfortunately, my idea found little favor with our bank and other possible sources of financing. They were willing to fund the construction of a central pool for all of Sils, but argued that a private pool for a single hotel was not economically feasible. Although I did not agree with them, I took the initiative and met with the town and the tourist office to form a task force. We worked out a fully detailed project for an indoor pool in the village and a financing plan. It all came to naught when the citizens of Sils, as owners of the commons, the public lands, refused to grant building rights for one sliver of land which the project would have touched.

By then, three valuable years had gone by. After the "no" of the citizens, I went back to our bank and the public Hotel Credit Corporation. This time they were willing to back us up. Otto Glaus expanded his pre-

Spring 1968: when the Waldhaus lost ... well, not its innocence, but the cupola on its turret. Maybe we will restore it someday. And the innocence? It wasn't part of the original design (Photo: Hans Plattner)

liminary concept into a handsome design which beautifully blends into our forest landscape and which incorporated the latest technological advances. St. Moritz architect Robert Obrist, formerly of Otto Glaus's office, supervised the construction work.

Difficulties arose right from the start. Much of the pool had to be blasted out of the bedrock. Our contractor entrusted that job to a subcontractor who was by no means up to the task. Because of insufficient safety precautions, the hotel suffered thousands of francs of damage to its windows and façades. A jagged rock weighing three ounces flew all the way to the town square, landing on top of a car parked in front of the town hall.

The local contractor, with whom we had worked for decades, let us down very badly. By Christmas of 1969, three months after we had broken ground, he was already two months behind schedule. We were forced to renegotiate. The contractor agreed first, to put his very best foreman in charge and second, to pay a sizeable daily penalty for each additional delay in the revised construction schedule. From the spring of 1970, when work resumed after the winter season, construction finally progressed at a good pace.

Further headaches were caused by a cost overrun of hundreds of thousands of Swiss francs. This was serious indeed, since the original estimate of CHF 1 million was already stretching our resources to the limit. Fortunately, the architect in charge always kept us up-to-date on the financial situation. To contain the costs, we shelved our plans for including a sauna, but we did not want to cut any corners regarding the pool itself and its technical installations. At the start of the 1970/71 win-

The indoor pool, opened in December 1970: preliminary sketch by architect Otto Glaus, 1966

ter season, it opened for business. The pool has fully lived up to our optimistic expectations; it became instantly popular with our guests, and within a short time it led to the hoped-for increase in our occupancy rate.

The remodeling and expansion of the dining room (1978)

The gratifying increase in our occupancy rate, with extended periods of "full house," meant that our lounges and dining rooms more and more frequently reached their capacity limits. In the case of the lounges, we solved the problem in 1973 by moving the children's playroom and the public bathrooms from the main floor to the floor underneath and creating the "Sunny Corner" in their place. This inviting room now serves as an additional lounge, but can also be converted into a meeting or banquet room as needed.

Yesterday's future is past, especially the ashtrays! Only the arch remains: the Sunny Corner lounge in 1973 (Photo: Hans Steiner)

For this project we engaged the services of architect Ferdinand Pfammatter of Meilen near Zurich, who is both an accomplished professional and a regular Waldhaus guest with a good understanding of our hotel, its character and our guests. It is much harder for an architect to create

When the wind blew from the east, the fun would stop. The inner dining room veranda (1908) in the 1960s. On the right: Bruno Bandini, the lion tamer (see p. 167)

The unloved 1970s, better than their reputation?! Architect Ferdinand Pfammater's outer veranda, added in 1978, with lamps by Roberto Niederer (Photo: Lukas Pfammatter)

something new in an old building, where it has to fit in with the past, than to build something from the ground up.

At Christmas, 1977, we commissioned the same architect to find a way to expand our dining rooms. After carefully studying the problem, he came upon an excellent solution. He proposed enlarging the principal dining room with an addition, 15 feet deep, along the entire length of 85 feet, which would leave the architectural qualities of the existing room intact.

The time between seasons for remodeling and construction work is always very short. Our guests are eager for renovations, but they do not enjoy the noise from construction. Pfammatter and his trusted on-site supervisor, Karl Hofmann, had exactly 60 days at their disposal after the end of the winter season. In that time, they had to remodel and extend not only the dining room, but also the staff bedrooms on the two floors underneath. To make matters even more difficult, the spring of 1978 was bedeviled by particularly inclement weather.

Although I had at one point offered to give them three more weeks, the work was completed right on time (if only just) for the re-opening of the Waldhaus on June 10, with lunch served in the new veranda at noon on opening day.

The new dining room, a model of simplicity, radiates light and elegance and delights our guests, our staff and us. With a hotel capacity of 220-250 guests, we can now seat more than 330 in our three dining rooms.

Palais du Garage

Early in the century, the Palace Hotel in St. Moritz built what must have been one of the world's very first indoor tennis courts. It was eventually converted to other uses. In 1983, the Waldhaus became the first hotel in the region to have a private indoor court again.

It is part of what I have dubbed our "Palais du Garage," the first stage of which was built in the spring and fall of 1982 and the spring of 1983 on the west side of our hotel below the Fex road. The plans for it were once again drawn up by Ferdinand Pfammatter, with Karl Hofmann supervising the construction. The building contains an underground garage for 60 cars and, in addition to the indoor tennis court, a new outdoor court. There are locker rooms, a little lounge, a billiards room and all the necessary technical installations.

In 1984 and 1985, the complex will be completed by two apartment houses for our staff. Up to now, most of our employees—few of whom are permanent residents of Sils—have lived in the hotel. Increasingly, some of them would prefer to leave their workplace at the end of the day and spend their free time in the comfort of their own apartment; but in a village full of condominiums for well-paying vacationers, it is virtually impossible to find affordable apartments for rent.

A Swiss franc of today is no longer the same as a Swiss franc of 1908, but it is worth noting that at CHF 5.5 million, our budget for the "Palais du Garage" is more than double what our ancestors had to pay for the entire hotel with everything in it, 75 years ago.

In the rocks, up to 10 m (or 33 ft) deep: "Palais du Garage" under construction, 1982. At the top on the left, the 1928 garage building where the family lived during the Depression (see pp. 127, 131)

This is your captain speaking …

The alpine climate at 6,000 feet and the growing complexity of our hotel's technical installations are a rich source of occasionally nasty surprises that keep our life from becoming boring.

One of the most exciting incidents occurred on February 22, 1971. That afternoon, my wife alerted me to water leaking into the corridor next to the laundry at the lowest point of the hotel. Our plumber and I tried unsuccessfully to find out where the water was coming from. We decided to have a mason come the next morning to open up the wall where the water was leaking out. On my next "tour du maître"—my routine rounds of the hotel—at 6 p.m., the great lounge felt rather chilly, although the control light indicated that the heat was on. With an uneasy foreboding, I hurried down to the boiler room and nearly fell into a pool of water. The room was flooded to a depth of more than four feet. The oil burners of two of the three furnaces were already under water, that of the third, which stands on higher ground, was halfway submerged. Here we were in the middle of winter, with 200 guests and more than 100 employees, and the hotel was without heat. Outside, the temperature was -5° C (23° F), fortunately there was no wind.

Thoughts were racing through my head. I absolutely knew repairs had to be made as rapidly as possible, or there would be disastrous damage from freezing and bursting pipes all over the hotel, and a mass exodus of our guests.

I summoned our plumber again, and we quickly saw that there had to be a break in the water main leading to the swimming pool, which starts near the boiler room and passes under the hotel forecourt. That would also explain the water leak near the laundry, which lies three floors below. By turning off a central valve, we were able to stop the water inflow. The pumping engine of the Sils fire department arrived in record time and succeeded in pumping the boiler room dry within an hour. The oil burner repairman from St. Moritz thought he could get the one burner which had not been totally submerged back in working order in about two hours. With it, we could at least keep the guest rooms and the indoor pool warm (as long as the outside temperature did not drop much lower) and also ensure our hot water supply.

The technician explained that the other two burners were beyond hope, and that replacements were only available in Zurich. This meant that the public rooms and various other areas of the hotel could not be heated! A call to a gentleman at the factory in Zurich revealed that—in the middle of Switzerland's biggest city (!!)—he saw no way to round up a car to bring the replacement burners to Sils in the middle of the night. After repairing the one oil burner, the technician from St. Moritz and our chauffeur of long standing, Oskar Frey, took off for Zurich, shortly after midnight, to pick up the replacements.

A touch of Steve Jobs! Apple was founded in a garage; the Waldhaus celebrated itself in one. Or rather, in the indoor tennis court at the Palais du Garage. Marthaler theater, June 2008 (Photo: Dorothea Wimmer)

Meanwhile, it occurred to me that we might be able to heat the public rooms by setting up the kind of giant space heaters used on construction sites. By 9:30 p.m., the men from our electrical contractor in St. Moritz were here, installing the heaters in the dining room, the great lounge and the bar. With that, the temperature in these rooms gradually came back up to 20°C (68°F).

Feeling like a general after a hard-won battle, I went to inspect the dining room. It was already dark and empty, but there was a new surprise: the heater had caught fire! Luckily, the firemen and electricians were still on hand, enjoying a well-deserved glass of wine in the staff dining room. They quickly put out the fire and repaired the heater.

At 1 p.m. on the following day, our two emissaries returned from Zurich with the replacement oil burners. Two hours later the entire heating system was back to normal. Our guests had scarcely noticed the whole drama.

← Felix Dietrich, Urs Kienberger, Maria Dietrich in the evening sun

The fourth generation

The next generation is a four-leaf clover. We have two sons and two daughters. Urs, the oldest, is an economist and a specialist in monetary theory and other arcane matters. He also moonlights as the youngest member of our board of directors, its only non-hotelier member. Our two daughters, Maria and Claudia, have trained in the hotel trade. Jürg, our youngest, whose interests include music, modern languages and art history, is studying at the University of Lausanne.

Maria is the only one of our children not born in a hospital but right here at the Waldhaus. Perhaps it was a sign of things to come! How she has now come back to the Waldhaus for good, after her schooling and further training, will be revealed shortly below.

I was chosen as the confirmation sponsor of a promising lad from St. Gallen by the name of Felix Dietrich. He often spent his vacations with us, first as a high school student and later as a bank apprentice. To earn gas money for his motorized "moped" bike, he would work as a cashier at the miniature golf, or temp in the dining room or office and in other departments. During a Christmas vacation, when he was 16 or so, we had just started to operate a refreshment stand at the ice rink at the request of the tourist office. Felix was put in charge and went down the hill every morning with a load

We were hotel children, we were not guests: Jürg Kienberger, about 1964

Urs and Jürg, 1980

of drinks, instant coffee, etc. The refreshment stand was not a hit, as the curling players preferred the restaurants in Sils to Felix's stand. The young entrepreneur was very unhappy with the meager sales so he decided to increase them by becoming his own best paying customer.

This episode and others prompted me to have a talk with Felix about his future. In fact, he said that after his bank apprenticeship, he wanted to change careers and enter the hotel business. At the end of his apprenticeship, Felix went to England to breathe some foreign air and to get to know the country and its language. Upon his return, he enrolled at the prestigious Lausanne Hotel School. The school's three-and-a-half-year program includes three five-month internships at hotels or restaurants, one each in the dining room, in the kitchen, and in the office. We regularly have interns from Lausanne and other hotel management schools at the Waldhaus. I offered Felix an opportunity to do his administrative internship at the Waldhaus, but asked him to spend another seven months with us as an assistant manager once he had finished his internship. In return, I promised to thoroughly acquaint him with our many-sided business with all of its advantages and disadvantages. He accepted, and I had every reason to be satisfied with my talented and enterprising assistant. What none of us had expected, though it now seems a beautifully logical development, was that he would also win our daughter Maria's heart. By December 1973, as his year with us was ending, they celebrated their engagement.

Felix and Maria Dietrich-Kienberger, January 11, 1975

"A Family Affair" in three stages. In 1930–1931, HEDY DIETRICH, nee Mäder (1913–2010), spent two seasons at the Waldhaus working as a maid for the owners' family. "I pitched in wherever I was needed," Felix Dietrich's mother told Andrin Willi in 2008. At Hedy Dietrich's recommendation, Rita Müller (later Kienberger; 1926–2006) came to the Waldhaus in 1948, to help out with the waitstaff for a few months. Rita and Hedy knew each other and were distantly related through their mothers. One thing led to another. And a few years later, Hedy Dietrich thought Rolf Kienberger would make a good confirmation sponsor for young Felix. "And he actually accepted."

For the next few years, the young couple alternated between jobs in other hotels in Switzerland and abroad and working at the Waldhaus. Felix also completed a series of management seminars organized by the Swiss Hotel Association, further strengthening his professional qualifications.

A heart attack in August 1977 forced me to take a break for several months. Our son Urs, who had just got his university degree at St. Gallen, took my place to supervise the remodeling of our main kitchen. Felix and Maria gave up their positions at a leading hotel in Interlaken and hurried home to help us. They settled permanently in Maria's parental home at the end of 1977. By that time, I had regained my health and was able to resume all my activities. I had had three months in which to contemplate how we two couples, and especially we two men, could divide up management tasks sensibly and efficiently. Rita and the younger generation agreed to my proposals. Since then and until further notice (wrote Rolf Kienberger in 1983), the two generations have been pulling together ... pulling, I am happy to report, in the same direction!

Felix Dietrich with film director Fred Zinnemann, who produced his final film, *Five Days One Summer*, in the Engadine in 1982

"The fifth generation, too, knows where to find us"

Claudia Klotz

With her parents and two, then three siblings, Rolf and Rita Kienberger's youngest daughter moved four times every year when she was little, from the Chantarella to the "Villa," to the Waldhaus, and back again, as Jürg Kienberger describes it on p. 260 "I loved moving," she says. "We moved to Sils permanently in the spring of 1963. It was my very first day of school, I can remember perfectly when Papa took Jürg, Maria and me from St. Moritz to the school in Sils. We first-graders started school at nine, while the older children started at eight, four grades in the same classroom, and since Maria was in fourth grade, she knew if I did something wrong. After that first day of school we climbed the hill to the Waldhaus, and that was where we stayed. It was the year in which the Waldhaus relaunched the winter season.

CLAUDIA KLOTZ, her husband Peter, their two daughters Beatrice and Manuela and their families can often be found together at the Waldhaus at family celebrations. Claudia Klotz did a hotel apprenticeship at the Sandi Hotel in Bad Ragaz and graduated from the Belvoirpark hotel school in Zurich. She worked at the Bellevue hotel in Braunwald and for one season at the Waldhaus. She and Peter, who grew up in Wolfsburg and Hanover, met when he was a chef at the Waldhaus.

In Sils we lived in the hotel. Urs and Jürg were in no. 30, Maria and I ... I don't remember the room number. I do remember Aunt Gertrud's efforts to give us a proper upbringing. She may be the reason we have such good manners. She was very strict with us, with others, not so much. Like Oreste Copes, who was her assistant in the cellar before he started working at the concierge desk. He could do whatever he wanted. Of course, we did try to provoke her sometimes. For example, we would make a point of going in the front door of the hotel, so that she would catch us and send us back out to use the staff entrance as we were supposed to. 'Do not run where there are guests,' how many times did we hear that? I did not like to sit quietly. Quite unlike my brother Jürg, who was two-and-a-half years younger. Nevertheless, or maybe precisely for that reason, I would often get him to join in. He may not have wanted to, but he had to come along, and then he would be scolded as well. Urs and Maria were the older children, and we the younger ones and that's how we were treated.

"As a child I wanted to be a farmer. When Aunt Gertrud informed me that as a farmer, I would also have to muck out the barn, I coolly replied that I would have hired hands to do that."

Many children in the village thought that we had it made up there on the hill, that we could do everything, eat with the guests every day, enjoy parties with them and so on. But we always had the same food as the staff. Our friends at school didn't notice that we were more or less just with our family, they couldn't really figure out what kind of life we had. For me, it was always something special when we got to mix with the guests, or when there were not enough children and we could join in the children's parties. Mr Knina, the band leader, let us join in, but we couldn't win any of the prizes, those were reserved for the guest children. We would have liked to win a prize, but we could live without them.

Our relationships as siblings changed over time. Today Maria and Jürg are closer, as are Urs and I. I don't know how that happened, but that is just how it is. I don't even know whether the others see it that way. I have never been sorry that my husband Peter and I, who both worked in the hotel/restaurant business, did not end up working at the Waldhaus. We are still all a close-knit family, if someone needs something, we are there for each other. For example, I help check the rooms at the end of the season. I go through all the rooms and make a list of what is missing or needs repaired, etc. I can do ten rooms in two hours. Maria helps, but she is much slower, as her beeper is always going off.

Brothers and sisters Jürg, Maria, Claudia and Urs Kienberger (from l. to r.)

I think it is important that those who are in charge of the operational side at

René's heroes. Executive chef René Zigerli and his team. 2nd from right, sitting: Peter Klotz, soon to be Waldhaus daughter Claudia Kienberger's husband

the Waldhaus are also the ones making the decisions. I usually agree with them. I don't interfere; it has to be right for those who work there. I think family members who are not directly involved in the business should not criticize too much, since the decision-makers are also the ones who carry the responsibility. Luckily, I am not one of the decision-makers. Otherwise the hotel would still be the same as it was a hundred years ago. Also, I would probably drive everyone crazy with my lack of optimism. The Waldhaus needs someone like Felix, like Claudio, confident of what has already been done rather than constantly aware of what still needs to be done.

Many people said that the family had made a grave mistake investing in the spa. But this investment was and is correct, and I strongly believe in and find it wonderful how Patrick and Claudio have managed to build on the successes of the fourth Waldhaus generation. We all know that things can quickly become very complicated and times can change, but up to now it has not happened. It isn't the dividends which are important to us, it is our shared interest that the Waldhaus continues to exist. If the hotel needs us, we are there. The fifth generation, too, knows where to find us."

← Pictured:
Paolo Tafuri

Working relations

Not only do we have loyal guests, our staff has been uncommonly loyal as well. Many of them have been with us uncommonly long. Some positions have passed from father to son, as was the case with Ugo Bianchi, our boilerman and mechanic from 1908 until the 1930s, who was succeeded by his son Antonio, who then held the same post for decades. It was true of our casserolier, our "scullery man" Giuseppe Vetti, who passed the job on to his son Giulio. There were the brothers, Peter and Josef Lipp, who worked for us right from the hotel's first season until 1930, the former as concierge, the latter as a doorman and driver. Peter Lipp was succeeded by Franz Waldegg, who started as a bellboy at age 14 and continued until he had to resign for health reasons in 1964. His sister Therese was one of the mainstays of our dining-room staff.

The record for length of service, though, is held by two cashiers and executive secretaries. Cécile Murith of Gruyeres (1870–1938) had been Josef Giger's secretary at the Du Lac in St. Moritz and throughout the construction of the Waldhaus. She continued working here until shortly before her death. Anny Reich (b. 1894) hardly expected to be with us for a good 50 years, when she joined us at the Palace in Lugano in 1924 as a governess and private tutor for me and my siblings. She eventually became Cécile Murith's successor and also, after the death of my parents, something of a substitute grandparent to our children.

To have employees stay with us for so many years has many advantages, but also may produce some problems. People can become very set in their ways and protective of what they perceive as their rightfully acquired status. A little episode illustrates the point.

On a quiet afternoon early in the season, two guests were sitting in our lounge. They had ordered tea from the *chef de rang* on duty. Recognizable by his black bow tie, a *chef de rang* is a senior waiter responsible for one dining room "station" with 20 to 40 covers. He has one or two assistants, called *commis*. On the afternoon in question, I noticed that after ten minutes the two guests were still waiting for their tea. I asked the *chef de rang*, who was idly standing there, why it had not been served yet. He averred that he was waiting for his *commis* who was just serving a bottle of mineral water to a room upstairs. When I suggested that he might actually walk the 40 paces to the pantry and get the tea himself, he was quite piqued in his professional pride!

We do what we can to prevent such on-the-job intransigence and further our staff's qualifications and motivation. We organize management training courses with external specialists for our senior employees. We also try to provide individual opportunities for seeing how things are done elsewhere, both in Switzerland and abroad. Our Executive Chef Rene Zigerli, for instance, has attended a "seminaire gastronomique" in Bordeaux and given guest performances at the Grand Hotel in Stockholm, the Hohenzollern Hotel in Osnabrück/Germany and the Dorchester in London (the CV of whose celebrated chef, Anton Mosimann, includes a stint at the Waldhaus kitchen).

Our efforts have been richly rewarded by many instances of dedicated and highly competent service, notwithstanding an occasional disappointment.

Cooking up a storm

The same winter season of 1970/71 that brought us the flood in the boiler room confronted us with one of the worst disappointments of its kind.

In the summer of 1970, our excellent executive chef, Albert Naef, told me that he wished to retire the following winter as his duties had taken their toll. To my disappointment, our search for a successor turned up

If you give them the right tools, they will give you good meals. December 1977: the Waldhaus kitchen after the first major renovation, with Chef René Zigerli (left)

only three candidates for what is usually a very coveted position. Based on qualifications and interviews, and after consulting a colleague who had employed one of the applicants for three years, I made my decision. He turned out to be a disaster. I had to summarily dismiss him after just three weeks. The man was a passable chef, but the atmosphere in his kitchen and his relationship with the head waiter and other waiters was abysmal. Also, he squandered supplies in an alarming manner. With the money he wasted during the unfortunate three weeks he was with us, my wife and I could easily have paid for a trip around the world. Albert Naef came to our rescue, postponing his well-deserved retirement until I succeeded in finding a worthy successor.

The birthday surprise

On the morning of February 10, 1978, my 61st birthday, our concierge informed me that Agostino, our hard-working but unpredictable engineer of several years' standing, had called from Italy to say that he and his friend Antida, a chambermaid who had also been with us for years, had left and would not be back. While Agostino had already expressed his intention of returning to his native Italy at some point in the future and had even begun to instruct a fellow employee in the secrets of his demanding and complicated duties, he had firmly promised to stay with us until the end of the season.

Rudi Knina: making more than music

For 23 years, from 1951 to 1974, Rudi Knina from Vienna was in charge of our little orchestra and delighted our guests and us with his music, his unflappable charm and his talent for getting children and adults alike

ANNI KNINA:
"My husband was the head of the Waldhaus trio from 1950 to 1974. I had a laundry in Heiden near St. Gallen. One day Mrs Kienberger asked me if I could fill in at the Waldhaus. I had already given up the laundry by then. That's how my husband and I came to be working together at the Waldhaus. Rudi had warned me, 'If they ask you about helping out, do not ever admit that you were a head housekeeper. Those are always the bad guys.' When I arrived in Sils, Mrs Kienberger said to me, 'Welcome, you'll now be the head housekeeper.'"

to just plain have fun (see p. 298). That the morale of our "troops" never sagged during the slow first winter season of 1963/64, for instance, owed much to Rudi Knina's infectious good cheer.

On one of the dreaded February or March weekends when there can be over a hundred arrivals and departures on the same day, I was making the rounds to see which rooms were ready to be occupied. To my surprise, I ran into the diminutive Maestro in a room which had just been vacated. There he was, changing the linens as if there was nothing to it! To be fair, I do have to add that his wife was our housekeeper at the time.

"Specialists can find a problem for every solution"

Guido Schmidt

"Each time I enter the hotel, I don't know what awaits me. When I came for the first time in April 1978, the dining room was being expanded. A major undertaking. Now, as I leave the Waldhaus 41 years later, the dining room addition is being refurbished with new windows and better insulation, and so I have come full circle. My predecessor had left in a mad rush. He just called from Italy to say that he wasn't coming back. This meant I had to teach myself one thing after the other. I had no idea where anything was; fortunately, the technology of the time was much simpler. The heating system consisted of just one group for the whole hotel. I couldn't believe that you could run and heat such a huge building with so many guest rooms and other spaces with just one heating system and a circulation pump. Today the system is divided up into various zones which can be controlled individually. There wasn't much of a ventilation system, in the kitchen the air was simply sucked out. Today it's a different matter: think 'filter,' 'heat recovery,' and so on.

My constant worry was the heating system, as the enormous steam boiler did not always function reliably, and you had to regulate the amount of water in the system very precisely. Many hotels had steam heat at the time, it dated back to when the Waldhaus was made ready for its first winter season. Some of the old double-paned windows from then are still in use, even though many of the windows and doors have been replaced during renovations. Another headache was the kitchen. I maintained all of the kitchen equipment, luckily the electric range was new and represented technological progress and a major investment, compared to the coal range it had replaced. I was inevitably and constantly in 'touch' with the new range, as there would always be one burner or the other out of order. A kitchen is especially subject to wear and tear. Nowadays that costs a lot more. I was able to quickly repair an electric burner, a cable, a switch on my own—but when it comes to an induction range, my hands are tied.

I could have used many hands when it came to the lighting. When I first started working here, there were only conventional light bulbs. I had to go through the public rooms at least once a week and replace bulbs, I usually did this at 5 a.m. A Sisyphean task. Like the daily winding of the master clock at the cashier's office. I restored all the Magneta clocks and got the system running again. This old clock downstairs still controls all the wall clocks on the floors, in the staff restaurant, the kitchen, the coffee kitchen, the *salon bleu* and above the elevator in the main entrance. A purely mechanical system which, by the way, has to be adjusted when the temperature changes. Truly ingenious.

GUIDO SCHMIDT has been our in-house engineer, with multiple tasks and talents, since April 13, 1978. The St. Moritz native, who also happens to be a passionate mountain-goer and photographer, did a precision-mechanics apprenticeship at Oerlikon-Bührle (an arms manufacturer) and then became a teacher and caregiver at a sheltered workshop for the handicapped. Now he is retiring. He will continue to look after some of his favorites at the Waldhaus, especially the 1910 Welte-Mignon piano (see p. 48).

The remodeling of the great lounge in 1991, when it was extended by six meters, 20 feet, into the forest, was also impressive. At the time, there was only one helicopter which could carry and place the long steel girders behind the hotel: a Russian Kamov with coaxial rotors.

The expense was worth it. Even now, the great lounge radiates a timeless warmth, and I enjoy that. Some other public areas and guest rooms have already been remodeled twice over during my many years working here. A hotel is a never-ending 'life cycle' of construction.

After countless renovations I am certain about one thing. Every planner, every architect, every specialist has a problem for every solution. That could sum up my entire working life here. The lowly in-house technician is no academic, but often experience is the best teacher. There are, of course, excellent planners and I can understand well thought-out arguments, but if somebody comes along and does not know the context, they will have a hard time convincing me. In construction, what appears to be cheaper today often brings higher costs in the long run, which one often fails to take into account. I have repeated this so many times, that even I can understand why the Waldhaus may sometimes be tired of me.

"The hotel was state-of-the-art, technologically speaking, when it first opened. There was the system for summoning maids and porters, a built-in vacuum cleaner and so much more. Things constantly prone to breakdowns. A never-ending repair process."

Sauna, indoor tennis court, parking garage, the second parking garage, staff apartments, more guest rooms, everything was renovated and enlarged, but it was still only Erwin, the in-house carpenter, and I who remained in charge of maintenance. At some point it got to be too much, and we were able to hire an additional person as technical staff. The systems, too, had become more complex. At first, we didn't have smoke alarms. No TVs in the rooms; the Waldhaus had exactly three sets for rent, but they were hardly ever in demand. There was one public TV set in the reading room, but neither the choice of stations nor the reception was particularly thrilling. Gradually the whole hotel was hooked up. I experienced the step-by-step advance of digitalization. In the old days, you had to wear slippers if you wanted to enter the room where the telephone equipment was, nowadays the phone system takes up hardly any space. Everything is constantly changing."

50 (or rather, 89) years ago, secretary at the Waldhaus Hotel

Adeline Burger

When in 1983 we celebrated 75 years of the Waldhaus, the *Neue Zürcher Zeitung* took the opportunity to publish a fine article. As a result, we were surprised a few months later by the following contribution which appeared in the *NZZ* of February 23, 1984. Unfortunately, we missed our chance to personally get back in touch with the writer. So we cannot add any further details to Adeline Burger's fascinating memories.

The NZZ *wrote: "75 years ago, on June 15, 1908, the Waldhaus Hotel in Sils Maria opened its doors: one of the hotels which have contributed to the worldwide reputation of the Swiss hotel industry. In 1924, the Waldhaus was open in winter for the first time. We received the following personal response to the article about this anniversary in* NZZ *no. 239 of October 13, 1983."*

"Even now, I can see myself as I was 53 years ago, coming through the revolving door with my suitcase in hand, shyly looking into the great lounge. I was dazed: all those guests enjoying afternoon tea, and the lovely music! A bellboy brought me back to reality with the question of what I was looking for. 'The office,' I said. 'Oh, you are standing right in front of it.' He opened the door and a nice lady received me. It was Mademoiselle Cécile, my boss. Male secretaries smoked too much for her taste, and so she had been granted a female assistant. And after receiving a cable that said, 'Will you accept secretarial position at Waldhaus Hotel Sils Maria?,' I was lucky enough to be employed by this grand hotel.

The Waldhaus was 'a model of the Swiss hotel industry' not only for its guests, but also for its employees. Even back then, its staff had decent accommodations, and Mrs Kienberger personally tasted the meals for the three staff 'tables' [divided by hierarchy]. No mashed potatoes that had turned sour and, after having been sent back, reappeared the next day as potato soup, with the cook tauntingly saying afterwards, 'Well, you didn't eat yesterday's mashed potatoes, but you did eat today's soup.' (Accommodations, too, were a problem in many places. At the B. Hotel in Andermatt, I first had to sleep on a sack of leaves and instead of a closet there was a piece of twine.)

The discrete entry in the September 1930 Waldhaus guestbooks for Comte et Comtesse d'Ourem et suite actually wasn't for Alfonso XIII of Spain with his wife, but Manuel II, the last king of Portugal. King Manuel (1889–1932) had to abdicate in 1910, and he and his spouse Auguste Victoria (1890–1966) lived in comfortable exile in Twickenham in west London. She was the sister of Friedrich Prince of Hohenzollern-Sigmaringen, whose family were regular guests at the Waldhaus.

The Waldhaus had many prominent guests. From my office perch, I could admire Elisabeth Bergner on her balcony. I took dictation for several guests during my break times. I particularly remember Professor de Quervain, whose wife would always come to get him, 'Come, let's go for a walk.' And the dictation would be immediately postponed to the next day. King Alfons of Spain with entourage was also there. They occupied the entire fifth floor, and the best waiter, wearing white gloves, had to serve them. Apropos best waiter: once, as he was serving the hotel manager and some guests, he stumbled, managed not to drop the tray but a chicken leg flew out from the tail of his tailcoat. Mr. Kienberger told this story with a grin, but the waiter was reprimanded.

King Alfons' car also left a lasting impression on me: a Maybach with an inlaid golden coat of arms on the doors. The chauffeur explained everything to the concierge and I was allowed to listen in. Once the maître d' came and got me so that I could look down from the mezzanine into the dining room. I had to see that. It was a nouveau riche couple who, it seems, had such terrible table manners that a screen had been placed around their table. That is what a first-class hotel is all about: they think of everything and protect guests from each other.

When I read that last year the turnover at the Waldhaus reached nearly six million francs, I remembered the first time that I had 10,000 in the daily ledger. I was so excited that Mr. Kienberger gave me a box of pralines like the guests were given upon departure. And for every additional 10,000 I would get another box! It added up to several boxes because as soon as the entries started to near 10,000, I would ask the bartender for an instalment payment. He settled up with the office every three or four days. It was an exciting time.

At the end of the season I was given a reference letter. It was so good I could hardly believe it. Mr. Stumm, for whom I sometimes took dictation, happened to be in the office. He advised me to run up and down the steps to the fifth floor for as long as I could and then return to the office. When I reappeared, out of breath, he said—Ms. Cécile had shown him the reference letter—that he totally agreed, except that he hadn't seen much of my 'calm disposition.' The letter of reference also said that they would be happy to hire me for the winter season.

Thus I came to spend the winter season 1930/31 there as well. At one time in the course of that winter, Sils Maria was completely snowed in and cut off from the world for a few days. The postal bus couldn't get through and the telephone lines were interrupted. It was wonderful and most of the guests enjoyed it. But there were a few who nearly despaired. Such as a Belgian stockbroker couple. It was admirable that the Waldhaus was able to feed all of the guests and employees as usual; they had that many provisions on hand. And it was also a sign of how well the hotel was organized. I worked a few more seasons in first-class hotels, but I most enjoyed my time in Sils Maria at the Waldhaus Hotel."

← From Waldhaus generation five (below and right) to six, on the preceding double page: Elias, Flavia, Selena and Christian, four of Rita and Rolf Kienberger's 13 great-grandchildren

What will the future bring?

With more than 40,000 guest-nights and annual revenues of CHF 7 million (in 1983), the Waldhaus appears set on a good course.

What will the future bring? The answer may lie in the hands of the seven dwarfs, our grandchildren, who are looking ahead with confidence and optimism..

In the next chapters, it is Urs Kienberger who resumes telling the story.

Claudio Dietrich, *March 27, 1977

Franca Dietrich, *August 7, 1978

Beatrice Klotz, *February 7, 1979
(Photo Fritz, Wengen)

Manuela Klotz, *August 25, 1982
(Photo Fritz, Wengen)

Patrick and Sandra Dietrich, *December 4, 1980

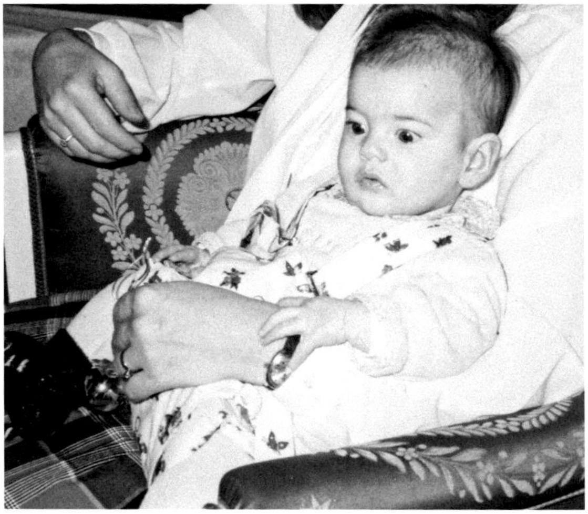

Carla Dietrich, *August 31, 1983

Lena Kienberger: three years after the 1983 book, Rolf and Rita Kienberger gave an equally warm welcome to grandchild no. 8 (*June 4, 1986)

1984–88: changing of the guard

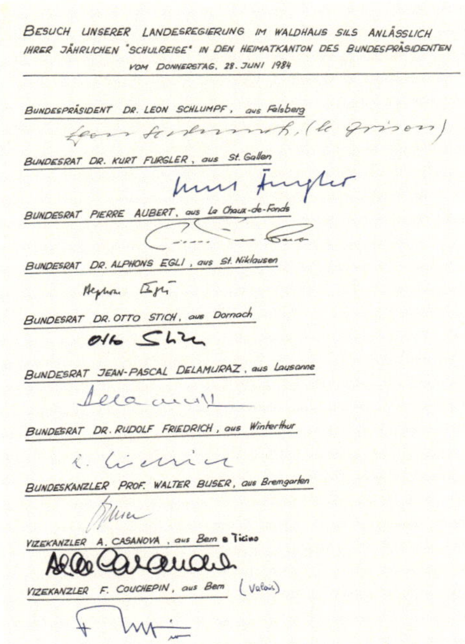

BESUCH UNSERER LANDESREGIERUNG IM WALDHAUS SILS ANLÄSSLICH IHRER JÄHRLICHEN "SCHULREISE" IN DEN HEIMATKANTON DES BUNDESPRÄSIDENTEN VOM DONNERSTAG, 28. JUNI 1984

BUNDESPRÄSIDENT DR. LEON SCHLUMPF, aus Felsberg

BUNDESRAT DR. KURT FURGLER, aus St. Gallen

BUNDESRAT PIERRE AUBERT, aus La Chaux-de-Fonds

BUNDESRAT DR. ALPHONS EGLI, aus St. Niklausen

BUNDESRAT DR. OTTO STICH, aus Dornach

BUNDESRAT JEAN-PASCAL DELAMURAZ, aus Lausanne

BUNDESRAT DR. RUDOLF FRIEDRICH, aus Winterthur

BUNDESKANZLER PROF. WALTER BUSER, aus Bremgarten

VIZEKANZLER A. CASANOVA, aus Bern e Ticino

VIZEKANZLER F. COUCHEPIN, aus Bern (Valais)

From June 28 to June 29, 1984, all of Switzerland was governed from Sils

From June 28 to 29, 1984, all of Switzerland was governed from Sils. That is, the entire seven-member Federal Council which forms our national government stayed at the Waldhaus. Each one of them is chosen in turn to be president for a year, and by tradition he or she gets to organize something of a field trip to his home canton for the entire Council in early summer. In that year, Leon Schlumpf from Graubünden was our president, and he chose to come here.

Such moments are proud and salient highlights of our history, no less than major building projects or prestigious awards. Some of our biggest milestones and proudest accomplishments are much less visible, though. The transition from Generation III to Generation IV at the Waldhaus was a fine example of that.

In 1987, when Rolf Kienberger was 70, Maria and Felix Dietrich became the sole managers of the hotel after ten years of shared management responsibilities between the two generations. The start of the ten shared years had been considerably rockier than what Rolf Kienberger describes on p. 188. Maria and Felix, aged 24 and 27, had hurried home

1978: Rolf Kienberger and Felix Dietrich are at one

after our father's serious heart problems of August 1977. Luckily, by the winter of 1977/78, Rolf Kienberger had recovered quite well, and he was ready to take back the helm. But now Felix was there, too. It turned into a very challenging season, with plenty of guests, but many unresolved questions between the two of them. In spring, when the season was over, Rolf and Felix got together and went on a spring outing which became a Waldhaus legend. They had a frank discussion of what had happened. Together, they managed to draw up a clear and intelligent division of labor. Carefully thought out, faithfully and systematically implemented, this plan became a harmonious and beneficial foundation for an auspicious Waldhaus decade based on mutual respect and hard work.

This was not automatically a Waldhaus tradition. We have already described the difficult and ultimately unsuccessful transition from Josef Giger, the worn-out founder, to his son Gustav, and in 1918, the brisk imposition of Oskar Kienberger as a new commander in chief. The second transition, a generation later, had not been all that much easier. 71-year-old Oskar Kienberger passed the management on to Rolf Kienberger (soon joined by Rita Kienberger) in 1950, but retained the last word in all major—and many minor—decisions, also holding on to his controlling majority of shares. It stayed that way for more than twelve years. The resulting much-delayed reintroduction of a full winter season, which O. K. resisted with all the force of his convictions and his personality, put the future of the entire enterprise at risk. And it was a miracle that Rolf and Rita Kienberger persevered and never lost patience through these many long and trying years.

Just as in the woods surrounding our hotel, the old trees have to make room for the young ones so that they can flourish. Figuratively speaking, this is what has happened in our family business, and I am pleased to say that we have succeeded. Since June 1, 1987, Felix and Maria Dietrich have taken command of our business. (Rolf Kienberger in the 1987 annual report)

« Nous pouvons vous recommander le Waldhaus à Sils Maria qui est situé à quelques km de St. Moritz seulement et qui dispose encore de chambres libres pour la période en question. »
In the difficult years, when the Waldhaus was finally open again for winter in the 1950s (but at first, hesitantly, only over the end-of-year holidays), Albert Candrian wrote this wonderfully generous recommendation to each and every guest on the Suvretta waiting list.

In 1987, by contrast, it was a very different story. A very successful decade of shared management was now followed by an equally harmonious and orderly next step. "Rolf K. retires. He remains chairman and delegate of the board. By agreement with F. D. and M. D., he remains in charge of bookkeeping and wine purchases; he will have a continued say in financial matters, investment decisions, and the hiring and compensation of managers and assistant managers."

Rolf Kienberger had not been chairman for long. His father had held on to this position until his death. Then our cousin Alfred Kienberger (1907–83), GM at the Trois Rois in Basel, took over, with Albert Candrian serving as deputy chairman. Albert Candrian (1904–85), GM of the Suvretta House from 1954 to 1968 and of the Seiler hotels in Zermatt before that, was also family; his wife Helene was the daughter of Mali and Josef Wolflisberg. With their wealth of experience and close connection to the Waldhaus, Uncle Fredy and Uncle Bert were valuable advisors and conversation partners for our parents, and provided indispensable support during many difficult days. Upon their passing, in close succession, Rolf Kienberger became chairman. Felix and I had been elected members somewhat earlier.

In this way, the Waldhaus has been the center of our work, our efforts, our passion and sometimes our struggles, from one generation of our family to the next. But also, the center of our lives, our home. In fact, in Sils, our family had always literally lived right in the hotel, with the lone exception of our grandparents moving over to the top of the garage between the seasons, during the impoverished years when the seasons themselves were so short. The family had no real apartment in the hotel,

1983: Rita Kienberger with the seniors of the Waldhaus board. From left to right, Rolf Kienberger, Fredy Kienberger and Albert Candrian-Wolflisberg. They were a good team for a long time

just a few rooms plus a private dining room on the mezzanine floor, and a handsome living room on the floor where the public rooms are. The sign on the door of that room said "Privé," and that is indeed what it was for us, our private space in the middle of hotel life. The setup was very practical. One door led to the hallway in front of the lounge, and another straight into the cashier's and the manager's office. Upstairs, our parents' bedroom had an internal window looking directly down to the entrance hallway and the concierge desk (falling asleep, you could hear the music from the lounge and the bar). The dining room overlooked the forecourt in front of the hotel, so we could see arrivals and departures even before the concierge would summon us. And on the way, you passed other windows which offered a look down into the main dining room. Obviously, our privacy was very limited, the hotel and the public areas were never very far away. Nor did we have very much space, and especially, we did not have a kitchen of our own. In the 1970s and 1980s, with three generations living side-by-side, Rolf and Rita Kienberger (and Aunt Gertrud, my father's sister) on one hand, and all the Dietrichs on the other—with one child, then two, then four and finally five—living conditions became rather precarious. Nowadays it is hard to even imagine how that worked. But help was on the way.

Our great-grandmother Amalia Giger, suffering from gout, was already in a wheelchair when the Waldhaus opened. Was that the purpose of all the windows that look down into the public rooms from the mezzanine: that she could always see what was going on and intervene when something went awry? That's what family lore says ... though architectural historians tell us that 110 years ago it may simply have been general practice to fit all enclosed spaces with a window or a skylight.

In 1985, the last stage of what we jokingly call the "Palais du Garage" (see p. 181) was completed. The final stage comprised two buildings with apartments and efficiencies, a first for the Waldhaus: in 1984, the Chesa Spuonda opened (spuonda meaning "hillside" in Romansch), and in 1985, the Chesa Godin (god is a forest, godin a little forest). They were intended for our staff ... and included an apartment in the Chesa Godin for Rolf and Rita Kienberger in their retirement. Another, large apartment in the same building was unexpectedly left over. It was intended for Executive Chef René Zigerli, but his family was, for understandable reasons, reluctant to move from the place they had rented in the middle of the village. So, the Dietrichs had the idea that they and their children could move into the new apartment. Grandma Rita welcomed the idea with enthusiasm. Rolf Kienberger, not so much. "A hotelier ought to live in the hotel and nowhere else," he sternly maintained; but gradually he came around, too. Both the Kienbergers and the Dietrichs would now have a real, private apartment.

The Chesa Godin got finished at the very last moment, just before Christmas. The family's rooms in the hotel had already all been promised, and rented out, for the upcoming holidays. So, they had to clean everything out and move in a mad rush. For our family, and for the Waldhaus, that was par for the course: the hotel and its needs come first, no matter what. But in the end, the change was a blessing, particularly for the Dietrichs. And it has had a lasting effect. Would Claudio and Patrick Dietrich still have decided on an apprenticeship as cooks, when the time came—laying such a sound and tangible foundation for everything that came later in their hotel careers—if they had not spent their childhood in an apartment that allowed them to get an early taste of helping out and experimenting in their own kitchen at home? It is telling that we four hotel children from the preceding generation, who did not have that experience, never really got into cooking, and in some cases still haven't—precisely because we grew up in the hotel, as paradoxical as that may sound. Funny, too, that Rolf and Rita Kienberger, who very much enjoyed their own new apartment, almost never cooked anything there. Their fridge was stocked with little more than breakfast items, plus plenty of drinks for themselves and their guests. And always, of course, something for their grandchildren, who never went away hungry.

"I thought that was so nice, a manager with a family and small children." DONATA WILLI (82) of the Posthotel Löwen—"the Lion"—in Mulegns on the Julier road, is Andrin Willi's aunt, and she worked for Rolf and Rita Kienberger ("under Rolf Kienberger," as she puts it) at the Chantarella Hotel in St. Moritz in the winters of 1958 and 1959. Urs, Maria and Claudia were six, five and two; Jürg was born in 1958. "When the weather was nice, the three older children and their nanny came to see me at the inventory office in the morning. They would knock politely and I would say, 'Come in.' Maria came in first, then Urs and Claudia. Every time, I would ask what they wanted. 'We'd like to have our sleds,' said Maria. 'Yes, here they are,' I said. They always left them with me because they were afraid that the 'ski man,' where the other sleds were kept, would rent them out. Then they took their sleds and went on their way."

How is it today? In 1996/97, a third annex with 17 apartments and efficiencies was built for our staff, adding to our options. Thus, Claudio and Cornelia as well as Patrick and Ursina with their children still live on the hotel grounds, while Felix and Maria, as well as Carla Lehner and my wife and I have moved to the village.

"Filling the children with enthusiasm for the Waldhaus"

Maria Dietrich-Kienberger

MARIA DIETRICH (*1953), nee Kienberger ("Generation IV"), has spent no less than 55 of her first 66 years at the Waldhaus. She was literally born in it, grew up in it and, in winter, at the Chantarella in St. Moritz and returned to the Waldhaus for good when she was 24. She managed the hotel with her husband Felix for 33 years. The mother of Claudio, Franca, Patrick, Sandra and Carla has always tried, and continues to try, to keep in balance both people and numbers.

"In the summer of 1977, after my father's heart attack, we unexpectedly returned to the Waldhaus. No one knew how things would turn out. Claudio was just a few months old. Felix was working as head of HR at the Victoria Jungfrau in Interlaken, where the season had started just a week after Claudio was born. Our little family didn't see much of him as his job was very demanding. I went to Sils by myself with Claudio, to pitch in wherever I could. Not to help run the hotel as I wouldn't have been up to the task at that time, but I was able to take over the treasury and also help my mother with other matters. It was a valuable time, and I learned a lot from her.

After the summer season ended and the winter season began, Felix joined us in Sils. My father was soon on the mend, and it was clear to him that we didn't need to stay. But, we wanted to stay! My father was 60, I was 24 and Felix 27, when we decided to join forces. The first season was a trial. Felix didn't want to take on just any job, he had clear ideas of how he wanted to help shape the Waldhaus. Papa saw things differently and continued to make all the decisions himself and ran the hotel just as he had in the past. This upset Felix. Luckily, the two of them went on a long mountain hike after the season ended and talked over what had gone wrong. They put together a plan, divided up responsibilities, and amazingly my father and Felix followed it. From that point on, all went well. From the start, Felix was involved in human resources management; one of his great strengths is dealing with people. Papa took care of purchasing and the wine cellar, and both of them looked after the guests. The wine cellar was one of my father's great passions which he enjoyed right up to the end of his life.

I didn't take on too many duties as we had our little family. I didn't want the children to be brought up by a nanny, I wanted to spend time with them myself. We could never have raised five children on our own. At the Waldhaus, though, with the support of my parents, that was possible, and it worked well until my father turned 70. At that point my parents retired, although my mother continued to work behind the scenes and was also a great help with our children.

We all ate together, we all lived at the hotel, we were very close and our children heard many stories. My parents filled them with enthusiasm for the Waldhaus. When we later set up our little museum, Carla in particular was happy that she could now see all the objects from grandma and grandpa's stories.

In our own childhood, our family went through some very hard times but our parents never let on. Once, Claudia asked our mother why we never took a vacation by the sea. My mother set out to say, 'because we don't have enough m...,' 'not enough time,' she quickly corrected herself. Uh-oh, we children thought, it's not just the time. Nevertheless, my parents were always upbeat, they never gave us the feeling that they were under pressure even though the Waldhaus was a heavy burden. They always made us and our children see the hotel as a great gift and showed us that investing time and effort in it was well worth it. We learned from my parents how to smoothly pass on the hotel to the next generation. My father had had a much more difficult time of it, as my grandfather did not give up control of the hotel until his death. We thus learned how to do it, while my parents had learned how not to do it."

← Maître d'Hôtel Walter Nana, at the Waldhaus since 1985, takes off. Also see p. 169.

A Cast of Thousands

If it says "family" on the cover, there must be "family" in it. This Waldhaus book confirms that in many ways; but it would be absurd to tell our hotel history only in family terms. The Waldhaus would not have survived a single day of a single season with just the family and without all of the other people who have contributed and collaborated and helped shape the hotel. This goes well beyond the trite acknowledgment that it takes many heads and hands for the hotel to function. A hotel, in its essence, is not just a physical entity, it is more than just an accumulation of bricks and beds. A hotel is also, and perhaps to a greater extent, the sum of the services it provides and of the people who provide them. With their time and effort, their lives, their personalities, their skills, their idiosyncrasies, their dreams and ambitions, as well as their worries and their own limitations, all of these people help to shape and define the hotel.

Like a small village behind the scenes. Mardi Gras 2013—a staff party after working hours

What's more, behind the scenes, the Waldhaus is something like a small village. With more than 50 staff bedrooms in the main building and nearly 30 apartments and efficiencies in the annexes, the Waldhaus is, at least during the seasons, not only a place of work but also a home to close to three-quarters of our staff. Beyond work, the hotel thus becomes a fixed part of their lives, and at the same time they put more than "just" their work into the Waldhaus. The hotel and the people who work in it are interwoven in a special way. At the risk of sounding rather pretentious in talking about what is, after all, just a hotel, we might go as far as calling it our shared destiny.

For obvious reasons, then, this chronicle ought to devote at least as much attention to those who work with us as to our family. There are many. Hollywood blockbusters like Ben Hur and Cleopatra used to boast that they had "a cast of thousands." It is not a statement that comes to mind when you think of the anything-but-gargantuan Waldhaus. Our payroll for the summer of 2019 comprises 161 names, not counting the eleven musicians who by turns make up our resident trio. And yet, if we were to include just those who have worked here at one time or another since the year 2000, when our current century began, we would already have one thousand names.

"The Waldhaus would not have survived a single day of a season without those who work for and with us." It was only during the slowest weeks at the beginning and end of the season during World War II, when operations were reduced to a minimum anyway, that the family literally did almost all the work by themselves. Our grandfather welcomed the guests at the front, our grandmother, already in her sixties, made the beds and the rooms, and plucky Aunt Gertrud did all the cooking.

Waldhaus aficionados, happy to recognize many of the same faces each time they return, may be surprised by this number. In fact, many staff members stay for years and years, and we can rightly say that the Waldhaus is not only our life's work but also theirs. But there are also those who only work at the Waldhaus for a season, or a year, or two, as part of their training or careers. In a seasonal business, moving on is fairly easy, you don't have to loudly and conspicuously give notice, you can just say: "Thank you, but I will be doing something else this summer." It is good that we have both. We are happy and proud of our veterans with their many years of service and are greatly indebted to them—but if we *only* had long-serving veterans, this would not be an easy place to run.

Whether our employees are here for a short or a long time, not everyone will take on an equally important role. For some, the Waldhaus is perhaps a mere episode without much weight, just as they may have only a small impact on the Waldhaus story; or they simply do not want

Udo scores. Udo Nagiller, the legendary barman. He first worked here in 1953, and left as the millennium came to an end.

For generations of guest children, she was the face of the Waldhaus. Anita Bryner at the children's club.

to become too involved even if they stay on. Many others, though, make a deep impression—sometimes in the shortest of times—with the force of their initiative, their abilities and their personality. All the more so if they stay for half their working life, or all of it. And some of the impressions are lasting even if they are unplanned and unintended.

The man who was supposed to park a visitor's expensive car and almost drove it over the high retaining wall that separates the forecourt from the Fex road, hitting the accelerator instead of the brake, will remember the Waldhaus for a long time, and the Waldhaus will remember him. Fortunately, he got stuck on the edge, with the front wheels already in the air; better not to think about what could have happened. Or, much worse yet, what could have happened to the young apprentice who fell out of a window at the very highest point of the Waldhaus, on a cold winter night, and survived almost unharmed—thanks to a double miracle: that the tower window from which she fell was the only one with a balcony under it, two floors below; and the room to which the balcony belonged was occupied that night, with the guests waking up and letting her in out of the life-threatening cold.

So many stories, so many men and women who have added to the Waldhaus story and earned our respect, affection and gratitude! Over the years, many of them have found a voice in the "Waldhaus News." It has been published once a year since 2002—16 times in just as many years, with versatile Waldhaus veteran Hubert Halter as editor-in-chief and me as copy editor and contributor of titles and subtexts: a total of 348 newspaper pages in that time, which would be the equivalent of close to 1,000 pages in this book. And, already, 36 more pages are in the new "111" anniversary edition that our management assistant Sandra Fuchs and Felix Dietrich have been working on. You can see the problem. 1,000 pages—who is willing to play the judge to decide whose voice and whose story should get into this book and what should not? We do not want to play this tricky game; we do not just appreciate a handful of employees but a great many of them. As a result, this book is largely limited to an arbitrary selection of conversations by Andrin Willi with "eye witnesses." One day we will do better, perhaps bringing out a collected volume from the Waldhaus News.

Meanwhile, who makes the Waldhaus team? As much as we strive to find first-rate and qualified staff and to provide them with the right conditions for their work, we do not arrogantly believe that "only the best are good enough for us." As Patrick Dietrich says on p. 309 ("Where are we headed?"), what counts just as much is how we function together as human beings, both among ourselves and towards our guests. This implies loyalty and commitment, which in turn are not just a one-way street. We do not simply change horses at the first sign of a weakness. As employers, we willingly accept the challenge of continuing to work with those who want the right thing but do not always achieve it.

Nevertheless, what the hotel requires is no walk in the park. To keep a five-star hotel in shape and satisfy its guests is a hard, intensive and demanding job. By and large, our approach seems to have worked fairly well. We often hear from guests that the Waldhaus is right on track with its team. That is what counts in the end: we have to deliver, things have to *work* for our guests.

There are plenty of related challenges, some particular to a family firm like ours. If we want a good, capable crew, it stands to reason that they in turn will not be satisfied if we just tell them to do this and do that. They will want to contribute their own ideas and use their own judgement as well, have some leeway in shaping their own work and, by extension, the hotel. Only then will they really feel at home, and only then will the Waldhaus fully benefit from what they are and what they can do. The difficulty is that our enterprise relies heavily on a triad of distinctive, interwoven factors: the strong family presence, an extraordinary sense of continuity, of remaining true to oneself over very long periods of time, and a conscious strategy of going our own way in many respects. We firmly believe in these principles, since they account for much of the hotel's charm and originality. What exactly that charm and originality is, is never easy to pin down, or to explain to others, but that makes it no less real.

I have spent much time contemplating this dilemma. How do we maintain our strong family presence and still leave enough room for our employees as well, particularly the best of them? We have to ensure that we do not block or demotivate them at every turn. At the same time, we should remain aware that their legitimate initiatives and the professional leeway they rightly claim might also cause the hotel to vacillate between one course and another, undermining its vital continuity. The natural tendency of those who are good at their jobs and want to simplify their work is to focus on the practical which can also gently and subtly undermine the hotel's character, make it more ordinary, banal and common. Conversely, we must ask ourselves at every turn how to keep this continuity, which we cherish so much, from turning into rigidity and immobility. And who keeps us on the right side of the fine line between "different" and "unworkable" or "too pretentiously peculiar"? We must remain open to a constant give-and-take with those who work for us, sensitive to these tensions and conflicting goals. We can neither ignore these conflicts, nor simply hope to get rid of them once and for all by following some glib textbook prescriptions from corporate organization theory. Instead, we have to tackle them again and again, with attention, honesty and an open mind.

The crucial role of those who work with us also obviously finds its reflection in our company's books. Nearly one of every two francs that

Gianni raises the flag. Giovanni Rosano (Photo Stefan Pielow, 2008)

we earn goes towards personnel expenses, broadly defined—for chefs and waiters and chambermaids, but also the entire management and the carpenter, the florist and the hiking guides, the masseurs and musicians. In 2018, the payroll absorbed 45 percent of our earnings. 2018 was a good year; in more difficult years the share is even higher, as you cannot simply reduce the labor input across the board in line with the occupancy rate.

This statistic gives expression to what we have said about the importance of our staff. But it also stands for a major economic challenge. Almost half of our income is already spoken for before the invoices for everything else arrive—ranging from all the supplies to energy and marketing, from the cost of the free guest passes for public transportation and (in summer) the cable cars and the boat on the lake, to many other things large and small, stamps, interest on our loans, insurance, or the profit-sharing bonuses for management at different levels. You can easily see what a challenge that represents, and how much of a struggle it is to set aside the roughly 20–25 percent of revenues for maintenance and investment which the Waldhaus ideally needs to ensure its long-term survival, so that one day someone else can write a sequel to this chronicle.

Housekeeping! (Photo: Stefan Pielow, 2007)

Why *is* it a struggle, continually challenging us, and our guests' ability and willingness to pay? You might rightly ask: if the Waldhaus really is such a good thing, as we keep claiming, shouldn't it by now have become a steady and easy moneymaker, after more than a century of existence? Speaking as an economist, I could give you a fairly simple (if simultaneously complex and intractable) reason for that.

Most jobs at the hotel are only marginally more productive than they were in our great-grandparents' time. A good chef does not produce umpteen times more tasty meals, a skillful and experienced waiter does not serve umpteen times more guests, a thorough and hard-working housekeeping employee does not make up umpteen times more rooms than their equally hard-working predecessors of the belle epoque. That's in the nature of these services and in no way implies that the hotel trade is simply stuck in the past. What appears on our tables, what we expect from those who wait on them, and what a five-star guest room should offer and what it takes to maintain and service it, has actually changed quite dramatically, be it in technical, social or cultural terms. And there have been technical advances and labor-saving devices in our trade, too, but they have in many cases been more than offset by new bells and whistles added to the "product." For example, housekeeping staff no longer have to empty chamber pots or keep providing pitchers of fresh hot and cold water, but each and every room now has an entire shiny bathroom of its own to be cleaned.

Renato, team player, umpire, coach. Renato Pellegrinelli, much more than "just" our Pastry Chef since 1986

In Switzerland as a whole, productivity has greatly increased during these past 111 years, and salaries and other working conditions have grown accordingly. In a fair and open society, the benefits from these advances cannot simply be limited to the sectors in which they arose. Working conditions and salaries in the hotel and restaurant industry cannot differ radically from those in the rest of the economy and in society at large. But what is the process by which they are adjusted, and how far must and should these adjustments go? That is never automatic or a simple given; but where and when it does occur, it inexorably drives up the "unit costs" of our services and puts us under permanent economic pressure.

The challenge would be great enough if it were just a matter of the relationship between various sectors of the economy. What makes it even greater is the fact that national borders and distances play less and less of a role. As a hotel, we are compared directly with countries and hotels which operate in completely different economic and social circumstances and with completely different conditions of production. That we are measured against each other is perfectly natural and legitimate, but it puts us in a hugely competitive environment.

Here, a dishwasher roughly earns a gross hourly rate of CHF 19.50 if you compute it on the basis of actual working hours (i.e. excluding vacations and all that), not counting social contributions paid by the employer. That is the contractual minimum. It is not a princely sum by Swiss standards. But at how many other holiday destinations which are now readily available to all of us will rates like these apply?

There is no point in railing against this state of affairs. Like the (for us) chronically unfavorable exchange rate, it is as much part of Switzerland as the beautiful scenery, the amazing public transportation network, and so many other things and achievements that we are all proud of. But the pressure is on. There is a reason why we are celebrating the 111 years of the Waldhaus with such fanfare. It cannot be taken for granted.

Ah well: salaries. For many years, our industry (at least in vacation hotels), stuck with a rather archaic wage system. Only those who were working behind the scenes, such as the chefs, received a fixed wage. Those at the front—waiters, chambermaids, porters, the concierge and his team—were paid only a very small fixed stipend, although that included free (if rather basic) food and lodging. Until and including 1970, the major part of their income came from a mandatory service charge added to each check, the total of which, the "tronc," was divided among the employees according to a complex system of points. Of course, there

Slightly bent, but still standing: Luca Cristiano, Paula Suhner, Dino Rosano and Jennifer Sigg at the end of their three-year apprenticeship, June 2015

were also voluntary tips in today's sense. Wages fluctuated enormously with the ebb and flow of business, as is still the case in part in the U.S.

The salaries, and the prices for rooms and food, only became fixed with the introduction of "service included" in 1971.

It was not much earlier that another, similarly profound change had begun. Up until that time, seasonal employees in a hotel simply did not get any days off. You had a job from this date to that and were expected to work, period. When the idea of having a day off finally came up, many employees were far from thrilled. "We are here to work, not to take time off," they said (and backward-looking hoteliers, who may hardly have taken a day off themselves, were more than ready to agree with them). What seems (on the part of the employees) a strikingly irrational response to a long-overdue innovation, of course, in reality had more to do with money—with tips, to be more precise. Everybody wanted to be there when the guests were leaving, so as not to miss the hoped-for tips, which played a much larger role in those years. At the same time, employees had hardly had an opportunity to pursue a life outside their jobs during the season. A life like that of Walter Nana's, today's dynamic and hard-working ruler of the Waldhaus dining rooms (pictured on p. 214 and interviewed on p. 169), who is a consummate athlete and passionate motorcyclist in his free time, would have been inconceivable back then.

Wages and working conditions have made great strides since those days. But some aspects have also become more onerous. Think of pension contributions, social security, health and accident insurance. The federal government also mandates minimums for what has to be charged for food and accommodations, which used to be included for free (and thus weren't taxable income).

Along with new and expanded laws—labor law, social security, etc.—and the effects of a competitive labor market, the peculiarly Swiss institution of country-wide collective labor agreements declared generally binding by the government, was another vehicle for changes. When unions and employers in a given industry negotiate a collective labor agreement, the government can declare this to be generally binding for everyone, not just the participating unions and employer associations. The hotel industry has had a succession of such agreements since the early 1970s. Despite his enormous workload at the hotel, Rolf Kienberger, who was at that time the Vice President of the Swiss Hotel Association, took it upon himself to help break ground by serving as chairman of the extended negotiations for the very first such agreement—demonstrating that the Waldhaus was willing to play an active and creative role in carrying our industry from the past into the present.

And so it goes on, a family affair profoundly shaped, far beyond the family, by so many others with their work and their lives. Shall we coin a phrase and call it a *work in progress*?

"Much was spontaneous"

Felix Dietrich

"As general manager, I was not a soloist, but a player who can be successful with his team. I have a feeling for which person should go into which position. That was helpful to me earlier in team sports and later at the hotel. I would never have been able to do alone what we achieved as a team. I knew that I had to get people on board to help me make the Waldhaus special.

FELIX DIETRICH is the son of innkeepers and bakers from St. Gallen. As a teenager, he was already impressed by the Waldhaus and what Rolf and Rita Kienberger did in and with it. Soon, the Waldhaus was also impressed by Felix. After his bank apprenticeship, he graduated from the Lausanne Hotel School, worked at hotels such as the Dorchester in London, the Du Rhône in Geneva and the Victoria Jungfrau in Interlaken. In 1975, he married Maria Kienberger, and the rest is Waldhaus history.

Creating offers that others can't copy, being a little unique, finding niches, producing experiences that are different, that is the secret of a successful host. I am convinced that the personal contact with people will not disappear. Robots may take over repetitive work in the hospitality industry, but they are unable to anticipate guests' wishes.

We do not offer off-the-peg service, but have created things that didn't previously exist. Planning is one thing, the courage to improvise is another. Once when we were meeting a group of Waldhaus guests at the Chur train station, I spontaneously asked a quintet of Mexican street musicians to play for us for about 10 minutes on the platform as a small surprise for the arrivals. Our guests thought we had planned it, but it was simply a spontaneous idea for welcoming them.

It was easy for me to find people to work for us. I always walk around with open eyes and ears. I first observe how people respond to me. If their reaction is positive, I ask a few questions, try to find out whether they have qualities that convince me. If I discover they have skills or talents that I can utilize in some way, then I try to keep in touch with them. I always have my little cards along (pulls out a business card). Good fortune is always there for us to pick it up. Much too often, we walk right by it and move on, because we are not living in the moment, missing out on the most interesting people, buildings, situations. I have the 180-degree vision of a seagull—sometimes I see and hear what is going on behind me. That can also be a problem. Faced with the huge range of products at a supermarket, I think of 20 different meals I could fix, and so end up buying enough food for a week instead of just a day.

"There are many former staff members who continue to spread the Waldhaus virus. And there were staff members whom I would have liked to keep forever."

Time and again, I have created custom-made jobs for people who were a good fit with the Waldhaus, or hired someone for whom there was no job at the moment. Such as the graphic designer whom we never ought to have put to work in the kitchen, but who did enrich our team, and with whom we were able to finally create a long-planned cookbook. Or the two American backpackers who, in off season, helped us pack 7,000 cardboard boxes with little bottles of pinot noir from Jenins for a guest mailing. Artists, musicians, waiters, writers, whoever: we were able to fill the hotel with life. I am only talking about 10 percent of all of our employees in this case; we have found the others in the normal ways. Although we once ran a 'help wanted' ad that more or less said we were sorry that the Waldhaus didn't have any positions to offer at present, explaining that most of our staff stayed on for a long time and so we also had to plan far ahead. That got a great echo, 50 responses, some spontaneously stopped by in person. Peter Durrer (currently GM of the Palace Lucerne) was one of them; he started his hotel career here. Our goal should be to turn all our staff members into Waldhaus ambassadors.

On the other hand, I have always found it hard to let people go. We gave them a second and third chance, and I often was reproached for being too kind. I had a lot of patience with apprentices and interns, as I think that they have so much to learn at a very volatile stage in their lives. I can say that almost everyone who had problems as an apprentice is now doing very well. I respected the fact that some of our managers no longer wanted to work with certain members of their teams. In some cases, I should have perhaps taken action earlier, but in the end, it was a joint decision not to renew a contract. What is certain is that you cannot run a hotel without 'willing accomplices.' Good employees do not have to be the best in their field, but they need to have a positive impact on their team and our guests. People who change careers midstream often have an enthusiasm that is infectious to others.

The Waldhaus has a staff of 160. I estimate that I devoted 20 percent of my time to them, 50 percent at my desk taking care of day-to-day business and 50 percent mingling with the guests. Despite all the work, I always found time for family and friends. The hotel also gave me the freedom to do PR work or spontaneous volunteer stints. Up to as late as 2000, I had no computer, preferring to personally pass on information from one department to the next. I always knew what was going on at the front, be it the concierge, the dining rooms, the bar, the reservations office, while I often got to hear that I wasn't keeping up enough with the departments behind the scenes such as the carpenter or the chambermaids or at the pool. Much of what I did was spontaneous.

Until I attended a workshop where a psychologist prompted us to take a closer look at ourselves, I even thought that my management style was participatory. As it turned out, our management staff thought I was authoritarian. That gave me pause. Well: they knew how to take me, and we were also usually in a hurry. Good employees are not always good at making decisions, so that, under time pressure, I would often make a decision for them. It appears that members of management were actually often glad that I did.

Over the years, I have learned that there is more than one road to Rome. I listen when someone tells me how something can be done differently, as it is good to try new approaches. It is always good to respect your vis-à-vis. I have learned how to recognize our employees' capabilities and how to utilize them. I find it fascinating that the fifth Waldhaus generation goes about this in a much more conscious and targeted manner. They lead by studying the abilities and responsibilities of the managers and giving them more of a role and more opportunities for development. I find that very good. At the same time, I am glad that I can still implement certain things and be of use to our business and family."

"I trained 47 apprentices at the Waldhaus"

Kurt Röösli

"Before I joined the Waldhaus as chef de partie in 1991, I had cooked on one of the most modern cruise ships in the world, the conditions in the kitchen were the best you could imagine. By comparison, the Waldhaus kitchen was pure Middle Ages. The high ceiling, the outdated appliances, the electric range, the heat, the rudimentary ventilation—really. I was dismayed. It took a few days to start feeling its positive energy and notice how well one could work in this kitchen. Modernity brings many advantages, but heart and soul often lie in the old. Over the years I came to appreciate the Waldhaus kitchen, as it was then, very much, it was the heart, the stomach of the hotel. And as it is today, it is a meeting place, a cathedral that still strikes me as new, very bright and clear, probably one of the most handsome kitchens in the world. The ventilation has not blocked the view, the walls are pristine, the lighting is incredibly elegant. But the old walls had stored up positive energy, and I understand that the new kitchen will need time until it regains its patina and can start telling stories again.

KURT RÖÖSLI had his first day of work at the Waldhaus on December 18, 1991. When he moved on, after a quarter century, he had fundamentally changed the Waldhaus kitchen and affected the lives of many people, not just in the kitchen. Since 2016, he has headed the kitchens and all things related to food and drink at the Wagerenhof Foundation in Uster near Zurich. Kurt also met his Austrian wife Sissi at the Waldhaus. She came as a service and F&B intern and became head of HR. She is currently responsible for Human Resources at the Savoy Hotel in Zurich. They have two adult daughters, Anna and Lena.

We were able to preserve and re-use the charcoal grill from the early days. If I could go back, I would ask for a small wood-fired stove next to it. Dishes such as polenta or risottos simply are better when cooked over a fire than on a cold induction plate. I also think that it would give young chefs an intuitive feeling for cooking over a fire, and I am certain that the guests would immediately pick up and love the story behind it.

HARTLY MATHIS (1926–2017): "In the summer of 1955, I was executive chef at the Waldhaus and in the winters of 1953–54 and 1954–55, at the Chantarella with Rolf Kienberger and his wife," Hartly Mathis remembered in 2008. He later became master of the Suvretta kitchens and, starting in 1967, brought sophisticated gastronomy to the high Alps at his own "Marmite" restaurant on Corviglia. "At the time, much weight was given to classic cuisine, we had to, as we had an older clientele. We could make some modern, lighter dishes, but basically, we had to focus on classic cuisine. For example, an entire saddle of veal. Or a Filet Wellington. The large pièces that were carved in front of the guests in the dining room were standard. And for lunch, there was a good pot roast, a bœuf braisé or a choucroute garnie. I could go on: duck, turkey, chicken, a lot of fish, lots of trout. The fishermen from Isola on Lake Sils brought us live trout and we had a trout tank."

I quickly became the right-hand man of then executive chef René Zigerli. He was tremendously knowledgeable, and I had a good personal rapport with him, it was like a father-son relationship, and I took on the classic role of an intermediary. It was a question of discipline and deference to the chef, but also of motivating the entire team and having an open ear for their concerns.

When I spent a summer working on a ship again in 1995, and someone filled in for me who had not internalized the necessary diplomacy to the same extent, things came to a head, and I was appointed as the new executive chef in the summer of 1996. Was that the right step? I spent a long time pondering that question. My personal relationship with René Zigerli was still very important to me, and I was full of doubts. I suddenly saw things from a different perspective, double-checked every order, there was so much to do, my days became quite long, and yet there was nothing I would have rather done than this job. At age 30, one tends to tackle things like a bull at the gate, but even I learned to delegate and to share trust, and I loved and continue to love my role as an educator. Over the years, I trained 47 apprentices at the Waldhaus and am still in contact with most of them. As their tutor, their master, you have a great influence on what they learn, above and beyond their official curriculum: we processed entire animals, made sauces, meat stocks and soup from scratch, an apprentice could explore every aspect of our work at the Waldhaus and could personally present dishes to the guests at the chef's table, at the breakfast buffet or at the big buffet dinners; a young chef has to learn poise and self-confidence.

In my time at the hotel, there were many changes. Felix Dietrich wanted to introduce service on a plate rather than on a platter, I wanted to show off our skills, so we introduced weekly buffet dinners with special themes, which continue to today. We began to consistently use local products, building up a network of suppliers and farmers, introducing our guests to the farms, at a time when the general trend to go local was still far off. At the outset we had been 20 chefs, by 2008, the year of the Waldhaus centennial, there were 26 of us.

HARTLY MATHIS:
"I never forgot how Rolf Kienberger's father Oskar Kienberger said, 'Whatever happens, we shouldn't try to cut expenses in the kitchen! We have a bit of a handicap with our rooms, as we are a little behind, they are lovely, but perhaps not what people now think of as luxury. The food should make up for it.'" Hartly Mathis was Kurt Röösli's pre-pre-pre-pre-predecessor as executive chef at the Waldhaus.

When I was an apprentice, working in a hotel or restaurant kitchen still was a kind of modern slavery. Nowadays, it's all about working hours, about eight-hour days. I would plead for a healthy mix. We all know that life as a cook has positive and negative sides, but if you put in a lot, you also receive a lot, and your enjoyment of work cannot simply be measured by looking at the clock. With this philosophy, our senior chefs often stayed for five years or more. My immediate successor Dennis Remo Brunner was there for 12 years in all. That also says something about working conditions at the Waldhaus."

sets
games
games

Records and challenges

Ich bin der Leiter des Hauses. It is not easy to convey in translation the calm confidence of the words with which Rolf Kienberger would introduce himself to new guests. He was more than the manager, he was in charge. The "boss," perhaps, though he would never have used that word.

In the summer of 1987, Felix and Maria took charge on their own. They had already shaped the Waldhaus and its life alongside our parents for a decade ("Changing of the guard," p. 207). Now, they were ready to give it their all. With enthusiasm, expertise and skill, they

"Ich bin der Leiter des Hauses." Rolf Kienberger (1917–1994) with Annie Reich (1894–1984), around 1975 (Photo: Toni Cavelti)

devoted themselves to a wide range of tasks. By now, they also were the parents of five children. Claudio, the oldest, was ten, Carla, the youngest, was not yet four. Maria was grateful that her own job at the hotel did not, at first, change as much as Felix's. Our mother, Rita Kienberger, was nearly ten years younger than our father and continued to work nearly full-time. This allowed hard-working Maria, for all her commitment to the hotel, to strike a good balance between her role as a mother and her duties at the hotel. But no one should underestimate her role in the management of the hotel, which would continue to expand as the children grew older. More about that later.

Felix, on the other hand, had very much on his plate right from the start. He took on these responsibilities with great zest, with vigor and initiative—be it reservations, marketing or the finding, motivating, guiding and training of employees; or special moments such as personally travelling down to Chur to welcome the participants of a large conference with an antique Albula Line lounge car, or organizing jazz concerts (previously unheard of at the Waldhaus) in our lounge or bar; or dealing with anyone from our suppliers to the workmen, young apprentices, professional colleagues, the press and of course, ever and always, with our guests.

While this was happening, the hotel climbed new heights. As reluctant as we are to reduce our success to a single number, let us for once do it anyway. After a somewhat subdued 1987, chairman Rolf Kienberger in his annual report for 1988 proudly reported results "such as we had long dreamed of but had never seen before." A year later, "revenues surpassed the 8-million mark for the first time"; the report for 1990 recorded "an increase of 12.2 percent," and for 1991, it said, "for the third time in a row, revenue increased by CHF 1 m and has surpassed the ten-million mark for the first time."

Maria and Felix had the support of a fine team. Now, and already during the preceding period of co-management with Rolf and Rita Kienberger, Felix was fortunate to be able to count on a succession of excellent and diligent management assistants. They included Patrick

Ghielmetti, who will reappear both in this book and in our history (see p. 317), or Ernst and Silvia Wyrsch, who went on to manage the Steigenberger Belvedere in Davos for many years, with Ernst, who is currently on the go as a happiness coach and hotel expert, also winning laurels as chairman of the Davos Hockey Club and (to this day) chairman of the Graubünden Hotel Association, or Marzio and Hanni Forni from Airolo, to name just a few. One of the things they had in common was: the more qualified and ambitious the assistant, the more likely he or she was to move on to a new career and assume the management of his or her own hotel.

In any case, Felix's broad shoulders quickly had more than enough to bear. At least in part that had something to do with how extensively Rolf Kienberger had defined his own role. Rolf Kienberger was no patriarch, nor an autocrat; if he had been, he would hardly have instilled so much admiration and fascination for the Waldhaus and for our trade in a person like Felix Dietrich. What he was, though, was a true *patron* in the old French sense of the word: calm, steady, human and with a fine sense of humor, but also strict and demanding, resolute, precise and disciplined. An authority who, with our mother at his side, dominated the hotel down to the smallest details with around-the-clock attention and an enormous capacity for work. (To be sure, his reluctance to rely much on others to run the hotel also owed something to the bottom line. For most of the years under his watch, the Waldhaus was engaged in an all-out struggle to catch up after the long years of enforced frugality during the war and in its wake, investing virtually every penny they could save, which made it imperative to minimize the costly "middlemen"—and middle women—in the running of the hotel.)

Ich bin der Leiter des Hauses. For all his admiration for Rolf, Felix did not intend to simply copy his role. The Waldhaus had strongly influenced him, but he had been around and had seen other role models and other ways to operate as well, both positive and negative ones. Besides, he had graduated from the Lausanne Hotel School with all honors (first in his class), and in his first years at the Waldhaus he had enrolled

1968. A year full of disruptions in the world. Things were calmer at the Waldhaus, if not always at the switchboard. Urs Kienberger, a summer job

in the valuable management seminars offered by the Swiss Hotel Association leading up to the title of "federally certified Swiss hotel/restaurant manager." In terms of his personality, he was no carbon copy of his admired father-in-law either.

Seeing Felix at work in full swing, people readily think of him as "a born hotelier"—even more readily, perhaps, than they would have thought it in the case of Rolf Kienberger, who at first glance often seemed an improbable candidate for the job, as brilliant as he turned out to be upon closer observation. Felix, in turn, brought a thorough expertise and obvious leadership qualities to the job, as well as an excellent head for numbers, but the first words which come to mind to describe Felix are "impresario" and—his own favorite expression—the "player-coach." The hotelier as impresario who thoroughly enjoys organizing things, pulling strings, putting up a show (not necessarily putting *on* a show; that's different), with a certain inclination for self-promotion thrown in for good measure. A player-coach who jumps right into the fray, but with a plan, leading, motivating, organizing—the way he already did, when growing up, in the boy scouts (or its Catholic counterpart, to be precise) as well as in team sports such as handball or soccer, where he eagerly participated even though he was never that much of an athlete. And in all situations, his innate ease, not to say compulsion, in reaching out.

This rich bundle of talents and inclinations threatened to quickly attract an equally oversized array of duties and responsibilities, all the more so in view of the expectations of family, guests and staff conditioned by Felix's larger-than-life predecessor. Everyone wanted Felix to be Felix—and simultaneously wanted him to be Rolf Kienberger, too.

Faced with this explosion of expectations and responsibilities, Felix and Maria were actively looking for a new, lasting partnership for sharing the hotel's management, thinking of duplicating and repeating the success of the "cohabitation" prior to 1987. For some time, they and I had even been discussing whether we should team up together. It was, to be sure, a pretty far-fetched idea. It is true that Felix and I had been friends since childhood, with a high mutual regard for each other's very different temperaments and skills. We also had in common a deep appreciation of my parents' work and values, and were both entranced by the Waldhaus, this extraordinary and attractive place. And yet ...

"A born hotelier" may perfectly describe my brother-in-law, but you would hardly apply it to me. Of course, I had grown up, together with my siblings, in the midst of the hotel, in the same way a farm child grows up on the farm or a circus child amidst the trailers behind the big top. In the midst of the hotel, we did not even have a real apartment. During school vacations, we were all put to work, and since early childhood, I had picked up and been fascinated by the endless stream of hotel stories told by my parents, my aunts and uncles and grandparents, and all the other people with whom we shared the hotel. Stories told at the family table, or while someone was arranging flowers, or in the evening in the Privé or on the way to church or on walks in the forest or hikes in the mountains.

I am a hotel child through and through—but one with two left hands, like when I dropped a tray with 16 glasses while clearing a table and all the waiters cheered. A hotel child deficient in much of what would be useful in the daily life of the hotel; a loner who at times walked down the hallways with bowed head, in order not to be noticed, more interested in books than playing games (I'm still no good with cards) and happiest when hiking alone through our beautiful landscape for days on end. It was no wonder that for a long time I did not seriously consider finding a useful role at the Waldhaus, as attached as I was to it. I went away, first to boarding school, the Collège St-Michel in Fribourg, relieved by a wonderful year as an exchange student with a farmer family in Iowa/ USA; then I got a degree in economics at St. Gallen. After that, I returned to the U.S. for graduate school and work as a teaching and research assistant, spent some time in Brazil and then came back to Switzerland, now happily married to Nancy Wiedeman from Peoria, Illinois, to an interesting job as a bank economist with Swiss Bank Corporation in Basel.

Nevertheless, over time I came to realize to what extent my heart still belonged to the Waldhaus. In spite of all those positive experiences, the Waldhaus and how it was doing continued to take center stage in my thoughts. But I knew that the hotel hardly needed lots of well-meaning ideas and advice from far away. It needed people willing to be there and lend a hand (and a head) from early in the morning to late at night.

"Messieurs, soignez les détails!" Napoleon kept admonishing his generals. (Let's leave aside for the moment that he still ended up losing at Waterloo.)

The years away from home had given me self-assurance and a greater ease in interacting with people rather than just books, as well as poise for appearing in public. Although my profession (which I enjoyed) was an academic one, my curriculum at St. Gallen and my job at the bank were by no means confined to the impractical abstractions of the ivory tower. And I now had more confidence to function outside of my natural comfort zone. On the other hand, I had very little management experience. From that perspective, Felix and Maria's offer to team up together had the special appeal that their range of skills and hotel experience would amply compensate the blank spots in my own CV, thus allowing me to concentrate on my strengths.

And I did have strengths that I could offer. The freedom and the opportunities to go my own way, which my years "on the road" had provided, meant that now, like Maria and Felix, I could commit myself to the Waldhaus with all my heart and without reservations, without having to fear that at some point I would regret missed opportunities. (What our move to Sils meant for my dear wife, an "urban child," who now abruptly found herself moored in a village in the mountains, is a different story altogether.)

What I could contribute in particular was an eye for precision, an eye for written and oral communication, an eye for atmosphere, for subtle differences, for complex—and often hidden—connections, and finally an eye for the limits of being soberly sensible. All of these traits have a substantial bearing on the success of our enterprise. The importance of communication, for instance, is obvious. If the Waldhaus wants to stand out by being different, it can only succeed if it manages to convincingly explain itself, again and again. But the "limits of being soberly sensible"? I do not mean this as a call to, literally, leave reason behind (although I respectfully remind you that the Waldhaus would not exist if our forebears had been more reasonable). But I was convinced that to preserve the hotel's charm, its magic and its special qualities, we needed at times to go beyond the purely practical and pragmatic, as essential as those things are for a hotel to function. Every hotelier worth his or her salt is basically aware of that; but in the practical pressures of day-to-day life it may sometimes require a bit of an outsider to speak up for this cause. The same is true for the cause of precision—be it for words or for figures, ranging from the accounts to recoding the guests' addresses and information and the editing of the daily menus.

The celestial mechanics which keep a satellite in place in space have an elegant clarity: an equilibrium of opposing forces, the interplay between velocity and gravitational force. Our "human mechanics" were not so orderly, they were arduous and fragile; but they, too, kept the Waldhaus on an impressive trajectory by subtly balancing opposing forces.

With all that, I was enough of a hotel child to know that what really counts in the end is to stay in touch with our guests, with them and their needs (without losing sight of those we work with in the process). I made this my first priority, no different from the other family members at the hotel. It is a priority you can only truly do justice to, in as many situations as possible, if you are firmly anchored in day-to-day hotel life. In my own case, I endeavored to find such an anchor by being intensely involved in reservations.

We did embark on the experiment: starting in 1989, we did team up together to run the Waldhaus. (Notably on terms that cost the hotel little more than a single GM would have cost under ordinary circumstances.) The impact on the hotel was clear and powerful. What we aimed for, and often achieved, was not so much to search for harmonious compromises, the lowest common denominator; rather, we hoped for creative ideas and decisions, for actions with a clear personal signature, but tested and tempered in discussions with each other. Our individual styles and character gave the hotel more dimensions, a far more complex and many-sided identity, than it would have had with just one of us in charge. It was a highly stimulating, fulfilling and successful way to operate, but also demanding and arduous. You could feel the tension—a tension which made the hotel more interesting and distinctive, and opened it to an even broader range of guests.

It was powerful. But the tension that enriched the hotel was there between us, too, as we were working together, particularly we two alpha males. Not being a musician, I do not know if the metaphor is really valid, but I felt we were something akin to an ambitious, hard-driving chamber ensemble practicing and performing together. “Management as chamber music”: beautiful results, but demanding, challenging and not without peril for those who engage in it. (Don’t try it unless you also have a Maria Dietrich at your table.) Time and again, you have to measure your goals and ideas against the questions, the skepticism of the others. In the process, your ideas become stronger and clearer and more articulated—or at other times you start realizing that they are far less brilliant and convincing than you first thought. That is never easy, even if, as in our own case, we fortunately had the strong bond of a shared understanding of what we wanted to do with the Waldhaus and what we wanted the Waldhaus to be.

A central motivation for our teaming up had been that with the three of us rather than two or one we would each have a somewhat lighter burden. But that’s not how it came out. With shared passion and differing views, we often energized each other. Where one of us may have been ready to leave good enough alone; the other one was sure to say:

let's try some more, we can do better than that. Ever driven to do more and accomplish more, especially the author of these lines, chafing against his own limits.

Long before the Internet put myriads of quotations at the fingertips of even the least literate, Rolf Kienberger ended his Annual Report to the Waldhaus shareholders' meeting in 1992 with a wonderfully apt verse by Wilhelm Busch, the German humorist. Here is our attempt to render it in English:

Never.
That which you desired so much,
You have now been given.
You triumph and rejoice a bunch:
"Now, I'm no longer driven!"
Ah, my friend, what words you speak,
Please tame your tongue.
Any wish, come true, will seek
To hatch the next one.

So, it was not easy. Was it worth it? It is true that Felix and Maria would have been perfectly able to manage the Waldhaus on their own, and in many ways their lives would have been easier if they had done so. All of our lives might have been easier, had we gone our separate ways. But if the three of us had not taken that dare of working together, so many interesting and beautiful things, so many highlights and special moments would never have come about. Let's just be thankful, and refrain from weighing pros and cons! The Waldhaus is such a fascinating place precisely because it holds so many unanswered questions. Just like life.

"It was supposed to get much easier"

Maria Dietrich-Kienberger

"Three years after our parents retired, my brother Urs came back to the Waldhaus; that was the winter of 1989/90. We had big plans, had asked ourselves who would do what, work was supposed to get much easier. It got more complicated. Urs became (in his own words) 'CEO for all that is not necessarily needed.' With his humor and his talent for writing, he has added a great deal to the hotel, our guests loved his sense of humor, but it did not tend to make life easier. Urs and Felix are so different from each other. They goaded each other into doing their best, which was incredibly good and an advantage for the Waldhaus but not for our family.

One thing I have learned is how infinitely important constant dialog is in a family business. In each generation, we must continue to respect each other. I myself have always tried to show the way. It is particularly important among siblings. And we have always extended it to the family members who are not directly involved in the business as well. Not always an easy task, but without communication we can't work together. It is hardest when there is rivalry. We should view and accept it as a normal part of life, in our own family no less and no more than anywhere else, and be aware that it can cause great problems.

> "Now, the hotel's strategy is much more clearly formulated. In our own time, much of it was just in our heads, but Claudio and Patrick have clearly set down their policies so that people outside of the family can see and understand them."

What I want above all is to give our sons trust and confidence for the future. Each of them will do their best and make the best of things. There will certainly be mistakes as well, now and in the future, that is a normal part of life; but if a family member were not prepared to do his or her best for the Waldhaus, then he or she wouldn't and shouldn't be working here at all. I would like to pass on this basic trust [in people's good intentions]. And I am happy that I do not have to retire completely yet, but can, like my parents, continue to do what I like and what I can do well."

Thoughts in autumn

What we have been trying to achieve together is complex and intricate, and it has never been easy to put it in a nutshell. In the autumn of my days at the Waldhaus, let's give it a try anyway.

Continuity—the underestimated challenge

Innovation and change are dynamic and exciting, while the patient and steady pursuit of long-term goals may seem passive and uninspiring. But impressions can be deceiving. Continuity in a dynamic world does not mean idly standing still. Deliberately staying in place when all around you everything is in flux and in motion requires a great deal of creativity, skill and hard work, as well as a trio of rather special qualities. You obviously need a clear appreciation and understanding of what already exists. Second, you need the skill to explain yourself. Continuity, by definition, is at odds with trends, and hence at odds with what everybody comes to regard as normal. If you do not want to simply follow a trend, you continually have to make a case for being different. And finally, as an entrepreneur you need a thick skin and a fair amount of self-confidence to accept with equanimity that people will often pat you on the back and compliment you for—seemingly—having done nothing at all. For the more you succeed in ensuring continuity, no

"It makes you cringe to see those monstrous old luxury hotels wherever you look, products of the most awful bad taste seen since the beginning of time," thundered the Austrian writer Hans Weigel (1908–1991) in 1962, in *Lern dieses Volk der Hirten kennen* (published by Artemis in Stuttgart and Zurich), a portrait of Switzerland otherwise marked by great affection for our country and a genuine understanding of its workings. Sometimes, the spirit of an age and the goal of continuity rather fiercely get in each other's way. Funny that in our specific case the target of his ire had precisely the same vintage as the author himself.

matter how much effort and creativity that may have cost you, the more they will think, in admiration or as a reproach: "Nothing has changed."

Continuity is thus no less demanding than rapid change and marked growth, or than simply going with the flow. It is a balancing act that requires endurance and imagination. The effort does have its own rewards, particularly at a time like ours, when many long for continuity and stability, and especially when our efforts are devoted to a product as strong as this wonderful hotel of our forebears.

Le pas-trop-grand hôtel

Our ancestors made no little plans. Even in its earliest days, the Waldhaus could accommodate as many as 250 guests at the peak of the season. Nowadays, that can rise to 290 or more in a pinch, when we host particularly many families with children (something that was less common in earlier times). By and large, though, our hotel has nary a bed more than 111 years ago. That may sound odd. Where would the world be if everyone had done the same, just stayed within the same limits

The Waldhaus in the snow, 1978 (Photo: Hans Steiner)

for generations on end? But this self-imposed limitation has allowed us to preserve what we see as possibly the most rewarding and important aspect of running a hotel: the personal interaction with our guests. I am talking about the pride and pleasure derived from creating ever new delights and experiences for people we actually know, rather than for some abstract, impersonal "clients." And with it, the opportunity to get immediate and direct feedback for what we do.

"It's all about people." On the face of it, this does not sound like a terribly original thought. Isn't that what just about any hotelier would say? Indeed, any hotel manager, no matter how large or fancy their hotel may be, would be there in person if, say, the Prince of Wales came through the door or the New York Times wanted to do an interview. However, our own idea is both broader and more radical: to consistently take an interest in as many of our guests as humanly possible, without first deciding who really counts. There is the cliché of the seasoned concierge or hotelier who can, with practiced eye, separate at a glance the wheat from the chaff, the interesting few from the uninteresting crowd. We do not go in for that; we would find it far too limiting and limited. Again and again, experience has shown us that people can turn out to be so different from what a first impression reveals, and that evident prominence and the appearance of a hefty wallet often tells you very little about the ultimate and underlying story.

"Now, if I would call it a flagship, that is simply too grandiose for the Waldhaus, which precisely does not want to be grandiose, but it is indeed an institution in the Engadine. In the war years, I worked in hotels in Davos, and I have to say: If you have worked in a hotel yourself, you immediately sense what kind of atmosphere a place has. And the atmosphere at the Waldhaus is special. It simply is special." MARCELLA MAIER (1920–2018), honorary citizen of St. Moritz, 2008 in a conversation with Andrin Willi.

This is not just lofty idealism or an obsession with the way things used to be. What guides us is a combination of sentimental ideals and down-to-earth commercial motives. Apart from the fun of giving free rein to our innate curiosity about the people who walk through our door (and certainly, to some extent, the vanity of taking center stage), we also have a tangible and material interest in trying to attract and engage as many guests as possible to and for our hotel. We could obviously let others do that for us, but we firmly believe that it creates far stronger and more lasting ties and gives the Waldhaus a more distinctive profile when we, as the responsible owners, personally give it a human face. Steadily and consistently, and if necessary, against all current trends.

To do this in earnest already posed a mighty challenge for our ancestors. They could scarcely have imagined how much more of a challenge it is today. With virtually the same hotel capacity, the 622 guests and 12,900 overnight stays of the—successful—first Waldhaus year, in 1908, with its one season of 100 days, have ballooned into the 10,800 guests and their 46,000 overnight stays of the summer and winter of 2018 with their total of 258 opening days. If personally interacting with our guests were our only ambition, we would have been well-advised long ago to concentrate our efforts on a much smaller and more exclusive hotel. But size matters, too. A good hotel needs a certain size in order to support a sufficiently wide range of infrastructure and services. Or rather, it comes at a very high price in a smaller hotel, where expenses would be spread across fewer people. We would then have to focus ever more on the heft of our guests' pocketbooks, with profound consequences for what we might call the sociology of our hotel. Even more importantly, reducing the hotel's capacity would affect its "sociology" in a second way. Only if there is a sufficient number and sufficient diversity of guests can you hope to get that fascinating blend of the public and the private, of intimacy and distance, that is the very mark of a grand hotel and one of its key pleasures and source of its charm.

JOHN KIRCHHEIMER: "I can walk through the lounge in my fishing boots and am just as welcome as if I were sitting there in a suit. And in the evening, when you sit in the great lounge, it is like an Agatha Christie film. You see the guests sitting around, each one observing the other one, hidden behind a newspaper or a book. One will complain that the lights are too bright, another says they are too dim, that is all part of the experience." John Kirchheimer (75) came to the Waldhaus for the first time in 1948. It wasn't his last visit.

Small enough to be run with a personal touch, but large enough to remain fascinating: a true balancing act. There you have it, the Waldhaus in nutshell.

Beyond the grand theories

When we talk about style and size, continuity and change, we do not want to forget that, before all other considerations, a good hotel has to *function*. The beds have to be made, the soup served hot, the chauffeur has to show up where and when he or she is needed. There is no way around this, not for us nor for any of our colleagues: a hotel is only good if it works. To achieve that is no trivial accomplishment, not something we could do blindfolded; it takes constant work, care and first-rate professional competence. At the same time, simply by functioning properly, a hotel does not yet become truly fascinating or memorable. I'd even go a step further and say once again, provocatively: let's watch out that for all the practical competence we need, we do not concentrate too exclusively on what's practical and pragmatic.

The consummate pragmatist looks into a room and sees at once, say, that the waiters are struggling. A hotelier with less of a practical bend sees that the lighting is too bright, or he will concentrate on a conversation with a guest rather than refilling his wine glass. For optimum results we need both. Reason and practicality set our limits ... but let us not forget that they, too, have their limits.

When it is called for, we must not forget to stand up for what's idiosyncratic or unreasonable, for wit and humor and a quirk here and there. Not just where no one will notice and it does not get in anyone's way. Guests rightly insist on comfort and service. Employees need the right tools and conditions to make their work as easy as possible. Craftsmen and artisans proudly replace the old with the new, suppliers take equal pride in innovating and throwing out the familiar. Architects, too, want to leave their mark, not simply maintain what already exists. All these ambitions are legitimate and understandable. But in the end, many will be glad and grateful, too, if we see to it that not everything becomes too smooth and even and normal, that the Waldhaus keeps its history and its stories, its wit, its soul and its character.

Change and continuity

111 years without a single dramatic change of course, while passing from one generation to the next four times over. This continuity, which we have already applauded, may be the Waldhaus's most distinguishing feature. If our ancestors suddenly came back, they would still easily recognize what they created.

A prime example is the generosity of the hotel's public spaces. "How nice," everybody thinks and is full of praise for the founders. At most, we who are here now get credit for having resisted the temptation to make these spaces smaller or use them for other, more economically productive purposes. Few will be aware that actually, our dining rooms and public areas are a full 40 percent *larger* than they were in 1908. That's 380 additional square meters (4,000 sq. feet). To wit: even as treasured and seemingly obvious a legacy from the past as the generosity of these public spaces in fact owes much to the efforts of subsequent generations.

The reading room and the Arvenstube were not there in 1908, but were added in 1929. More recent alterations, in 1999–2000 and 2012, enlarged the Arvenstube, added the foyer in the rocks which complements the reading room, and created the handsome smokers' lounge. The dining room veranda dates from 1978. In one go, it enlarged the dining rooms by more than a quarter. Likewise, there was an addition to the great lounge in 1991. The Sunny Corner, where the—much too small—original bar had been located until 1929 and where the children later used to play, has had its present form and function since 1973. And the 40 percent that we mentioned do not even extend to the new conference rooms and the children's playroom underneath the public rooms.

If we think about it, it is not so surprising that such changes went largely unnoticed. The reason that the Waldhaus so visibly remains true to its founding concept does not necessarily indicate that very little has changed. Rather, many of the changes and additions that did take place have been guided and inspired by the same goals that our forebears followed. This reflects the quality of their concepts, which have stood the test of time in terms of their prudence and foresight. And it also reflects the benefits of uninterrupted generational succession. It is the primary reason why the original qualities and the belief in them still exist. It is not as if we had a hidden vault with the carefully guarded writings of our ancestors, which we take out from time to time to study and interpret by candlelight. Rather, the principles have stayed present in our day-to-day lives, passed on (quite naturally) at the family table and in our joint, intensive work. We are less likely, then, to shake our heads and ask at every turn, "What on earth were they thinking?" We are still prepared to invest money and effort in the goals from the past (such as the generosity of the public spaces). We certainly have no more money than other hotels (on the contrary), but we have had the courage and conviction to invest it in different ways.

It is interesting to approach the Waldhaus for once with a question that seems decidedly un-Waldhaus-like: what has actually changed over time? Quite a lot, as it turns out, although few of the changes are very visible at first glance. We have just discussed a primary reason for this lack of visibility: that the new often neatly fits in with what there was, as it reflects the same principles and ideas. There is a second and more pedestrian reason: Much of what has changed and been added is not conspicuous simply because today's guests expect it as a matter of course, in this and in any good hotel. Criminologists know the phenomenon perfectly well: people do not see what seems normal. We would only notice, or be bothered, if it were missing.

November 1992
Dear Waldhaus Guests
We always hope that nothing happens—but we cannot count on it. That is why the 1908 Waldhaus inventory included 290 chamber pots. It also explains why our electricians spent countless long and costly working hours installing a new fire alarm system with 313 smoke alarms this year. (Photo: Guido Schmidt)

And yet, the path to what our guests now take for granted was often long and difficult, and therefore plays a much greater role in our own recollections than in the perception of our guests. Bathrooms are a prime example. In 1908, as noted on p. 38, we were way ahead of the pack, with some 40 private bathrooms (plus 17 public restrooms and a half-dozen public baths). Getting to where we are today, with more than 150 private bathrooms—with 117 bathtubs, 106 showers and 159 toilets—was the work of generations, greatly pressuring and challenging us until quite recently. For decades and for generations of our family, building bathrooms was an ongoing quest, a passion, an obsession, so much so that, starting on p. 269, we are devoting an entire chapter to the topic.

What else has changed? In hindsight many of the changes seem hardly worth mentioning. Such as a TV in every room. Starting in the 1960s, there was a transmitter on top of Piz Corvatsch, which broadcast two or three channels. For years, then, we had just a single television set in the hotel. It sat in the reading room—rather to the annoyance of those who wanted to read or write. We Waldhaus children were delighted, on the other hand. Of course, the reading room was off limits, with or without the TV, but in off-season, the magical box stood on the large safe in the cashier's office, where we could all gather in the evening during the three or four months a year when the hotel was closed.

Televisions in the guest rooms only became a fixture in the 1980s. At first, it was only upon request and for a surcharge; after 1990, they were in all the rooms. This was a bigger step than you might think, and we went about it with some hesitation. The 150 TV sets themselves were a relatively minor investment. A single new bathroom would have cost more. But the massive walls of the hotel blocked the signal from Cor-

Ski school

vatsch, which meant that the rooms on the west and north sides had only poor or no reception. In a laborious and costly operation, all the rooms had to be wired. More than that, we were concerned whether and how TVs in all the rooms might change the behavior of our guests. Would they all retire to their rooms, to the detriment of public life at the hotel? That was a pretty crucial question. We firmly believed then, and still do, that our public spaces and how they are utilized and experienced play a very central role in determining the charm and purpose of a hotel such as ours. Fortunately, the attraction of the public rooms proved strong enough to minimize the impact of television on our guests' habits. We are happy and relieved to report that this seems to hold equally true today, as regarding the many added enticements of the internet and other new media.

Before TV, Waldhaus guests had access to the world thanks to an ingenious and typically Swiss facility called "Telefonrundspruch," a system broadcasting six radio programs by way of the telephone network. It was very Swiss in its goal to provide first-rate radio reception no matter where you were in the country, at a time when the mountains and the periphery were less well served by wireless programs. And it was also very Swiss in its content, which was both diverse and inclusive: you got the three Swiss national programs of "Beromünster" (German), "Sottens" (French) and "Monte Ceneri" (Italian), plus three other, cleverly compiled programs called "Classic," "Light" and "International."

The useful radio receivers with their six buttons were in every guest room (and in our own living room, the Privé). Sadly, Telefonrundspruch went off the air in 1997 (shall we say, it reached the end of the wire?).

We used to ...

In the Waldhaus of our childhood, in the 1950s and 1960s, we were often told about things that "we used to" have and "used to" do. In the 1950s and 1960s, the Waldhaus guest lists were particularly impressive, with an exceptional concentration of famous names, but at the same time the hotel was struggling with huge economic challenges due to the long-delayed reintroduction of the winter season and an investment backlog that had built up since 1930. There was simply no money for all kinds of services and amenities which had been routine in prewar times.

We still had our resident trio. It remains an important Waldhaus tradition, never interrupted, one of the hotel's defining features (even if we, as teenagers, would have opted for very different kinds of musical entertainment). But there were amenities of the past that we only knew from hearsay, such as the barber and hairdresser's across from the chapel, or the role of Henry Hoek, a prominent mountain climber, ski pioneer and author, who had served as our resident hiking and ski tour guide. The Waldhaus had had its own ski school, and a sled run in the forest, prepared with ice and banked curves, for the enjoyment of adults as much as children, and its own bakery deep in the bowels of the hotel. There had been a "Maître de Plaisir," a kind of cruise director on firm land, organizing entertainment and parties for the guests, or the chocolate shop by the main entrance, a Gift Shop "avant la lettre," and the

Defying the Depression with resourceful innovation: "thé dansant" in the park. As there was no money for appropriate lawn chairs, the chairs from the dining room were carried outside in the afternoon and back inside in time for dinner.

billiards table which, until 1929, had stood in the bar. In our childhood, even the hotel library had gradually gone into hiding behind curtains and cupboard doors.

This makes it all the more satisfying that, eventually, we were increasingly able to move back in the opposite direction. In 1984, within the "Palais du Garage" (p. 181) a hair salon was installed, and next to the new indoor tennis court there was now space again for the billiards table. In 1993, we gave new life to the tradition of a summer hiking guide. In the same year, a fancy new bookcase was installed at great cost in the reading room, allowing us to unearth the hotel library, which regained further visibility after the year 2000 with the reactivation of the bookcases in the bar and additional shelving in the Sunny Corner and on the bel etage on the way to the pool. (However, we readily recognize that our thousands of books could still use more space and a thorough reorganization.) There has been a small gift shop next to the spa for 25 years. Relying instead on the Corvatsch Ski School, we have not reintroduced a ski school of our own, but for the past 20 years we have had a ski instructor installed every evening at the front desk to provide information and advice, a valuable service for all skiers. All of these were unspectacular, but heartening steps and initiatives to recapture "what we used to have," the various comforts and glories of the past.

Some things are gone for good. Brave attempts to revive the popular afternoon "thé dansant" (as you can see in the illustration, there was even dancing outdoors, at the height of summer) came to naught; fashion and customs have changed too much. New bridge weeks (reflecting that the Waldhaus also used to have a bridge hostess) were not a lasting success. And the fact that our bakery now harbors part of our quirky little hotel museum, rather than turning out rolls and croissants, has the practical reason that nowadays a baker would have both too much and too little to do at the Waldhaus (he or she could easily bake more than what our 200 or 280 guests need, but couldn't be there seven days a week). Besides, the impressive oven was badly damaged in 1939, when some water was inadvertently left in its pipes at the end of the season, which ruined the oven when it froze in the unheated winter.

We should not linger too long, mourning such losses. Instead, let's rejoice about all the additional things we now have, attractions that, mostly, no one would even have thought of in the past: the spa with its baths and treatments and all that goes with it, the amenities and activities for children, the great many cultural events. You can hardly say that today's hotel life is poorer or less interesting than in the good old days. All the more so since I confidently think that the Waldhaus has been able to maintain the intangible essentials which have given it its true character since its earliest days: its management by the family, its independence, the personal welcome, the generosity of its spaces and spirit, our steady concentration on just one "core product," the Waldhaus. There is its serene and happy calm, its relaxed and unforced sense of community, its typical restraint. A hotel with class and without airs—a "one-class hotel" in the sense that, to the maximum degree possible, we want to put the emphasis on what the hotel can offer all, rather than just some, of its guests. All these traits are always under pressure. But we are pretty obstinate when it comes to the Waldhaus.

FAITHFUL COMPANIONS
Switzerland as a tourist destination already had an amazing infrastructure early on: hotels, trains, steamers, and so on. Much of it is still here. For a long time, though, few took much pride in that historic heritage. It was just for tourism, after all, and anyway who wanted to be seen as old-fashioned? Gradually, some devotees and experts started to question and counter that general neglect—such as the architectural historian and preservation expert Roland Flückiger, Beat and Dorothee Kleiner with their private "Hotel and Tourism Museum" (closed in 2008) and the hikers and writers, Ursula Bauer and Jürg Frischknecht. ICOMOS Switzerland began bringing preservationists, tourism professionals and interested hoteliers together in specialized conferences and started awarding a prize for "Historic Hotel of the Year" (the Waldhaus received it in 2005, plus a special anniversary edition in 2015). Our most active connection with historically-minded colleagues is "Swiss Historic Hotels," which we helped found in 2004.

All gone

Admittedly, we Waldhaus children, now grown old, wistfully remember quite a list of lost rituals, traces and special places that shaped our own childhood, even if no one else will have noticed that they are gone. When I enter the lower garage and the indoor tennis court, I remember the meadow, which they replaced with a fenced-in area where the laundry was hung up to dry. I remember the sleek rowboats on the lake. You can still find boats there, but they seem wider, heavier, more ungainly by comparison. The old service elevator with its wire cage, replaced in 1976, which opened up splendid views towards Maloja as you rose. The fountain behind the hotel, which had once served to catch the overflow from the hydraulic guest elevator (see p. 40) and the traces of which were still visible in our youth. The many, alluringly mysterious storage rooms all over, in the attic, on the floor underneath the public rooms, in the basement and other hidden places. The chaise longues (recamieres) which used to stand in very many of the guest rooms and then became more and more of a rarity. The curious short ski lift, which in the 1960s led from the plain to the hotel, with its rather awkward downhill run through the forest.

"My craziest assignment was when the GM came to me and said, 'We have to do this quickly.' He meant that we had to remodel the entire fourth floor. There were staff rooms there and now they were supposed to be dismantled, the walls taken out, the windows refurbished and the rooms turned into guest rooms. And I, I was supposed to make all the new doors. A mere forty of them!" If anyone knows that the time between the seasons is no longer a "quiet time," it is ERWIN BRUNSCHWILER (82), who was an in-house carpenter at the Waldhaus for 36 years. Those were the years when we were investing left, right and center, trying to catch up with the backlog from hard times past. Once, when all of us were sitting around swapping stories, Erwin said, "I could tell a lot. But I won't."

When reintroducing the winter season, Rolf Kienberger thought it essential to have an offer for skiers close to the hotel, particularly children. It was a lift with only two T-bars; the lift would not run continuously, but carry a single skier or two to the top and then stop, while the other, empty T-bar arrived at the bottom, ready for the next taker. Every spring the entire lift would be dismantled and stored away, and then laboriously set up again at Christmas—the same seasonal ritual of dismantling and rebuilding as with the ungainly wooden winter porch in front of the main entrance (you can see it on p. 266), and—in reverse chronology—the miniature golf course, which was stored away in a garage during the winter and then reassembled every June.

Those were not the only rituals related to closing down for the time between the seasons and reopening for the next. The most complex operation was that until 1963, i.e. in the years when there was no winter season or just a very short one, all water and heating pipes in the hotel had to be drained to prevent the water in them from freezing in the sub-zero temperatures because the hotel (except for the offices and the family's apartment) was not heated between the seasons. Some water was almost always left somewhere by oversight, creating leaks when it froze and expanded, which then led to nasty and messy surprises when the water and the heat were turned back on.

The actual time between the seasons, which began and ended in such a laborious and ceremonious fashion with all these rituals, had a different feel from today as well, it was, or seemed to us, much quieter than it does now. Fittingly, we all called it "the quiet time"—the term, and the reality behind it, has pretty much disappeared. The seasons have (fortunately) become much longer and more intense and the time in-between correspondingly shorter, filled more and more with work and bustle, which owes more than a little to the advent of "instant communication."

Even so, the transitions, the ebb and flow of the seasons, remain a good and treasured aspect of our life at the hotel. Our years do not simply slip by in an uninterrupted stream, they always contain a structure and a certain positive tension. And the changes that gradually took away the quiet from the "quiet time" were not all bad; the "quiet" of days gone by also contained the menace of "eternal rest," the Waldhaus could not have survived in the long run on such short seasons and with so little investment. Thus, there are two sides to everything, even to this hotel that takes pride in not having a back and a front.

Quiet time. Notes from a hotel child

Jürg Kienberger

JÜRG KIENBERGER is the only one of our generation to really have moved away from the hotel. In decades as a musician and actor, he has inspired theater-goers on large and small stages throughout the German-speaking world and sometimes far beyond. It can rightly be said that he is the only one of us to have a real profession. But the Waldhaus has not let him go. Many of his productions consciously or subconsciously draw on his hotel memories, and he continues to have strong ties to the family business (he was a member of our board of directors from 1999 to 2018).

"It did not bother me, the youngest, that our family moved four times every year. I, the youngest, was not bothered by the fact that our family moved four times every year. My two oldest siblings, though, had to completely recalibrate every few months, as they were already going to school.

From Christmas to Easter we lived in St. Moritz, high above the town at the Chantarella Hotel, which my parents managed in winter for several years. After the winter season ended, we would move 50 meters closer to the ski runs into a rented house, the Villa Chantarella, where we spent the time between the seasons, which we fondly called the 'quiet time,' and played at being a 'real' family. Mama cooked, Papa didn't wear a tie, and we four children didn't have to speak in a whisper or tiptoe around all of the time. In May we would move everything we had 10 kilometers upriver along the Inn to Sils Maria, to our real home, the Waldhaus. At the time, the Waldhaus was only open in summer. After the summer season, we would move back to our off-season house in October and then, finally, to the Chantarella Hotel just before Christmas, having thus survived our fourth move.

The language of instruction at the St. Moritz elementary school is German, whereas in Sils the children are taught in Romansch. At the time, it hardly seemed worth noting that in Maloja, only another 5 kilometers away, the children were Italian-speaking. We picked up Italian at the hotel from the staff. What's more, first-graders in St. Moritz were taught to print, while the Sils first-graders wrote cursive. My siblings had to learn both; and not confusing 'zweiundvierzig' (42) with 'vainchaquatter' (24) is not exactly easy, even if you are not dyslexic. The one consolation was that Sils had much longer summer vacations, given that it still had a substantial number of farming families who needed the children to help with the hay harvest in summer. In St. Moritz winter vacations were longer, so my siblings got to enjoy two sets of longer vacations. Besides, recalibrating keeps you on your toes; to this day, both of my oldest siblings are very good with numbers.

Drawing on a lifetime of hotel expertise and experience, my 61-year-old great-grandfather built the Waldhaus in 1908. My grandparents took over after him and managed, in the roaring 1920s and until war broke out in 1939, to complement our summer business with a series of fairly successful winter seasons. During and after the war, the British, German and Canadian winter-sport enthusiasts stayed away, and it was no longer possible to open the hotel in winter.

Only in 1955/56 did they dare to try reopening in winter, and already in February we at the Chantarella received word from Sils that 'he has stopped eating.' My grandfather was refusing to eat as he was so worried about the miserable occupancy rates. In deference to his health, the family decided to close the hotel immediately. Over the next few winters, the hotel was only ever opened for a short time, over Christmas/New Year, when it filled with guests who hadn't found rooms in St. Moritz.

St. Moritz was well-equipped for winter sports, while Sils still didn't have any lifts. The effort for these short winter openings was enormous. The hotel, where the temperature had fallen below freezing, had to be heated up weeks in advance, and there was the difficulty of finding staff for just three weeks. For the kitchen and dining rooms they hired the entire brigade from the Splendido Hotel in Portofino, as the bathing season there didn't start before March.

In 1963/64, my dad convinced my skeptical grandfather to make another attempt at opening the Waldhaus for an entire winter season. We moved for the last time. The Chantarella had to find other managers. It was torn down in 2002, some fancy vacation homes have replaced the venerable hotel; the villa, where we spent our beloved "quiet time," is still standing.

In Sils, everything went well over the end-of-year holidays, but by Epiphany (January 6) at the latest, nearly all of the guests had left.

The time of the dreaded "January hole" was upon us. Over the following three weeks, four to at most seven guests wandered around the large hotel. They were taken care of by 13 chefs, their executive chef and the pastry chef, 15 waiters, five chambermaids and just as many assistant maids, four floor porters, the head housekeeper, a first and second concierge, a night porter, a switchboard operator, three doormen and bellboys, a chauffeur, seven people at the office (including an intern), the person in charge of provisions and her assistant, the person in charge of the coffee kitchen, the cellar master, two dishwashers, a seamstress, a presser, four launderesses, a head laundryman, a house technician, a carpenter, a snow shoveler, the bandleader and his two fellow musicians.

To make the lonely existence of the few guests in the large public rooms more bearable, we as the owners' family discretely joined them. For once, we ate in the guests' dining room, and we children were even allowed to invite friends over and played parcheesi in small groups at various tables during the afternoon tea concert so that the lounge didn't look quite so empty. I liked to listen to Rudi Knina's trio, who played the same Viennese waltzes that I already knew from recordings at the Chantarella ice rink.

In February, the number of guests went up again, our family modestly withdrew to our private dining room, we went back to eating the same meals as the staff and, as ever, were called to greet or say good-bye to all arriving or departing guests, be it Sunday evening or in the middle of the all-important 12.30 "Beromünster" radio news. My grandfather had always wanted to personally greet and say good-bye to each guest, and this tradition continues unabated. When Easter came, the hotel unexpectedly filled up again and had 304 guests, including 80 children, partly sleeping on extra beds which we borrowed from other hotels which had already closed. A few days after Easter, my parents shook the hands of the last departing guests who would hopefully be back next year, and the off-season had begun. We children loved this, as the hotel finally belonged to us. Wrapped up in winter jackets and wool scarves, we rode our tricycles down the long, unheated corridors and through the empty public rooms. The carpets were rolled up, the furniture put away and everything covered with sheets. A wonderful place to play hide-and-seek. A badminton net was set up in the great lounge. My sister Claudia and I once got up to 1,024 volleys in a row, which took more than 20 minutes, and I even succeeded in blowing my nose with my left hand without having to put down the racket. Sometimes I secretly played the grand piano, until my fingers nearly froze despite my gloves. Back then, the "quiet time" justifiably and worthily earned its name.

January remained a fearful and yawning hole in our guest statistics for seven years, and the fully-booked Christmas and Easter holidays alone did not make it possible to earn enough money in the winter season to cover the urgently needed renovations.

Only in 1970, with construction of the indoor pool, for which my parents very courageously went hugely into debt, did the winter season begin to recover. The Furtschellas ski area was built and gradually the "January hole" was closed and renovations could begin. From now on, the "quiet time" would be replaced by construction noise, which began the minute the last guest departed.

At the moment, in 2019, Jürg K. performs and tours with Barbara Frey's *Die Toten* (based on James Joyce's *The Dead*) at the Zurich theater as well as the wonderful Christoph Marthaler productions of *Tiefer Schweb* for the Munich Kammerspiele and *Bekannte Gefühle, gemischte Gesichter* for the Volksbühne Berlin (also in Paris and at the Ruhrtriennale), and, finally, also with his solo productions, staged in close collaboration with his wife Claudia Carigiet, about Swiss reformer Huldrich Zwingli's childhood (*eingerockt+ausgesungen*), honey bees (*ich Biene-ergo summ*) and, now and again his classic, Waldhaus-inspired *Ich bin ja so allein,* along with Robert Walser's *Der Spaziergang* with Ueli Jäggi and *Novecento,* a Manfred Ferrari "resort k" production.
Jürg Kienberger and Claudia Carigiet live near Basel over the French border and have a daughter, Lena Kienberger. Lena, as you might guess, works in hotels.

Of the employees, totaling 135 by now (that is, by 2006), some 24 also continue living and working at the hotel during the off-season. The hotel is flourishing, and my siblings are satisfied—if somewhat pale and exhausted.

The year after next (in 2008), I will turn 50, the Waldhaus 100. I, too, now look older than our hotel, although I didn't become a hotelier. As part of the family, I have apparently also been infected, a hotel child who longs for vacations—for a long-lost quiet time."

"Quiet time. Notes from a hotel child," published in German in 2006 in the magazine Du *(vol. 66, issue 768: "Mythos St. Moritz")*

Travelling (back in time)

Car-free Sundays: If that rings a bell with you, you are probably Swiss, or perhaps German, and no longer quite young. In 1973, in the wake of the Yom Kippur war, the world lived through its first major oil crisis. Germany and Switzerland reacted by instituting countrywide Sunday driving bans for private transport. They lasted for only a few Sundays, but started to change people's minds about public transportation. In the preceding boom years, the future had more and more seemed to belong to private transportation, while public transport was relegated to the back burner. Now, people began to realize that the two need not be mutually exclusive and that an attractive public transportation system could benefit motorists, too, by reducing pressure on the roads.

Our region and the Waldhaus even had a leg up on this shift in attitudes. Before the crisis had hit, our region and the Swiss postal service (as the operator of the public buses) had come to an agreement to introduce a much-expanded winter service for that very winter, with buses connecting the towns and ski areas of the Upper Engadine at 30-minute intervals. As recently as in 1967/68, for example, there had been a total of only eight daily connections from Sils to St. Moritz (and all of five per day in off-season), only one of which did not involve a transfer if you wanted to get from Sils to the Corvatsch cable car. Until 1973, the Waldhaus had no choice but to rent a private bus with its driver from the lowlands every winter, to make the trip to and from Corvatsch and St. Moritz on a fixed schedule a couple of times a day. Now, we decided to simply offer our guests a free pass for the new "sport bus" and provide a van service between the hotel, the Sils bus stop and the newly opened Furtschellas cable car.

What many hotels have started doing quite recently, offering the free use of public transportation, thus has a tradition of almost half a century at the Waldhaus! At first, it was only in winter. Starting in 1997—once more, way ahead of others—we added a free summer pass to the cable cars and lifts, followed in 1999 by a free pass for the buses and trains in the region, all the way down to Soglio and Chiavenna, up to Alp Grüm and over to Zuoz and—if you dare to pronounce the Romansch names—S-chanf and Cinous-chel. (The economist who writes these lines notes with some dismay that the cost of the passes has continued to rise, notwithstanding the growing participation of other entities and hence the decline in exclusivity.)

Quite early, too, we took another symbolically important step. When Sils opened its large public underground garage in 1995, and began to seriously focus on reducing traffic in town, the Waldhaus decided to join in by introducing a—deliberately moderate—outdoor parking fee of its own for the first time. Without that "green tax," we would have risked that more and more of the premises of the hotel would be co-opted as parking spaces. ("This is the Wald Haus, not the Park Hotel," we quipped in German). Concurrently, we did away with the rather substantial charge that guests travelling by trains had had to pay for being picked up and dropped off by our chauffeur at the St. Moritz station when they arrived and departed (even at the time, it was CHF 44 for two people and CHF 64 for four, for instance.)

Meanwhile, the two Waldhaus underground garages which were opened in 1983 and 1999, both hewn out of the bedrock at considerable cost, show that we are not trying to get rid of motorists, we are just trying to do some nudging when it comes to private and public transportation.

Speaking of arrivals and departures: guests with the bad luck of having to drive up or down the hill right when it is snowing, risking their composure and their fenders and, all too often, enriching the auto repair shops in the Engadine in the process, will always view the ascent to the Waldhaus as a challenge and an imposition. While it's snowing, there really is little else you can do except put on the chains or wait until it stops. Otherwise, though, there is no comparison anymore to the hassle of winter driving conditions as they were in the past. What a blessing vehicles with four-wheel drive are, especially our own. We used to have to try everything to master the steep incline: put more weight on the wheels by putting heavy marble slabs in the trunk (actually, the

Around 1925, yet untroubled by the automobile: horse-drawn sleighs in front of the Waldhaus

marble tops from the old dressers in the guest rooms), install differential locks for the rear axle, spread sand and, over and over again, put chains on the tires.

In winter, the horses used to pull real sleighs. So much more pleasing to the eye than the plain and pragmatic all-weather coaches of today with their rubber tires, but for the sleighs to slide, the town crew had to keep shoveling snow into the road leading up to the hotel, which of course made it all the more difficult for cars. For many years, the Waldhaus fully lived up to its reputation as possibly the first grand hotel in the Alps with a Darwinian touch (a natural selection of motorized guests who made it versus those who did not), all the more so because the village streets and even the highways were plowed without the use of any salt. Today hardly anyone would be prepared to risk such conditions. Spreading salt, basically, does make the roads and paths somewhat easier to travel or walk on—alas, not always; with very low temperatures, it is just the opposite. Ice at low temperatures is actually brittle and much less slippery, but the salt lowers its melting point and makes it slippery anyway. Aesthetically, in any case, the salt is a disaster. It leads to brown and dirty winter streets with unsightly sidewalls and unfortunate, even destructive consequences for our splendid rugs in the hotel. There are times when we just want to join the Luddites and, well, steer back into the past!

← Waldhaus Spa, looking into the stone-pine bath

How to square a bathroom

How did we get from 38 bathrooms to 150? Adding and rebuilding bathrooms is like open-heart surgery, a complex spatial, technical and architectural challenge. The hotel needs intelligent, attractive and inviting bathrooms, and as many as possible. Along the way, you want to lose as few bedrooms as possible. You don't want to decrease hotel capacity or end up with less attractive and less practical floor plans. You have to have water, obviously, and right where it is needed, and drains, ventilation and heat. You also need enough electricity: where there is a bathroom, there is a hairdryer. How well we remember those years when we had more and more bathrooms, with the effect that at the peak of the season, at night just before dinnertime, when everyone was doing their hair the master fuse would blow! The range in the kitchen would grow cold, and in the bar the guests were suddenly sitting in the dark with their cocktails (or with wet hair in their equally dark bathrooms).

These challenges are exacerbated by the way in which this lovely old hotel is constructed: no concrete, but load-bearing walls made of quarry stones with an inserted framework of wood and iron, the floors underlaid with wooden beams and iron girders. Everything is sturdy and well-conceived, but every structural change, even just moving a door, turns into a costly and time-consuming exercise—which is all the more of a problem because of our long seasons and correspondingly short construction periods. You always had to think very carefully before deciding on any change.

Not to mention the money. Often, much was needed and little was available.

> *"Look," my father said, leaning over to lift the edge of the carpet. "If we had some money lying here, I would build a dozen bathrooms in no time." But there was nothing there except some dust, of course. It was around Christmas of 1967, I believe, and everybody in the family was talking about a big and lucrative convention we expected to get in March ... except that the participants all wanted rooms with bathrooms, while half of our rooms (and most of the ones still available) did not have any. Would the convention end up passing us by? Ever the impatient 15-year-old, I had said, this is impossible, we really have to build more bathrooms and fast. The image of my father's response, stooping down with the edge of the rug in his hand has stayed with me all these years.*
> *Despite the lack of bathrooms, the convention and the entire season turned into a resounding success. It was our first really good winter since 1930, and my father, steady go-getter that he was, continued building bathroom upon bathroom as rapidly as he could. And, my own impatience? It hasn't changed a bit.*

Building bathrooms is like trying to square a whole bunch of overlapping circles. Very Swiss, if you think about it, this continual search for balance between conflicting objectives! We have devoted ourselves to it with a passion, for generations. The results are rarely perfect to a casual observer, but that is just the point: conflict and balance. Rolf Kienberger, who almost always designed our hotel bathrooms on his own, became a true master. His eldest, the author of these lines, has followed in his footsteps, always traveling with a pencil and a tape measure in order to analyze good or bad solutions; or mentally moving walls and placing tubs and toilets even when taking a walk in the forest or a shower in the morning.

The very first attempt to add more bathrooms to the Waldhaus dates back much further ... and did not go terribly well. Unlike their counterparts in the other corners of the hotel, the attractive corner rooms 94, 144 and 194 at the front of the west wing did not originally have bathrooms of their own. In about 1923, they did get them—sort of: a small cube in a corner of the room (actually, a rather threadbare wooden construction, plastered over with a layer of reeds and wire netting), placed directly on the oak parquet. It contained only a tub and a toilet, perched on top of some linoleum, and was lit by a skylight high up in the wall. A double wash basin was installed in the guest room itself, and in order to regain some of the space lost, the stand-alone closet was set into the wall, with its feet still visible at the front. Family lore has it that this peculiar ensemble was the brainchild of Uncle Gustav and Aunt Mali, Gustav Giger and his sister Mali Wolflisberg, in those years of transition after World War I, when Oskar and Helene Kienberger had already been made general managers, but were still running the Palace Lugano (see p. 101).

Starting in 1925, Oskar Kienberger took over full-time, and under his aegis and in fruitful collaboration with architect Karl Koller more than a dozen additional, more satisfactory bathrooms were built and others renovated during the prosperous years leading up to 1930. No one foresaw at the time that 32 years would go by before we would be able to add any more.

Even the semi-successful experiment in rooms 94, 144 and 194 would stay in place for nearly a lifetime. What must Vivien Leigh have thought of it? She and her then-husband Leigh Holman spent two weeks in room 194 over the turn of the year 1936–37 (before she had filmed "Gone with the Wind" and a few months before Laurence Olivier became her lover). Only in 1986 were these lovely rooms finally paired with bathrooms elegant and generous enough to do them justice. To that end, we sacrificed the front of the public hallways with their windows looking west. For once, we gave the demands of individual rooms precedence over the quality of the public spaces. We do not do this lightly, as is illustrated by all the trouble we went to in 2005, spending a lot of money and giving up one guest room on each floor, in order to correct a misstep from the 1980s, when a series of new bathrooms were added, which protruded into the main corridor.

Spring 2005

Dear Guests,
Swiss hotels need new hallways! We have decided to show the way. This spring our spacious main corridors are being restored, the final and most visible part of a major two-year renovation which includes the remodeling of 24 rooms and bathrooms.

Of course, we don't really believe that anyone comes to the Waldhaus simply because of its corridors. We are convinced, however, that a good, attractive resort hotel is more than a mere assemblage of junior suites and wellness facilities. A lovely, old grand hotel like ours has many qualities that are no less important for being hard to measure. They can't be measured … but they can be carelessly destroyed; or conversely, they can be maintained and strengthened. That is precisely the goal of our current efforts. With the help of architects Miller & Maranta, we are going to great lengths to preserve the traditional character of our old corridors or to recapture it. As for the guest and bath rooms (architect Armando Ruinelli in cooperation with Eva Lamberti), we want to regain the generosity of the original floor plans, without, of course, doing away with the comfortable bathrooms and other amenities.

There were other detours and wrong turns along the way. In the 1970s, 80s and 90s, we were finally able to build or renovate numerous bathrooms, putting in kilometers of new pipes in the process. In the aftermath we discovered that the alloy from which these pipes were made did not agree with our water. Particularly in the hot water circuit, the water heavily corroded the pipes, and our celebrated spring water from the Fex Valley often came out of the faucets brown and cloudy to our and our guests' great dismay. Not all of the time, and exasperatingly, by no means always in the same place, but over and over again. Improved, more suitable grades of steel were already on the market, but our local plumbing contractor who had been building our bathrooms and had done a good job for many years, lacked the facilities to work with that material. Sadly, then, we had this new and obstinate problem on our hands precisely where we had invested so much. It took decades and many additional investments until we were gradually able to rid ourselves of the problem; today we are nearly there. It is sobering and disturbing to think what a disaster it would have been if that problem had, instead, emerged during one of the many times in our history when we'd simply have had no money at all to fix it.

Good is good, but better carries it. That is as true for bathrooms as for much else: what was good enough yesterday, may not be good enough for today. To avoid falling behind with our bathrooms, we have enlisted excellent and experienced help from outside. It started with the architects Miller and Maranta, whose first commission at the Waldhaus was the restoration and modernization of seven large vintage rooms and bathrooms in 1995. And over the past twelve years or so, architect Armando Ruinelli from Soglio has already renovated close to 70 bathrooms and many guest rooms as well.

← Thomas Demand, Alexander Kluge, Sir David Chipperfield

A hotel with culture at the core? Well …

No, we did not include the Bavarian beer festival held on Furtschellas, although it was fun. In summer 2018, we counted some 80 cultural events open to the public at the Waldhaus: lectures, concerts, readings, book launches, discussions with authors, excursions, and performances. (In the fabulous summer of our centennial in 2008, there were even half again as many.) There were the Hesse Days, the Sils "Kunst-und-Literat(o)ur" Days, the Resonanzen Festival, the Nietzsche Colloquium, Arthur Godel's long-established readers' circles, guest appearances by "Origen" and the Engadine Festival; we had choir weeks and dance classes. A very lively and varied program, much to our own liking as well. These Waldhaus events are complemented by countless public events and guided tours elsewhere in town and in the region.

Does this make the Waldhaus a "hotel with art and culture at its core," a *Kulturhotel*, as one would say in German with its predilection for compound words? People who call us that mean it as a compliment. But we have always been reluctant to define ourselves in this way. We find it too limiting; it falls short of what we want the Waldhaus to be. At least if "culture" and "art" are too quickly and too narrowly understood as cultural and artistic activities.

Children and families, sports, seminars, vacations, the incredible scenery and the views, the historic hotel, culinary pleasures, luxury: Luckily for us, a wide variety of reasons exist for visiting us and for liking our hotel. Some of the reasons may even be at odds with each other; you can read a book and a hotel in more ways than one. The very feature that one guest will seek and value most may be entirely secondary to others, or they may not even see that it's there. In general, the one thing that we and most of those who visit us primarily want is the Waldhaus as a *hotel*—as a functioning, good, inviting hotel. If there is one art in which we and our employees most hope to excel and for which we hope to be praised, it is that we know how to take care of our guests. That is an art, it is more than just craftsmanship and infrastructure. What counts for our guests is not just what we do but the way in which we do it. In other words, a question of culture, too. "Corporate culture": management textbooks are full of it. At a hotel, though, it goes beyond any textbook meaning; it carries its own weight and is part of the product. In a good hotel so much depends on the style, the culture of the place. This includes the way we deal with each other—ideally with attention and competence, with seriousness and a light touch, i.e. without overbearing solemnity and solicitude. It is the furnishings, the architecture, the engaging tension between old and new and the way in which we handle it, the quirks and rough edges, whether wanted or unintentional. It is a willingness to accept patina without getting caught up in it. It is the hidden chapel on the ground floor and salon music in the lounge. It is our steadfast refusal to make every corner of the hotel economically productive. It is our interaction with the environment, both the natural and the cultural, human one. All of that is part of our hotel culture.

We are in the "hospitality industry," but it is an ambiguous term. The art and culture of making guests feel truly welcome is our profession, and we are proud of it. Call it a mission, a passion; but is it hospitality? Wouldn't that have to be free? In a hotel, there is almost always a bill at the end. That need not diminish the value and beauty of our task. We make every effort to do justice to it, just as a musician aims to do justice to a Beethoven sonata. It is telling that Rolf Kienberger placed a marvelous 200-year-old quote by Brillat-Savarin at the beginning of the 1983 German edition of the "Waldhaus Sils-Maria" book: *Convier quelqu'un, c'est se charger de son bonheur pendant tout le temps qu'il est sous notre toit.*

And an essential part of this culture is, always, our guests. They are not mere consumers, nor mere audience, as in a theater; they play a key role as co-creators of our "production."

I am sure that our great-grandparents Josef and Amalia Giger, who founded the Waldhaus would have had little patience for such fancy talk. And yet, our discussions give a fair description of what they actually did in their daily life and work, as does Brillat-Savarin's charming definition of what it means to host someone. The hotel that they created was exceptionally cultivated and cultured right from the start. They practiced what they didn't preach. And the guests, whom the Waldhaus, just like Sils in general, was able to interest and attract from its earliest days, had a wonderful cultural pedigree. There are names which still have a prominent ring today: the great publisher, Samuel Fischer (with or without Hermann Hesse in tow; Hesse himself, who became a loyal Waldhaus regular many years later, in his old age thought he recalled an early Waldhaus visit at Fischer's invitation, although there is no trace of it in our guestbooks), or the Visconti family, or Katja Mann Pringsheim with her parents and probably a short first visit of her husband's as well. Our early guest books also show many half-forgotten luminaries that a knowledgeable reader might recognize, such as banker Carl Fürstenberg, known for his spirit and wit, or the businessman and patron of the arts, James Simon, to whom Berlin's great state museums owe Nefertiti's bust and many other treasures from ancient Egypt. A patient Google search would surely reveal many other interesting backgrounds and stories.

If Sils and the Waldhaus truly had culture at their core, it was mainly in light of our guests. This is still true today. Some years ago, a winter guest told me as he was leaving that he had brought along five books to read during his vacation—and in the course of that vacation he had spotted all five authors right here at the hotel, some of them actually staying here, others just visiting someone. (Or maybe it was only four out of five? We hoteliers always tend to embellish our stories.)

The German scholar, Paul Raabe (1927–2013), wrote a wonderful and eminently readable house-by-house report of interesting and famous Sils visitors from the past, *Spaziergänge durch Nietzsches Sils-Maria*. Arche published it in 1994, and reprinted it five more times until 2005, but it was out of print after that. Fortunately, Felix Dietrich's tenacity, support from a generous friend of the author and the willing cooperation of its former publisher with a new one (Wallstein in Göttingen) has now yielded a new edition, comprehensively revised by Mirella Carbone and Joachim Jung. If you read German, don't miss it! (If you read French, look for *Sur les pas de Nietzsche à Sils-Maria*, Edition Les Trois Platanes, adapté de l'allemand par Françoise Autin.)

"I take time to relax"

Alexander Kluge

Alexander Kluge and his family have been guests at the Waldhaus for more than a quarter of a century. We asked him five questions, we could have asked 500.

Is the Waldhaus more of a meeting place to you, or a peaceful haven?

Both. You can seclude yourself in this large hotel and find your peace and quiet. Or, in just a few steps, you can be with the other guests. Peace and quiet do not necessarily require solitude. Getting together with friends who return to the Waldhaus year after year like migratory birds creates a positive sense of time, too. And this is exactly what we mean by peace.

ALEXANDER KLUGE (*1932) is an intellectual powerhouse, not only as an author and filmmaker. His production company, for example, is responsible for an independent TV cultural journal which is broadcast by such networks as RTL. He has been traveling to Sils for 60 years, first coming on account of Theodor W. Adorno, who for a long time was a loyal, critical, fractious Waldhaus regular.

What encounters do you remember?

I have met people at the Waldhaus whom I might never have directly met anywhere else. I was aware of my contemporary, Gerhard Richter—born, like me, in February 1932—only through his famous paintings (i.e. abstractly). One day I was sitting in the Waldhaus bar writing my stories, and Gerhard Richter approached me spontaneously. Thanks to this encounter we have written two lovely books together and are friends.

Every year my children, my wife and I meet the extended Chipperfield family, and Nana and Thomas Demand. Since our first meeting at the Waldhaus, the Demands have added two children. There is little reason to retire to your room, although you could at any time.

Do you ever find time to relax at the Waldhaus or are there sometimes simply too many culture enthusiasts at the hotel?

I take time to relax. I need such quiet times, too, as I don't just vacation at the Waldhaus, but also work on my stories. Many of my texts were written here.

"111 years Hotel Waldhaus: Why?" That was Urs Kienberger's first choice as a title for this book. Have you also asked yourself that?

111 years Waldhaus! That is not a "why" question. It is an expression of wonderment. My children have been here nearly every year of their lives. They don't ask why. They find the Waldhaus a happy place. I find it amazing that so much time has gone by since 1908. My mother was born in 1908.

What do you like about the Waldhaus and what makes you return?

I passed the threshold of the Waldhaus for the first time in 1956. As a young lawyer, I brought some official papers from Frankfurt to Th. W. Adorno and his wife Grete. My attachment to this hotel continues up to the present. I keep returning, not out of inertia or mere habit, but out of affection.

← Johanna Staemmler, Armida Quartet

The leased Parnassus

When the Waldhaus scarcely knew where to turn during World War I, facing shortages of guests and money and labor, and short of food supplies as well, they had the idea of leasing some summer pastures from the village, including the cows (see p. 113). In World War II, when things became terribly difficult again, they chose to bring in Wilhelm Backhaus and Dinu Lipatti and other great musicians. 1941 saw the launching of the Engadine Concert Weeks, at the initiative of Ernst Schulthess (1899–1990), the enterprising and admirably well-connected protestant minister of Silvaplana and Sils. Excellent and acclaimed musicians gave first-rate concerts in return for a vacation.

In the beginning the concerts and recitals were concentrated on Sils and Silvaplana, with the Waldhaus as a natural focal point, since many other large hotels in the region were closed during the war. The concert series, which continues to this day under the heading of "Engadine Festival," quickly became a magnet for famous names, a kind of little sister to Lucerne: pianists Clara Haskil and Edwin Fischer performed, cellist Pierre Fournier, flutist Peter-Lukas Graf, oboist Heinz Holliger and his wife, the harpist Ursula Holliger, as well as ensembles such as the English Chamber Orchestra under Pinchas Zuckermann, the Collegium Musicum Zurich under Paul Sacher and later (in St. Moritz, of course!) the Berlin Philharmonic under Herbert von Karajan.

But curiously, the Waldhaus would organize almost no cultural events of its own for a long time to come. It was certainly not for want of the right guests or the right hotelier. The guest lists were a virtual Who's

Who of the cultural elite of the time, and hotelier Oskar Kienberger was exceptionally well-read, well-versed in music and had wide-ranging interests. Possibly, most guests were simply looking for peace and quiet. The main factor holding back cultural activities was probably quite mundane: the depression and wartime years, and the austere times that followed, simply left the hotel with no scope for anything "extra." The following Waldhaus generation, too, personified by the subtly sophisticated Rolf Kienberger, whose cultural affinities were pretty much on a par with his father's, deliberately and uncompromisingly concentrated all efforts on the nearly impossible goal of bringing the old family business back to a new and sustainable flowering.

Only when Rolf Kienberger was actually able to pull that off, against all obstacles and in the face of the experts' unalloyed skepticism, was there, quite literally, more room to play. Providentially, at just that time, a person came on stage, soon followed by a second one, who were ready to exploit this new potential to the very fullest. The first was Felix Dietrich. My brother-in-law came without much of a cultural background, but with a wonderfully open mind and capacity for enthusiasm, a born organizer ever ready to get practically and tangibly involved, in cases where others would hesitate.

And then I arrived, the one who would try to structure and communicate, take up other things on my own, sometimes put the brakes on, too. But let's not give credit where credit is not due. What Nietzsche, the most famous Silser, once said, that "one must still have chaos in oneself," could sometimes be my motto as well. If I talk about "structuring," I mean it intellectually and not necessarily in an operational sense. I wanted to understand and articulate, see connections and build bridges between works and artists, and ourselves and the public, particularly if the topics and events were out of the ordinary and less than obvious. In a modest but mostly productive way, it was a symbiosis between the two of us, my brother-in-law and me, if tinged with a dose of rivalry, stressful and exhilarating, a most fertile ground for a lavish bouquet of magnificent and often highly original offerings.

It has now become quite fashionable for hotels to "do" some culture. As a guest you sometimes face an over-abundance of choices. In the not-too-distant past, though, only a few had this idea (just as many grand hotels used to pay relatively scant attention to families with children, or local products, or public transportation). Early or late in the season, in particular, our program at the Waldhaus sometimes accounted for half or more of the entire Upper Engadine events calendar. If it hadn't been for the Laudinella in St. Moritz, to which we respectfully tip our hats, the predominance would have been even more pronounced.

When we pause to reflect, we remember thousands of special moments and thousands of special people to whom we would like to express our gratitude. Here are just a few which spontaneously come to mind.

In 1982, when the Austrian writer Ilse Aichinger was awarded the Petrarca Prize established by the German publisher, Hubert Burda, an illustrious crowd gathered at the Waldhaus. Hermann Lenz was there, as were fellow writers Urs Widmer, Peter Handke, Lars Gustafsson, Peter Hamm. Michael Krüger gave the laudation. To mark the festivities, Felix organized a memorable banquet at the outlandish Palazzo Castelmur in Val Bregaglia, which nobody had done for ages. At the decisive (i.e., most inopportune) moment, a severe thunderstorm came up, and whoosh the electricity went off. But our Farkaš trio steadfastly played on, Felix and his team calmly gained control of the chaos behind the scenes, dinner was served by candlelight. A dream of an occasion.

"O man! Take heed! The philosophers are coming!" It was in 1982, as well, that the industrious Professor Peter André Bloch of the Nietzsche House brought a meeting for Nietzsche experts and other interested parties to the Waldhaus. It had already taken place in the village once or twice. Named, programmatically, a "colloquium," it wanted to be more than just a series of top-down lectures. The Nietzsche Colloquium soon became a fixed institution in our fall calendar and continues to today. Every year it keeps us on our toes for four days and time and again provides us with very special moments (admittedly, also some moments where we laypersons don't understand a word). On the occasion of the 2011 Colloquium, a generous sponsor and board member of the Nietzsche House from Britain brought the great András Schiff with his breathtaking performance of Beethoven's Diabelli Variations to the Waldhaus. Miraculously, the maestro returned three years later, independently of the "Nietzsche connection," for a second and equally splendid piano recital.

Another, entirely different moment which left a lasting impression on me was the 1990 Colloquium, just after the fall of the Iron Curtain. Taking as its theme Nietzsche's reception in the GDR and the Soviet Union (to the extent that Nietzsche was a topic there at all), it brought together participants such as Jurij Archipow, a Soviet Germanist, and Ralf Eichberg, a young philosopher from the East German city of Halle an der Saale, as well as the Lutheran minister from Röcken and even a railway worker from the city of Naumburg. Nietzsche's father had been pastor in Röcken; upon his early death, his wife and the two children moved to Naumburg. The railway man happened to live in the very house to which they moved, and in which Nietzsche's sister would later establish the first Nietzsche archive. (The house is now—once again—a Nietzsche center ... run today by Ralf Eichberg.) It was a great and imaginative idea to bring these disparate people together. To hear how the four had, independently from each other and partly without any prior background in the matter, discovered with open minds the legacy of the great philosopher ostracized by the regime, and how, with courage and cunning, they had helped to salvage and protect that legacy, changed and broadened my view of East Germany and its history.

One of the most unusual of our many unusual visitors, or at least one whom you would not automatically associate with the seemingly calm and sedate Waldhaus, was the Appenzell artist Roman Signer. He has won fame as creator of ephemeral, elaborate and whimsical (and sometimes explosive) "time-sculptures." The uncommon and memorable encounter, in July 2003, arose from our own curiosity and the intercession of a common acquaintance. It included a public evening at the hotel and an expedition across the border to Italy to purchase, second-hand, an iconic three-wheeled "Piaggio" delivery van, marking the outset of a special trip that would end on a ski jump near Zakopane in the native Poland of Roman Signer's wife.

"Can we show you something?" asked two creative guests, independently of each other, in the 1990s. We have heard that before; it immediately puts us on our guard. Jürg Amann (1947–2013), the Swiss writer and winner of the Ingeborg Bachmann Prize, who had gotten to know us well on regular stays at the Nietzsche House and visits to the Waldhaus, had been inspired by many stimulating hours in the Waldhaus lounge to write a play: "Hotel. Ein Stück". With 60 characters (well, you rarely have a hotel all to yourself). And, of course, he had the conviction that the Waldhaus lounge was the very place where that play would have to be staged. Then there was the prominent German photographer A. T. Schaefer, who had been a Waldhaus regular with his family since the 1980s. One day, he showed us photographs and said he intended to make something that (in his view) had not been done before: a real portrait of a hotel—of this hotel—in the form of a book. Not some kind of PR exercise with a few vainglorious shots, but a big, focused, carefully composed book, of the kind one might put together to portray the city of Venice or Greta Garbo.

Needless to say, we knew that neither would work. A full-grown play in the middle of the great lounge, not just for one evening, but eight, ten times? And, how to justify at the drop of a hat, commissioning such a fancy and expensive book?

And yet, we found both proposals very tempting. Their authors had evidently taken a very close and serious look at the Waldhaus, and what they had come up with reflected the hotel in ways which we recognized and shared. (That happens far less often than you might think.) In addition, the projects appealed to our spirit of adventure and experimentation. Now then! In 1998, the Waldhaus would celebrate its 90th anniversary. We had toyed with the idea of celebrating that milestone in a suitable way. Much was going well for us at the moment, and we were in good form; who knew how it would be when the 100th anniversary came around? We also figured that, with the new millennium coming up in 2000, everyone and his sister would vie for public attention with grand projects. If, instead, we did something now, we would have the limelight to ourselves. (You see: a hotelier thinks like a ringmaster. Just without the lions and the elephants.)

So, we made a bold decision: we would do both! It took an inordinate amount of work and money and nerves. And our employees, too, were stretched to their very limits, as they mastered all the demands with valiant professionalism. But our travails were rewarded with unbelievable success, both as artistic achievement and in terms of publicity. Around 2,000 people saw the play, with six actors expertly dividing up the 60 roles, prominently among them our brother Jürg Kienberger and his wife Claudia Carigiet; even their daughter Lena had a small part. The splendid coffee-table book by A.T. Schaefer, who had devoted no less than 85 days of hard work at the Waldhaus to the photographs and had consented at our request to enrich it with ten clever essays by prominent guests, was a hit—to such an extent that we started calling the Waldhaus, tongue in cheek, "the hotel from the book."

"One day I am going to do something with the Waldhaus, too," Christoph Marthaler, the celebrated and unconventional Swiss theater producer, boldly stated. So, before we even started gathering and developing ideas for the 2008 Waldhaus centennial in our family get-togethers with the next generation, it was almost a foregone conclusion that it would feature a play as well ("The new generation steps in," p. 301). Christoph Marthaler, with his close-knit circle of actors, which had included Jürg Kienberger for many years already, had been a Waldhaus guest for a long time and had become a close friend. The same was true for many of those who worked with him.

Now, Christoph kept his word, and how! What he and his team thought up in spring 2008 went well beyond the relatively intimate play of ten years earlier, as big an undertaking as that had seemed to us at the time. They developed and rehearsed their play here at the hotel in

the time between the seasons. That in itself was already a big challenge, with them finding themselves alone with us in the empty hotel for week after week, as if on a remote island. Like a tsunami in Marthalerian slow motion, the play co-opted our entire premises, spreading out into the underground garage, the hallways, the reading room, the lounge and the dining room. The hotel and the play were so intensely interwoven that even we had a hard time seeing where the play stopped and hotel life began. When, in 2009, the Waldhaus play was nominated and chosen as "one of the ten most notable performances of German theater in the past year," which usually goes hand in hand with a coveted invitation to perform in Berlin in May, the participants unanimously decided that it could not be transported—to the great irritation of many in the theater world.

The Marthaler play was just one facet, although the most visible one, with which we drew attention to our centennial year. The family council had done an excellent job, as had our staff. Once again, we published a book, although with a different focus than the one from 1998. There were historic excursions with a 1948-vintage post bus, programs and offerings for children (Claudia Carigiet's children book "Gian and Gianna" was created for the occasion, as well as the Waldhaus children's pillow with Bravin, the squirrel, on it), artist Giuseppe Reichmuth made our little hotel museum a little less serious than it had been, and we initiated the tradition of a weekly chef's table in the imposing Waldhaus kitchen. Almost as an afterthought (I'm exaggerating), we spent close to CHF 10 million on one of the largest and most complex renovations in our history, all behind the scenes—to balance out the play, you might say—fixing up the kitchen, all of the adjoining working and storage areas and our staff's living quarters.

We drew only two red lines when we were planning the anniversary. As a matter of principle, we wanted to avoid as much as possible simply repeating what other hotels had already done. And, particularly, we were not going to have any fireworks. That was too noisy, too big, too ostentatious, too hard on nature. Christoph Marthaler and his actors knew that, too—and proceeded to take us for a glorious ride. At the very end of their play, the entire cast stood behind the net in the indoor tennis court, holding medicine balls of all sizes. Soon, they began dribbling the balls, gently at first and then harder and harder. The incomparable Graham Valentine took center stage and began to whistle through his fingers. And so, the 100-year-old Waldhaus still got its fireworks, acoustically perfect, touching and amazing!

The hotel comes first. This iron-clad principle applied even during the 2008 anniversary year, despite all of the cultural highlights. A simple statistic proves it: 244 paying guests. That was the daily average in that year's winter season, from the first to the last of the 114 days of that season. In the summer season, too (which lasted for 132), there were an impressive 183 guests per day. Our ancestors would have appreciated how improbable these figures were and how much work stood behind them. For a long time, 1929 had marked a high point never again attained, it was the measure of all things. From mid-July to the end of August 1929, the Waldhaus was permanently full, with an average of 242 guests. But that was the high season. With the slower start and end of the season, the 1929 average for the *entire* summer with its 113 days came to 154. And now, in that winter of 2008, which happened to have about the same length, it was 244. And in the summer, 20 days longer yet, it was 183.

A few years later, another Christoph, the untiringly resourceful Christoph Homberger, asked: "How about a cycle of Beethoven piano sonatas?" Hombi, sometime member of the Marthaler universe (he had been very much part of it in 2008) and a tenor, actor and theater producer in his own right, had brought us other fine highlights in the past. What he now had in mind was pretty crazy, though: a performance of all 32 piano sonatas, or even 36, if you count Beethoven's Op. 6 for four hands and three early works—but, not spaced across a year or two. No, all in one day, or rather, in one night, to be played one after the other by twelve respectable and in some cases quite prominent pianists. Crazy. Of course, we took the bait, and against all odds it became a first-rate musical experience. The Beethoven Night began at 9 p.m. on June 16, 2012 in the great lounge, with a full house. The audience was free to stand up, leave, get something to eat or drink, go for a walk, go to bed and then come back. Even in the wee hours of the morning, 30 people were still there; as dawn broke, more came back, and eventually the lounge was all full again, a rapt audience. Instead of simply following the chronological order, Christoph Homberger's artistic partner Christoph Keller had had the skill and good sense to work out a perfectly choreographed sequence of the sonatas and the interpreters, mixing and weaving the different keys, the different periods of composition and the individual styles of the performers into a riveting tapestry that provided a unique view of Beethoven's body of work for solo piano as a kind of monumental and fantastic pianistic landscape. The last note faded away at around 10.30 a.m. (it was Op. 81a, "Les Adieux," of course). It still echoes in our memory.

Some highlights come thundering in the door and test all limits. Others just calmly and softly drop in. A friend who keeps showing us that is Arthur Godel with his readers' circles. They are another stroke of luck, of the many we have had. Arthur Godel is a musicologist and literary scholar, who for many years was in charge of programming at SRF2, Switzerland's national German-language radio network for "classics and culture." He came by one day 16 years ago and proposed a series of reading seminars, comprising four days and three nights at the Waldhaus, for loyal SRF2 listeners who were members of the "SRF Kulturklub." He would accompany them with attractive events open to all guests: top-class authors' readings, classic chamber music, discussions or film presentations. That first, tentative series has turned into an institution. We have had 60 such seminars so far with hundreds of satisfied participants and numerous fascinating events, and six more are planned for this summer.

We do not want to leave the impression that we are primarily interested in organizing ever larger and ever more spectacular events. On the contrary. If we do something on a large scale, we usually have a special reason for it. But they are the exception. As a rule, we are far more set on surprises and special moments that are simply and harmoniously integrated into the hotel's daily life. They are both ordinary and extraordinary at

July 19, 2012. Not a gag—a brilliant and highly original evening. But the sceptics stayed home. That can happen, too.

the same time. I think of occasions such as Gisela Zoch-Westphal's presentation of Rose Ausländer's demanding poetry (in October 2000), or filmmaker Birgitta Ashoff's documentary about the composer Luigi Nono and his rather austere and complex music (January 2018), actually finding a big and attentive audience. Or an occasion with the intellectual firepower of a discussion between the authors Alexander Kluge and Durs Grünbein and publisher Renatus Deckert which was scheduled for April 2008 ("Das erste Buch"). In the event, Alexander Kluge unfortunately had to cancel at short notice for health reasons. Which shows that things don't always work out. Such as on the night of April 17, 1999, when the sinking of the Titanic fell through. There was too much ice. Or rather, snow. Producer Mathias Balzer wanted to bring actor Max Rüdlinger to the Waldhaus in a one-man play called "The sinking, according to the Titanic"; but they were stuck in Savognin because it snowed relentlessly and the Julier Pass was closed. At least, you get to hear Mathias Balzer's father Aldo here in the book on p. 109.

Let's stop reminiscing. I could go on for many pages. So many moments, so many creative people who initiated them! Don't try too hard to bring back the magic that was, our brother Jürg and his wife Claudia Carigiet always remind us. These highlights, the grand exclamation points and the quiet moments of bliss, derive their power precisely from the magic of the moment, from being transitory and unique. Trying too hard to bring them back by repeating or recording them or celebrating them in a book like this one is usually in vain and may even diminish and trivialize them. Better concentrate on the next project, the next highlight, Claudia and Jürg and others who live for live music and theater, keep telling us.

We will try to heed their advice. Highlights are shy companions. If you try too hard to hold them fast, they run away. What we should do is keep our door as wide open as possible—stay curious, receptive, enthusiastic and adventurous. And I think we can best succeed if we focus on our specific strengths.

Our hotel's tradition as a marvelous meeting place creates an incomparable cultural network of interesting personalities with a personal connection to us. This, in turn, generates countless constellations and topics for possible events and activities. All we have to do is be prepared, take chances, take up the ball, show an interest. To be sure, living with this happy surfeit also means navigating all the traps and pitfalls set by the necessity to choose and select. But the surfeit also has the lovely side effect of, very often, blurring, if not entirely suppressing, the usual distinction between those who are in the audience and those who happen to be in the spotlight. This, too, gives many events at the Waldhaus a special flair.

A guiding principle of our cultural commitment is something which, quite generally, informs much of what we do at the hotel. It is the principle of being serious with a light touch. As seriously as we take the hotel, we generally have a preference for the playful and almost incidental; we do not necessarily want to celebrate culture in a grand and solemn manner—a few exceptions notwithstanding. Our ideal is to offer events which simply, very naturally, fit into and enhance the daily life of the hotel, without making a show of it. Mind you: playful and incidental does not have to mean "lightweight" and "harmless," and there is often a good deal of expense and effort behind what we do and what we offer.

Are we immune to arbitrariness, lazy reruns, conventional mainstream and vain prestige in our cultural programming? You bet we aren't. Our deeds do not always match our words. Or, to give it a more positive spin: we always reserve the right to ignore our own rules—just because we feel like it. One important element of culture—our culture, at least—is indulgence.

A foundation for culture at the Waldhaus

Culture as an indulgence. That is not just a question of money. But money does play a role. We of the older generation vividly remember times when the Waldhaus had very little money or time for such indulgences. Lately, the environment in which we operate has become tougher again. We must not be too surprised by that. It would be presumptuous to expect the winds of change affecting traditional tourism in the Alps to leave the Waldhaus entirely untouched. It would be sad, though, if that obliged us to once more focus too exclusively on whatever pays for itself. At the initiative of Felix Dietrich, the pragmatist, we have therefore established a foundation, "Kultur im Waldhaus Sils." We founded it in 2015 to solicit support "for what is not necessary," from those who know and appreciate what we do. ("In a word: for what's most important," we brazenly added.) It has already had a gratifying echo.

Let's be clear about this: if you come to stay at the Waldhaus, you can rightly expect a hotel with "culture" as described in the previous chapter, meaning the culture which should imbue how we operate the hotel and how we treat and welcome you. It would be pretty absurd to solicit special contributions for that. It does not come for free, but the price for it shows up on your and everybody's bill.

Our cultural activities, as illustrated by the examples we have given, are a different matter. Few of them came about simply because the hotel had a need for them. They came about because we began to realize what a great natural crucible for those kinds of activities this hotel is. It is a bit like the Eiffel Tower, where they discovered a few years after it was built how great a platform it was for sending and receiving signals of all kinds. With the slight difference that the antennas on the tower in Paris became a very lucrative business, whereas our cultural activities depend on our willingness to help finance them. That dependency can turn into a problem. Every contribution to our foundation helps lessen this dependency and helps us to utilize the potential even more broadly. And the effect of the contributions is very direct. The Foundation is less intent on building a large capital base beyond the initial funds provided by us and some of our close friends than in putting current contributions to work immediately.

If the foundation's aim is "culture at the Waldhaus," that should not be taken to mean, too narrowly or too pedantically, activities that have to do with the Waldhaus or necessarily take place at the Waldhaus. What counts is the hotel's role as a natural crucible and catalyst for cultural activities, be it within its walls or radiating out into our surroundings. That is how it has been and so it should remain.

Talking about the foundation brings us back to the debate with which we started. The Waldhaus is a hotel with culture at its core, we stated, which primarily reflects the community of its guests. Every contribution to our foundation, coming from our guests, gives virtual expression to that fact.

"Behind the scenes, too, challenges and new beginnings ruled the day"

Martin Müller

MARTIN MÜLLER and IRENE MÜLLER (nee Ryser), he as F&B and Assistant Manager and she as Head of Human Resources (always ready to pitch in elsewhere, too), were at our side during the 1998 and 2008 Waldhaus anniversaries and the heady years that preceded and accompanied them. It was in no small measure due to them that the cultural pinnacles of those years went hand in hand with many professional and gastronomic highlights.

"During the time I worked at the Waldhaus, which began with an internship in the Food & Beverage sector in the winter of 1994, there were many changes. A new executive chef. A new culinary philosophy. A new head waiter. A new type of dining-room service. A new delivery entrance. A new kitchen. New wines. A new cashier system, and much more. The guests did not always notice the changes, but behind the scenes challenges and new beginnings ruled the day. My time at the Waldhaus had a strong impact on me, and my wife Irene and I look back on it with pleasure. Starting in 1997, both of us lived and worked at the Waldhaus, having been together before.

MARTIN MÜLLER and his wife IRENE spent 15 and 13 productive and creative years working at the Waldhaus and won the affection of many of our guests in the process. They met at hotel school in Thun. Their two sons Lars and Timo share a birthday, though Lars always stresses the fact that he is three years older. Martin and Irene went on to run the Bellevue Hotel in Adelboden, before becoming the managers of the Castell Hotel in Zuoz on April 1, 2015.

My intense association with chef Kurt Röösli, who was increasingly turning to local products, also inspired our offerings of wines and spirits. In 1995, for example, we began to contact select wine producers in Graubünden, the Valais and the Ticino directly. We were thus able to differentiate ourselves from other hotels, with a wide selection of local wines. At first there were about 190 wines on our wine list, by 2010 there were around 500. Between the seasons, Kurt and I would take the Waldhaus Toyota van and visit the various wine producers in Graubünden to purchase wine. The van would be filled with bottles to the brim, the drive back over the Julier Pass was iffy with the van just barely able to make the climb. On a number of occasions, we got lost in Gian Battista von Tscharner's wine cellar at Reichenau Castle ...

We also made the Waldhaus wine cellar more accessible. We launched the 'Keller in the Cellar' series, which still continues. Stefan Keller's public talks with well-known wine producers at the large cellar table attracted an illustrious crowd. Over the years, many of our business contacts with wine producers have turned into personal friendships, and this was all thanks to the Waldhaus. With Felix, I had frequent exchanges about structuring our offer, as well as about pricing. What I enjoyed particularly was the depth of vintages in the cellar, surely something that Rolf Kienberger would have favored, too. Meaning, I was able to buy wine that we aged at the Waldhaus. Nowadays that has become rare, as tying up a large amount of capital is frowned on in the capital-intensive hotel industry. Around CHF 300,000 was stored in the Waldhaus cellar in bottle form and some of these bottles, as I said, were only meant to be sold years later. It stands to reason that our wine stewards were happy to praise such wines and also to sell them.

Things were also happening in terms of the service. Walter Nana followed Roberto Schilirò as head waiter, and for a variety of good reasons management decided to do away with the platter service and all the clattering that went with it. Most chefs can arrange the food on a plate more attractively than waiters and waitresses can, and since the waiters did not need to carry every side dish to the guests at every table in a covered silver dish, which then had to be carried back to the kitchen, the service became simpler and faster and the food quality improved. Unfortunately, the distances are still just as great.

When the kitchen was renovated, the pantry, the 'office' area in hotel-speak, was also redesigned, enabling us to optimize operations, and we introduced a cashier system. Until then, waiters and waitresses would write vouchers, which were used to place an order, and then these vouchers were individually entered and booked to the guest rooms at the cashier's office. A very error-prone system, not only because of the handwriting that had to be deciphered. The changeover turned out to be difficult for many of the waiters and waitresses and programming the cash registers was also hard work. Once everything was up and running, though, inventory management suddenly became simpler.

"Well, when it comes to IT, the Waldhaus never played a pioneering role. In reservations, for example, they were still cheerfully working with cardboard plans. You could pencil in entries, or erase them again. It's amazing that not more errors were made with this antiquated method."

Either way, the Waldhaus, the values and personal contact with the guests which are practiced there had a strong impact on us, and we continue to pursue many of these Waldhaus values."

← Patrick Dietrich and Claudio Dietrich

From 2010: a new generation steps in. And up.

In 2010, Felix Dietrich, though still remaining very present and visible at the Waldhaus, stepped back and management was passed on to his sons Claudio and Patrick, first in a threesome with me, and after a few years, when I would follow Felix's example, on their own.

Claudio and Patrick are seconded by other family members, including their sister Carla Lehner, who currently heads the new spa, and Claudio's wife Cornelia, who is responsible for marketing. Their mother Maria Dietrich—still and always aiming for balance, whether it is with numbers or with people—has gradually reduced, but by no means ended, her own intense involvement in accounting and many other areas.

The generations come and go; the family remains. That's the Waldhaus way, isn't it? In fact, it is not as obvious and automatic as it appears. Our transitions from one generation to the next have never just simply fallen into place. The first transition was nearly a disaster (see "Uncle Gustav" and "Capital, revisited", pp. 98 and 115), the second was painfully protracted and only succeeded because the incoming "Generation III" showed admirable and extraordinary patience and an unshakeable belief in the future of the Waldhaus. Only the third transition proceeded smoothly and productively, after a few initial hitches (See "Changing of the guard," p. 207). And now, the fourth transition, from our generation to the fifth Waldhaus generation. The final verdict will have to wait until we're all gone and all is done, but from the current perspective, it seems to have gone remarkably well, borne along by good fortune and the productive collaboration between the generations.

It was Felix who set the ball in motion. He had let us know for a long time that he wanted to step back from his management role at age 60, in 2010. He and Maria had taken on a heavy dose of responsibilities at the Waldhaus at a very young age, first alongside Rolf and Rita Kienberger, then on their own, and soon (successfully, but strenuously) with me at their side. By 2010, they had been working at the hotel for a third of a century, a very long time for such a passionate, intensive and unrelenting commitment with very little private space. Stepping back, of course, calls for someone else to step up. Felix convinced all of us to seriously and systematically address the question of succession at an uncommonly early stage (though by no means too early!).

Basically, our prospects were good. Felix and Maria had done an excellent job of passing our fascination with the hotel and our commitment to it on to their children. At first glance, that may not sound like much of an achievement. Who wouldn't be fascinated by such a lovely inheritance? But in reality, it was a challenge, and not a small one. It is true that in principle a resort hotel lends itself very well to serving as a center of family life and an object of identification. Unlike a factory or some other abstract business, even as a child, you can experience and understand it. It is something you can visit, where you can stay or even, as we and the Dietrich children did, make it your own home. But it also holds a few tricky risks.

When you run a hotel, you want it to outwardly dance and sparkle like an enchanting game. It is only human, then, if behind the scenes and in private you are all the more tempted to stress all the pressures, the worries and hard work that it also entails. By doing that, though, you risk thoroughly discouraging the next generation from going anywhere near it when their own time to choose comes.

A second risk is the disparity between our visitors and ourselves, the ones they visit. A hotel aims to offer its guests (many of whom may, anyway, have a great deal of money) a life of luxury, comfort and leisure. We offer them what we ourselves do not have, or that, if we did seek it for ourselves, would soon get us and the hotel in a lot of trouble.

How can you make your own children understand and accept this disparity in good faith? Especially, if in the bustle of everyday life and work, you may often be tempted to placate them by offering them the luxuries of the hotel instead of the time you do not have?

Despite all the worries and risks, my sister and brother-in-law have obviously succeeded, as our parents did in our own case, in giving their children (and their nieces) a balanced and positive picture of the great and fascinating job of running a hotel. They managed to show them that the hotel gives us a lot, even if it is very different from what it does for our guests: we get fulfillment and a life's work, a fantastic playground for our abilities and creativity and imagination. The fact that four of the five Dietrich children—and their three cousins Beatrice, Manuela and Lena—ended up going to hotel or tourism schools speaks for itself. Not all of them have stayed in the business, but none have turned their back on the Waldhaus. It should be said that our parents, too, played a big role in helping to build such deep bonds between the fifth generation and the Waldhaus. I, too, did my best to contribute, but my skill in this regard is limited; too often I play the role of the stern guardian of what's right and proper, rather than the cheerful motivator.

If you've got money, you can enjoy yourself here. And if you don't, you have to provide the music.
RUDI KNINA (1904-1991), the beloved Waldhaus bandleader of our childhood and youth, knew what he was singing about, when he launched into this old Viennese ditty. A trained classical cellist and a born entertainer, he came from a well-off, Viennese Jewish family. After the Nazis arrived, he escaped to Switzerland (and to harsh internment in a refugee camp).

So, we had a new generation genuinely interested in the hotel. But there was still some way to go. Could their individual expectations and wishes be brought together into a whole? Would what each sibling and cousin wanted, and what they expected, add up to what the hotel needed? Or might it even add up to too much, an "oversupply," more players than roles? What about the timing: who would be ready and when, what would be needed and when?

We set out to tackle the many open questions. In October 2004, we had a first family weekend and intense generational exchange in Flühli in the hinterland of Lucerne. More such encounters, at which we continued and deepened our discussions, followed at yearly intervals, 2005 in Zurich, 2006 in Solothurn, 2007 in Constance, 2008 in Paspels in Graubünden and 2010 back at the Schweizerhof in Zurich. For good reason, we met away from Sils, so that we could give each other our undivided attention. "We" meant us four Kienberger siblings from Waldhaus Generation IV (we were born between 1950 and 1958) and our spouses and the eight descendants of "Generation V" = 5 Dietrich, 2 Klotz and 1 Kienberger Carigiet (born between 1977 and 1986), again with their spouses or partners. At times, we were coached by an experienced professional advisor.

It came in very handy that, along with the central question of succession, we had a second specific issue to discuss. We wanted to develop and implement a program for our 100th anniversary in 2008-2009. Together, we came up with a splendid, wide-ranging list of events and ideas. Above all, this second, practical topic was valuable as it provided a tangible context for our discussions of succession and helped to keep them from becoming too vague and abstract. Developing and implementing the 100th anniversary program, as a task we shared and solved together, led us right into such topics as what our shared view of the Waldhaus was and how our roles should be distributed in the future.

What came out of these efforts in the end? Everyone who has visited the Waldhaus lately has seen the beneficial results. Let's call it "2 + 2 + F": Claudio and Patrick Dietrich are in charge at the hotel (that's the first "2"), with Carla Lehner and Cornelia Dietrich at their side (the other "2"), with the solid consensus and support of the entire family as a firm basis and background ("F"). We can happily report that this family basis is not limited to the core family; we have the equally firm backing of the wider circle of our shareholders, which includes the descendants of our grandmother's two sisters and of one of our grandfather's brothers.

Thomas Mann, our celebrated visitor of days gone by, famously described the rise and decline of a bourgeois family over the course of four generations in his *Buddenbrooks* novel. Here we are, in generation five, seemingly putting paid to that formula. Thomas Mann might have been irritated (he often was). Granted: we seem to have left the realm of the probable quite some time ago.

Beyond the realm of the probable. If that applies to the circumstance that the new generation continues to be interested in the Waldhaus and identifies with it, it is just as true for the particulars of Claudio and Patrick's role. As resolutely as both of them had embarked on a hotel career, it was far from certain that they would be willing to commit to the family's own business. It takes courage and self-confidence to stand up to the constant comparison with the work of your parents, your uncle, your ancestors (basking, as they will, in the warm afterglow of hindsight), and to take the helm in a firm so deeply marked by many cherished traditions. With these considerations in mind, they might have had it easier to work somewhere far from home instead.

It was also courageous that they were and are ready to team up together and share management. The era of our generation, and the transition to it, clearly showed that having this sort of "management as chamber music" rather than a single CEO at the top can let a hotel take wing and give it entirely new colors and dimensions. But our experience has also shown that it is a demanding and challenging model, rife with risks and possible frustrations. Claudio and Patrick's decision to work together has the same potential, in either direction.

They showed courage, too, in embracing a great, but time-consuming and demanding tradition which has become increasingly rare. It is the old tradition of the hotelier operating not as a fairly aloof executive, but willing and ready to be deliberately and systematically present in day-to-day hotel life.

Hoteliers in more than name only

Claudio and Patrick did not simply get their jobs by birthright. Both began their careers with apprenticeships as cooks and then worked as chefs. They graduated from first-rate hotel management schools and gathered further professional experience at renowned addresses both in Switzerland and abroad during their studies and afterwards. And, of course, at the Waldhaus!

And, who's pulling the cart now?
The fifth generation on Oct. 11, 1986. Standing: Franca with Lena; Beatrice, Patrick and Claudio. In the wagon Sandra, Manuela and Carla

Claudio (1977) did his apprenticeship at the Margna Hotel in Sils-Baselgia, became a chef at Mosimann's in London, graduated from the Lausanne Hotel School after internships in Taiwan, Ragaz and France. For three years, he was Food and Beverage Coordinator at Badrutt's Palace in St. Moritz—so close to Sils, and yet so far away—and, for two and a half years, manager of (on-board) "inflight" development for business and first class of the intercontinental routes at Swiss, the airline. He has been married to Cornelia Ryser from Celerina since 2013.

After a school year in French-speaking Neuchâtel (Institut Lasalle), Patrick Dietrich, born in 1980, did his chef's apprenticeship at the Ermitage-Golf Hotel in Schönried near Gstaad, went on to cook at the Rathauskeller Zug and graduated from the Lucerne Hotel School after internships which included the Schweizerhof and the Hiltl Restaurant, both in Zurich. The next steps in his career included stints at the Swissôtel Le Plaza in Basel, the Wheatleigh in Lenox (Massachusetts), the Parkhotel Vitznau on Lake Lucerne and the Park Hotel in Bremen. He married Romansch-speaking Graubünden native Ursina Planta from Fuldera in Val Müstair in 2012; they have three children, Elias (2013), Selena (2015) and Rafael (2017).

Windows of opportunity and life plans

Given the solid professional foundation that Claudio and Patrick brought to the job and their willingness to take on a big challenge, our family meetings and discussions with and among members of "Generation V," which had started in 2004, quite quickly came to a consensus that the two brothers would be the ones to take charge at the Waldhaus. The timing was pretty good, too. In 2010, Claudio would be 33 and Patrick not quite 30. If they had had to take over any earlier, it would have reduced their chances of proving themselves and gaining experience in

The fifth Waldhaus generation in the summer of 1985 in front of Christian Zuan's "fat boulder" (p. 23). Not there yet: Lena Kienberger

30 years later—all accounted for!

other places. Waiting much longer would have increased the risk that their careers would already be at a stage where a return to Sils became more difficult and less attractive.

However, what about the other members of their generation? It is, after all, fortunate and remarkable to what degree Sils and the Waldhaus have left a lasting mark on every one of them. It is what helps keep our family together.

For Franca (1978), Beatrice (1979) and Sandra (1980), it was already fairly clear that their lives would move in a different direction. At the time, Franca Dietrich (now Nugnes, married to Rino Nugnes from St. Moritz) was a qualified nurse and already a mother. She and Rino now have two children, Lara (2003) and Fabrizio (2008); they live in Sils and Franca heads a counselling center for critically and chronically ill persons and their families. Beatrice Klotz (now Kintzinger), a trained chef with many talents and interests, had emigrated to Canada. She is now on the verge of returning to Switzerland with her two children Ashton (2007) and Lindsay (2008). Having retrained, she plans to work as a teacher/therapist. Patrick Dietrich's twin sister Sandra (now Palli), incidentally an active ice hockey player, has a Bachelor's in Tourism and Hospitality from HTW in Chur. Before she gave birth to her three children Gion-Mattia (2012), Flavia (2014) and Dimitri (2018), she rose to become assistant to the CEO of a Swiss retail giant. Now she lives in Fribourg, the hometown of her husband Frédéric Palli, and works part-time for an up-and-coming communications agency.

The younger members of the generation, Manuela (1982), Carla (1983) and Lena (1986), understandably declared that it was too early for them to decide once and for all for or against taking an active role at the Waldhaus. They were not thinking of one day replacing their two brothers or cousins at the helm, but did not want to prematurely exclude the possibility of finding a position at the hotel at some point in the future. This was a bit of a quandary. We could hardly give Claudio and Patrick "conditional" responsibility and explicitly oblige them to leave a door open for those who might come later. We tried to react with pragmatism, establishing that, as in our own generation, a future collaboration was entirely possible, but only if the two brothers agreed to it.

We are glad to see that, in the end, this became a reality where Carla Lehner and Claudio's wife Cornelia are concerned. Carla has always stayed close to the Waldhaus, with 22 Waldhaus seasons already behind her, between making a commercial apprenticeship at the Albris Hotel in Pontresina, earning a high school diploma (Berufsmatura) and giving birth to her son Christian (2010).

Manuela Klotz (now Heuri), a trained chef like her sister Beatrice and her cousins Claudio and Patrick, was Commis Entremetier in the Waldhaus kitchen in 2003–04, and our Demi-Chef Saucier in the following summer. She came back for a summer in 2008 and took an active part in our anniversary program. Now she and her husband Michael Heuri with their two daughters Elina (2011) and Annica (2013) live near Olten, half-way between Zurich and Berne. A keen skier and ski instructor, she has made children the focus of her life, both in her own family and in her work as the head of a playgroup.

The Dietrichs, of course, grew up right here, and Beatrice and Manuela are daughters of a chef. Their cousin Lena Kienberger, by contrast, has parents (our brother Jürg and his wife Claudia Carigiet), who took a different path entirely. And yet Lena, too, chose a hotel career. She was a commercial apprentice at a hotel in Basel and then graduated, like Patrick, from the Lucerne Hotel School. Currently, she works as event manager at the Euler Hotel in Basel. We said it before: Sils and the Waldhaus have left a lasting mark on all of us. It is what keeps our family together.

"Oasis of tranquility in a hectic world"

Claudio Dietrich

CLAUDIO DIETRICH and his brother Patrick have managed the Waldhaus of their forebears since 2010. Both learned and lived the hotel business from the ground up. Claudio's career began with a chef's apprenticeship at the Margna Hotel in Sils-Baselgia. He worked as a chef in such places as Anton Mosimann's in London, graduated from the Lausanne Hotel School, then worked in Taiwan, France and Switzerland, at Badrutt's Palace and for Swiss, the airline. Claudio is married to Cornelia Dietrich-Ryser, who is head of marketing at the Waldhaus, and he is the treasurer and deputy mayor of Sils.

"Sometimes I find that things at the Waldhaus move too slowly, then again I think that slowness is the key to steady improvement. It is our good fortune that we bring together such a diverse set of experiences. It pays to listen carefully, particularly in the case of renovations, and then work our way backwards from the intended goal to a precisely planned sequence of steps leading to the final result. That calls for an overall strategy, always with the idea of creating and maintaining a sense of generosity at its heart. In whatever we are working on, we keep that generosity, which our guests cherish, in mind, aware that the exact meaning of it is in constant flux.

For instance, while 15 years ago a booth for mobile phone calls may have been appropriate to meet the needs of working guests, it no longer serves that purpose today. Today's guests work wherever they happen to be. They are used to working and making phone calls even when on a family vacation. As people are no longer bound to one place, they work more intensively, live more intensively, enjoy their vacations more intensively. They need an unobtrusive infrastructure to fit it all in. If we succeed in offering an environment for intensive relaxation, while at the same time providing opportunities for intensive work, we can fully exploit our unique advantages. Then the Waldhaus can continue to be an oasis of tranquility in a hectic world, and we will always be able to find new guests who are looking for exactly that.

In what we do, I am not so much influenced by other hotels, I look at exciting companies, no matter in what field, and ask myself how they keep their specific promises. I am convinced that we need to create elegant co-working spaces in order to allow our guests to organize and optimize their own short breaks not *from* but *for* work, these time-outs from relaxing and being on vacation. It should also be possible to create an inspiring meeting room where you feel like you are in the midst of a forest. We would like a larger library, and are thinking about how to create other new, original spaces in tune with the Waldhaus. The Waldhaus is not simply a hotel for spending the night, it is a place where you should be able to vacation, relax and work at will, all at the same time.

When it comes to our culinary offers, it also doesn't make sense to simply copy others. We would rather look for products and concepts which fit the Waldhaus, systematically involving our staff and their specific know-how. Our Arvenstube restaurant is a good example. Even after years of promoting regional cuisine, we are still discovering new products which perfectly complement our offer. Our Executive Chef Gero Porstein developed the new Arvenstube concept, the only requirement was that it differ from our main dining room. Vacationers do not want multi-course menus every night. Sometimes they may want a simpler, less complicated dinner. In any case, our guests enjoy this new offer. I do not think that in our case an outright gourmet restaurant would be a significant step forward, given the Waldhaus' relatively remote location, which is both a liability and an asset. It makes our own guests glad to stay in; at the same time, it does not make it easy to get guests from St. Moritz to come here for dinner. Instead of 'fine dining,' I would much rather build a simple cabin in the woods and celebrate the art of simplicity there. Fondue in winter, a rustic touch would undoubtedly be an appreciated addition.

Thinking about our strategy, we have also considered whether we should acquire satellite businesses. We keep an eye out in our surroundings. If we were to take over a business, it would have to complement what we do at the Waldhaus. We do not have to force it, because we don't want to fragment our efforts and want to keep our focus on the personal touch. The presence of our family in the hotel is a major asset, alongside the many long-time staff members who also generate a feeling of trust and familiarity. As our guests get to know them personally, they and the family give the Waldhaus an identity and the assurance that despite all of the transformations the hotel remains true to itself.

Given that our guests' stays have become shorter, it is ever more important to mark the difference between the hectic pace of day-to-day life beyond our walls and these moments of relaxation under our roof. For the same reason, we will continue to devote much attention to cultural events, as they are an important puzzle piece in the vacation experience of Waldhaus guests. We do not want to become a narrowly defined art-and-culture hotel, but whenever you come to the Waldhaus, you should be sure, without having to study the calendar, that you can, if you feel like it, see or hear or experience something unique on our premises once or twice a week, and also that there is a wide range of inspiring cultural offerings in the surrounding area. That would-be guests continue to have this assurance is one of our main concerns. Our network of artists keeps growing. New creative artists with exciting ideas thus find their way to the Waldhaus. It's too bad we can't implement all of the projects proposed.

One of the greatest challenges for the future concerns our own roles. How can we unite the entire family, which has grown larger over the generations, behind the Waldhaus, so that the hotel can continue to be their hotel? All of them should be proud of the Waldhaus; we have to continually work together and include all family members to make sure that this is the case, otherwise the hotel will be difficult to manage in the future. The sixth Waldhaus generation now counts 13 family members, that is a little different from the more easily manageable conditions we had in the past, when there were fewer of us. It is clear that we will have to face difficult choices and decisions concerning the distribution of shares if we want our enterprise to continue to be nimble and project the stability and calm which is at the very heart of the Waldhaus."

"You cannot simply delegate the contacts with your guests"

Patrick Dietrich

PATRICK DIETRICH joined the Waldhaus when he was 29. Following an apprenticeship as a chef, he worked in that position at the Rathauskeller in Zug. He graduated from the Swiss school for hotel management in Lucerne and worked in leading hotels in Switzerland and abroad. His wife, Ursina Dietrich, grew up on a farm in neighboring Val Müstair and came to Sils as a teacher. With their three young children Elias, Selena and Rafael, they live directly across from the hotel.

"We certainly appreciate our many repeat guests. They account for 70 percent or more of our total. Many of them have come here again and again. I don't like to distinguish too much between 'regulars'and 'others,' though. We want the Waldhaus to be open, not a private club of long-established guests.

The personal touch remains very important to us in the fifth Waldhaus generation. Our staff, too, have a key role to play in making our guests feel comfortable, long-time regulars and first-time guests alike. It is not that we ask those who work with us to put on a show; we would rather practice and encourage an authentic friendliness, we are no fans of artifice. Charm and character are important hiring criteria for us. Professional skills are obviously relevant, but someone who is highly qualified, but just does not fit in in terms of character, will not last long at the Waldhaus.

I value my interactions with our guests, I love talking to them, and hearing from them makes me see the value of our efforts. It may sound odd, but for me it actually feels like receiving guests at home. Their feedback motivates us and makes us feel good, a feeling which I can pass on and return. Claudio and I complement each other well, he is more structured, I may be more patient, which helps me in my relationships with our staff and guests. We are just in the process of reconsidering our division of responsibilities to align them even more closely with that. My job will become less tied to the operational side, our management team will assume more of the management duties so that I can devote more of my time to our guests. Our reorganization underlines the fact that you cannot simply delegate the contacts with your guests and that we take guest relations very seriously. My job begins with the reservation, the room assignment and with direct contact with the guests from the moment they arrive until they leave.

The last few years have taught me a lot; I have learned to avoid the natural tendency to lend too much weight to negative comments. They are obviously important in showing us where we can improve; however, I also see my job as constructively softening the negative, introducing an upbeat view, emphasizing what is working well and what is fun.

Guests' reactions can be hurtful, and in my Waldhaus career there have been situations where I didn't feel comfortable. Luckily people who think that money can buy everything do not tend to feel very much at home at the Waldhaus. Sometimes you notice even during the reservation process that someone is looking for something other than the Waldhaus; you sense whether he or she will be happy here or not. That is why it is doubly important that I always keep an eye on the reservations.

To be clear: guests have every right to make demands, and we are prepared to meet them, but I do have trouble with people who think they are the only ones who matter. In such cases it is important that the management take a clear stand, and in general we shouldn't think it beneath us to get involved, to listen and find solutions. Understanding and communication are important in difficult situations. Speaking of that: I personally answer written comments—a rather intensive undertaking in the era of TripAdvisor and co. We systematically evaluate our questionnaires, of which we receive about 2,000 a year. We keep the data on file and can statistically evaluate every one of our services or also put together the feedbacks on a particular service. It wouldn't be right to ask our guests questions without valuing their answers, as happens sometimes in our industry. It is important to know our guests' wishes so that we can take better account of them. This is not just empty talk.

Together, Claudio and I can make our business succeed because we are so different from each other. We treat one another not only as brothers but also as business partners. We aren't always patient with each other. Within a family, one sometimes pays the least attention to those who are closest. In any case, it is good and helpful to not only turn to our own family but to include the opinions of our managing team.

I like to throw out ideas. The feeling behind an idea is also important to me, trial and error, the courage to simply try something new. Claudio is more factual. He first analyzes a situation and if he proposes an idea, he has usually thought it through from A to Z. Another of his strengths is his pragmatism. That is good for both of us, it enables us to try new ideas without dismissing them from the start.

We totally agree on the core values of the hotel. Financial success is relevant to all that we do, but numbers are not the only criteria. When you become a father you notice all the more that there are other dimensions. Finally, I also hope that my family can view the Waldhaus not as a competitor but as something rewarding. To wrap it up, I am well on my way to finding a balance between hotel and family, even though the hotel carries a lot of weight in my life. This is only possible because I can work with pleasure and conviction. I would find it much more difficult if I were forced to do a job that didn't give meaning to my life.

We don't yet know what the future will bring, but I find it useful to look back in order to understand what I would like to do differently in the future."

422

← The author with his hotel and his story—our hotel, our story

The overture to our new era

The composer of the overture to our new era was none other than Wolfgang Amadeus Mozart.

Spring 2010

Dear Guests,

June 26 to July 10, 2010

"Opera St. Moritz" at the Waldhaus Sils

An experiment

Opera at a grand hotel—a fine, impractical, tempting undertaking. With great spirit, an Engadine tradition enters its eleventh year despite many challenges. This time in a new location: here in our indoor tennis court! Dating from 1983 and so discretely carved into the side of the hill that many people have not yet discovered it, the indoor court is our biggest room by far, 6 meters and 20 feet high and with almost double the volume of our great lounge. It has surprising acoustic qualities, as we discovered during our anniversary theater in 2008.

W. A. Mozart: Le nozze di Figaro

Artistic director and conductor: Jan Schultsz. Director: Eva Buchmann. Impresario: Martin Grossmann. With the Hungarian Symphony Orchestra and excellent young singers from Russia, the Netherlands, Spain, Serbia, Italy, France, Rumania and Graubünden. Waldhaus liaison: Felix Dietrich.

Seven performances between June 26 and July 10, dress rehearsal on June 24

Count Almaviva's (tennis) court: Figaro at the Waldhaus, 2010 (Photo Giancarlo Cattaneo/Opera St. Moritz)

The beginning of our 2010 summer season was an emotionally charged and exciting moment. It was the start of the era of Claudio and Patrick Dietrich, with my sister and me still on the bridge for the time being. For the first time in 33 years, Felix Dietrich explicitly and officially was no longer on that bridge. How would we and he cope?

The intention was clear, but would he, would we succeed? After 33 years of intense commitment, would Felix really be able to leave the operations to someone else? That is where we got help from unexpected quarters. For ten years, we had watched with admiration, but also with some skepticism as a few aficionados and intrepid movers and shakers succeeded against all odds in putting together a full-grown opera production at one, then another of the large hotels in the region, annually in early summer under the name "Opera St. Moritz." They had repeatedly tried to convince us to hold it at the Waldhaus, but we kept our distance. There were just too many potential conflicts between the opera performances and our own "production," meaning the Waldhaus as a vacation experience. Finally, though, we agreed to try it. One does not always have to be sensible. We did insist that it be held in our indoor tennis court, not only because it had the necessary dimensions, but also to safeguard the ordinary life of the hotel. And we had an ace up our sleeve: Felix Dietrich. As a full-time liaison, he was prepared to ensure that both hotel life and the opera production were given the attention they deserved and would not get in each other's hair, both during the actual performances and in the run-up to them, when all had to be set up and rehearsed.

The results were marvelous. Skillfully and at considerable cost, the producers and artists of Opera St. Moritz fully utilized the hidden potential of the indoor tennis court, conjuring up an imaginative and very creditable performance of Mozart's "Marriage of Figaro", with a 45-piece orchestra, first-rate singers, a choir and all the technical accoutrements, and seating for 420 people. A large, purpose-built tent served as a foyer on the old outdoor tennis court in front of the indoor court. The only unexpected hitch was a heavy snowfall which temporarily brought down the tent just days before the premiere.

With his energy, his natural authority and his skills as a negotiator and organizer, Felix played a key role in making the experiment succeed. This big and demanding task came at exactly the right time for him and for us. It helped all of us to make a clean break with his previous role at the Waldhaus right at outset of the new era.

In light of our positive experience with "Figaro," we agreed to have Opera St. Moritz back in 2011, this time with Donizetti's "Anna Bolena," with Felix again at the forefront "from and for the Waldhaus." And once again, it was a resounding success.

Nevertheless, to the organizers' disappointment, we had insisted up front, "All good things come in twos." Much as we enjoyed and admired the production, it remained a balancing act. Seven or eight performances in a row, with more than 400 spectators and 60 participants—that was simply a couple of sizes too large for our hotel, even if everything was well-organized and

"Starting in May, they will be here," we wrote at the time. "Claudio Dietrich's main responsibility is everything that has to do with eating and drinking: service, the kitchen. He is also in charge of administration. Patrick Dietrich oversees accommodations: reservations, the concierge desk, housekeeping. And jointly they will ensure that the hotel continues to have a face and its own very personal character. Our guests will continue to be welcomed personally, just as they have always been."
A new generation at the Waldhaus for the fifth time: will everything change?

took place in the tennis annex rather than in the hotel itself. And while we were attracted by the idea of realizing a production of this sort and magnitude, which would normally be confined to a city, here on the periphery, we also found it somewhat paradoxical. All this effort to transport an intrinsically urban art form to the mountains—for an audience who, to a considerable extent, came precisely from those cities, for the occasion, for a night or two in the mountains.

"The Waldhaus: current and relevant"

Patrick Ghielmetti

"For me, the Waldhaus was a case of love at first sight. In 1984, I worked at the bar as an intern from the Lausanne Hotel School, with Udo (Nagiller) as my boss. Felix Dietrich proposed that I come back as an assistant manager, working with him and with Maria Dietrich and Rolf and Rita Kienberger, once I graduated from Lausanne two years later. I was very eager to get out into the world, but to return to the Waldhaus was the best decision I could have made at the time. Afterwards I did set out to explore the world. I have remained good friends with the family, a relationship which became more demanding in 2016, when Felix asked me to become 'associate coach' for the transition from the fourth to fifth generation and to keep an eye on the process. I have experience in leadership training, it is part of my job as a consultant. To assume such a role at the Waldhaus gave me a very special feeling. I never had to dissemble; and it was very important to me to win Claudio and Patrick's trust. It also formed a good basis for my new mandate as chairman of the board, which I wanted to be more than simply a favor between friends.

PATRICK GHIELMETTI is the new chairman of the "Hotel Waldhaus Sils-Maria" family corporation. In 1984, he came to Sils as a hotel school intern and returned from 1986-1988 as assistant manager, the beginning of a life-long friendship with the hotel and its family. Afterwards the Bern native set out to see the world. After a brilliant international career with Four Seasons Hotels, he now works as an independent consultant, based in Chicago, but active throughout the world as Global Experiential Leadership Trainer & Behavior-Based Executive Coach for prominent hotels.

Generational transitions are never easy; they, too, call for trust and courage. Letting go is easier said than done. The shift from the third to the fourth generation, at least how I experienced it, had been more of a hierarchical process. Times were different then. Nowadays people are more likely to speak their minds to each other, to express differences of opinion, the spirit of deference of the old days is less feasible today. Rolf Kienberger was a benign authority. A figure of respect, highly regarded by everyone—including myself. Felix was my 'guru.' His assurance had superstar qualities, and it is good that he is sometimes missed here and there. Claudio's strength is his overall HR management skills, Patrick's his social interactions with the guests, and together they, as the new generation, have an appreciation for the needed transformations. They are smart enough to keep what is good while pushing for the changes a new business model requires. The ability to differentiate is the basis for success, i.e. to remain new and to adapt to the times what has become irrelevant, or to dispose of it. The fifth Waldhaus generation recognizes that some transformations are necessary. It is not a case of 'I told you so,' but of putting one's finger on problems and in some cases making unpopular but appropriate decisions. I confidently feel that the hotel's positive down-to-earth qualities and its natural elegance are not being lost. That which makes up the kindness, warmth and very special *savoir faire* of the Waldhaus is firmly fixed in the fifth generation's DNA.

I have great respect for the 111 years of this family business. There are very few stories like this one anymore. And it is not a case of a business simply ticking along, with the family going through the motions while lining their own pockets. Every penny is reinvested. That is not a normal state of affairs. Total commitment to the hotel is a deeply ingrained core value of the entire family.

High occupancy rates have been a constant for a long time. But the fifth generation has to remain aware of the ever-present risk of an aging guest structure. To be fair, I should say that this was already just as much of a topic in 1984. The fact is that the guests who come to the Waldhaus bring others along, and that is passed on from generation to generation. I cannot say whether this fragile system will be sustainable in the future, but I am amazed by the amount invested in marketing activities and cultural events. I know of few hotels that are so steadfast in investing in cultural events and activities that keep the hotel relevant and in the public eye. The Waldhaus is current and relevant. It is an elegant, stylish 'old lady' that is very well preserved, not some moribund, old and dusty shadow of its former self.

> "It took a lot of courage for the family to name someone from outside as chairman of the board of a family corporation."

There are perfect, but often soulless hotels throughout the world. The Waldhaus has a soul and a big, beating heart! It has a unique character, combining luxury with comfort. It is an affordable five-star hotel without pretensions, and yet one in which you might run into a statesman, a star conductor, an artist or well-known writer. The intelligence of the Waldhaus is not aloof, it is open to everyone.

The Waldhaus even has its own orchestra. It already had a 'corporate sound' long before the concept existed. The Welte-Mignon piano? Unique! The quirky Waldhaus Museum? Unique!

The Waldhaus truly is and remains a unique experience."

← Patrick Dietrich with Elias and Selena

Where are we now and where are we headed?

Having Mozart in our ears and before our eyes, we had now genuinely begun a new era at the Waldhaus, with the transition to the fifth generation. Would everything now change? That is what some were hoping, while others feared it.

By now, we know the answer. Much has gone well, much has succeeded. We are proud and happy about what we have accomplished. The transition and the changes were gentle at first, but are now becoming more visible, as they should be. After the first big challenge, how to deal with Felix Dietrich retiring, yet staying on in the midst of his life's work, the next question was the future role of the other two members of our generation, meaning my sister and me. We, too, have now passed on to Generation V not only the bulk of our duties and worries, but also the center of the stage and the leeway to make their own decisions. All three of us are still active, but we can fairly say that the two generations are largely managing to stay out of each other's hair.

Maria nominally retired in 2017, when she turned 64—the official retirement age for women under the Swiss pension scheme. She continues to play a strong and supportive role much appreciated by the fifth generation, be it within the family or in accounting and as Claudio and Patrick's stand-in for guest contact, particularly when it comes to the tradition of greeting guests upon arrival and departure.

My own story is a bit more complicated. Being a little younger than Felix and having started working at the Waldhaus considerably later in my life, I had not really intended to step down from management in

2010 (at least not before 2017, at age 65—the official retirement age for Swiss men). Claudio and Patrick were ready for the three of us to work together, and we set out in good faith. Unfortunately, I soon noticed that I was no longer able to deliver all that I wanted to deliver. Decades of never letting up, driven by my ambition, passion and commitment to the "cause" of this special hotel have left their traces. My ambition, passion and commitment are still here, but I have irreversibly slowed down. (Those who have worked with me on this book could tell a tale or two about that.) This increasingly interfered in our joint management duties. I thus stepped back somewhat sooner than I had planned. The reader will notice my regret. In the end, though, this, too, was one of the lucky turns which helped us to carry out the transition from our generation to the next, fully and in good time. And the Waldhaus sees to it that none of us is idle or in any danger of becoming bored.

Two building projects during these years offer a good example of the interactions and the differences between our generations. One project arose from the need to more clearly separate non-smokers from those not yet not smoking. No big deal in such a large hotel, you would think. But it was! In such a carefully construed layout, adding or reconfiguring one part is very hard to do without bringing another part into disarray. Provisionally, we had declared the bar as the smoker's lounge, delighting some and annoying others, since the handsome room plays many different roles in day-to-day hotel life. A great deal of thought and money were needed to find a better solution, carefully embedded in an overall concept for the future of all the public rooms. Even the Sils building code had to be modified for that purpose, supported by a show of hands at a town meeting and subsequently approval by the state government. Our 1929 à la carte restaurant, the Arvenstube, which we did not want to lose or devalue, was shifted eastward, turned by 90 degrees and then reassembled in a different form. This made space for Miller & Maranta's new smokers' lounge, a real gem, without losing or adversely affecting any other part of the hotel. And the bar, which Miller & Maranta had meticulously restored and remodeled twelve years earlier, again became fully available for a wide variety of uses and occasions.

This complicated undertaking, carried through in 2011–12, still bore all the traits of "fourth-generation" thinking and of my own way of operating. Intricate, artful and refined, it was guided by the ambition to take into account a plethora of aspects and concerns while being integrated into the Waldhaus with such care that the end result of the big intervention—at a cost of over CHF 2.5 million—would look almost effortless. Is that a good thing? And, doesn't such sophistication also contain a risk that things unravel when any of the prerequisites on which the undertaking rests change in the future?

Be that as it may, the time came to take on a formative milestone which would alter the Waldhaus in a much more conspicuous way. It was a project rendered all the more important, and simultaneously more difficult, by the fact that 2011 rang in a period of six long years in which traditional tourism in Switzerland and, thus, the Waldhaus faced unusually strong and stubborn economic headwinds. This project and its success were now unequivocally the new generation's responsibility.

In response to evolving guests' needs, and in fierce competition with each other, resort hotels have been engaged in a virtual arms race in building new spas and making them ever bigger and more elaborate in recent years and decades. Back in 1970, the Waldhaus had been at the forefront of an earlier trend, when it added a very attractive indoor pool. The pool is still a great success. We complemented it 24 years later with saunas and more, and in 2006 architect Patrick Blarer of Samedan carefully overhauled it. Even so, it was no match for the world of today's spas. Our generation had grappled with the challenge for quite some time, but apart from our general reluctance to simply copy others, we got bogged down in the many obstacles. By this time, other hotels had created an almost impossibly large spectrum of examples and options. What really made sense for the Waldhaus, what was necessary and feasible for a place like ours, what could, should, did we want to afford? It was all the harder for us to answer these questions, as "wellness" had not really become part of our own personal lives. We also faced the challenges of building in a protected landscape with all its rules and restrictions, of working around an existing pool that we very much thought worth preserving, and of how to place a new annex right in front of the historic hotel without damaging its own position in the landscape and its treasured views.

At this point the new generation came to the fore and made this project a clear and central priority—a generation much more at home in the new world of spas than we, prepared to tackle these difficult questions head-on. Together, we embarked on an intense planning process, carried through a capital increase within the family and won the backing of the authorities and our lenders (UBS, as today's de facto successor to the "Bank für Graubünden" of days gone by, and the Federal Corporation for Hotel Financing). And thus, the feat was accomplished. In what were, effectively, little more than 12 months of construction work spread across 2.5 years (with work being concentrated on the times between our seasons), a splendid CHF 11 million spa was created—giving visible expression to the skill of our architects Miller & Maranta, and the energy and creative drive of Claudio and Patrick Dietrich and their sister Carla Lehner. A further addition, to incorporate what we learned from the new spa, is already in the works. And then we can—no, not sit back, but tackle our next project, and the one after that, and many more to come.

What next? Some years ago, I took part in a panel discussion in front of a large audience. It was the kind of event where each participant has five minutes to make his or her case, and no one sticks to that time limit. My turn came. I had brought along my mother's old egg-timer. I set it for five minutes and when it went off, I stopped. In the middle of a sentence. Dear reader, this book is not finished. But why should it be? Fortunately, the Waldhaus is not finished either. Certainly not "finished" in the sense of being at an end; these were just the first 111 years. But also, not finished in the sense of being completed; we hope it never will be. A good deal of its charm derives precisely from that. Seemingly ageless and constant, and yet somehow never completely finished, you can never entirely pin it down. If you want to know what happens next, you will have to come and see, and each visitor will see it a little differently. Not least because, in the process, we all also become part of this curious, unfinished story of a lovely and special hotel, “le (pas trop) grand hotel.”

Appendix

From our guest books

If you get right down to it, a hotel is, really, the sum of its guests. Fittingly, our modest first hotel history of 1983 ended with a wide-ranging and serendipitous glance at our guest books of days gone by. "For the sake of discretion, the list stops in 1979," we wrote back then. It would be very interesting to update it here, but we simply ran out of time. So, we are just reprinting the old list; if the opportunity arises, the author would be happy to sit down for a cup of coffee and a chat about other remarkable visitors from the past.

At the end of the arduous road of writing this book, the first names which come to mind are those of authors, of course, who have always been very present in Sils and at the Waldhaus. And, obviously, of those who produce and issue and distribute their books, the publishers. We might call them the hoteliers of the book realm.

Already in the old 1983 list, publishers' names such as S. Fischer, Ullstein, Kindler, Piper, Klostermann, Brockhaus, Ulrico Hoeppli and André Deutsch catch the eye, and it hasn't stopped, especially if you know your way around the German-speaking publishing world. Siegfried and Ulla Unseld of Suhrkamp, both Wolfgang and Hans Dieter Beck of C. H. Beck, Peter Schifferli of Arche, Egon Ammann, Benedikt Taschen, Hendrik te Neues, Markus Hatzer of Haymon, Andreas Rötzer of Matthes & Seitz, Georg Siebeck, Michael Klett, Gerd Haffmans, Anja Schutzbach of weissbooks, Sabine Dörlemann, Elisabeth Ruge and many more. And, always, Daniel and Anna Keel of Diogenes, at least two dozen times. Now, a new name has joined the list: Thomas Kramer of Scheidegger & Spiess. Actually, he has not come yet—but without him you would not be holding this book in your hands!

But let's get back to the 1983 list. "What do the widow of the discoverer of Troy (1908), the wife of the author of the "Little Prince" (1938) and Mr. James Bond of Philadelphia (1961) have in common?" we asked back then.

And Bernard J. H. Haitink (1962 f.), Alexander Mitscherlich (1962), Léon Rothschild, Bruxelles (1961), Peter Drucker (1970), Pierre Jean Jouve (1965, 1966, 1967, 1968), Paul Klecki (1967), Jean Simmons (1967), Prince et Princesse Boncompagni Ludovisi, Rome (1935), Neville Chamberlain (1935, 1937), Hermann Rothschild, Frankfurt (1935), Wilhelm Kempff (1936), Italo Balbo (1935), Dr. and Mrs. Werner Oetker (1936), S.E. Ahmed Abdel Wachab Pacha, Cairo (1936), Princess Menaka of Cooch Behar (1937), Vivien Leigh (1937), Richard Strauss (1928, 1937), Swiss Federal Councillor J. Baumann (1937, 1939), Princess Ratibor (1938), Manuel II of Portugal ("Comte d'Ourem", 1930), Baron Albert von Rothschild, Vienna (1910), Seine Excellenz Graf Bismarck-Bohlen, Potsdam (1910), Princesse Colonna et suite, Rome (1911), Arnold von Siemens, Berlin (1912), Sir Henry Lunn (1912), M. le Prince Argoutinsky-Dolgoroukoff, St. Petersbourg (1912), Prince et Princesse Lucedio Carrega, Sala Baganza (1912, 1913), Excellenz Th. von Bethmann-Hollweg, Reichskanzler, Berlin (1913), Sidney M. Brown, Baden (1915), Walter Boveri (1920, 1921 et al.), Max Reinhardt (1917, 1925), Otto Klemperer (1918, 1919, 1924, 1925, 1928, 1929, 1947, 1951, 1955, 1958), C. G. Jung (1918, 1926), Ms. Lily Abegg (1913, 1967, 1968, 1969, 1970, 1971, 1973, 1974). Mr. & Mrs. John T. Underwood, Brooklyn/NY (1923), Claudius Dornier (1957), Mr. & Mrs. H. M. Bentley (1948), M. et Mme. Antoine Bréguet (1964), M. Charles Christian Heidsieck, Reims (1966), Carl Duisberg (1924), Hans Erni (1946), Swiss Federal Councillor E. Wetter (1932, 1947), Pierre Fournier (1947, 1948, 1949, 1950, 1951, 1952, 1953, 1961), Prof. Fritz Stern, New York (1973 and then many more times), Dr. Bernhard Vogel (1974/75, 1975/76, 1976/77), James MacCracken (1972), William McChesney Martin (1972), Maurice Couve de Murville (1975), Ralf Dahrendorf (1970/71, 1973, 1975 ff.), Friedrich Ebert, Königsberg (1909), Emil Rathenau (1909, 1910), Carl Fürstenberg (1909, 1910, 1911), Gräfin Schlieffen, nee von Luck (1910), Otto Bally (1909, 1910), Dietrich Bührle (1939), W. R. Kern, Aarau (1926), Carl, Henry, Robert, Oscar, Hans, Georg Sulzer (1926 ff.), Iwan Bally (1946), Baron Louis Rothschild, Vienna (1912), Fritz Thyssen (1914, 1919, 1926), Karl Münchinger (1951, 1959), Richard von Weizsäcker (1960), Fred Zinnemann (1955, 1978), Bernhard Wicki (1966), Joseph Beuys (1969/70), Henry Morgenthau (1934), Karl Ulrich Schnabel (1947), Josef Keilberth (1956), Pierre Guerlain, Paris (1952), Josef Kardinal Frings (1954), Erich Kästner (1954), Georg Solti (1952, 1960), Albert and Else Bassermann (1925, 1931, 1934), Lya Mara (1924, 1925), Jean-Michel Frank, Paris (1931, 1932, 1939), Luchino Visconti (1910, 1911, 1912, 1913, 1919?, 1949), Duca Marcello e Duchessa Xenia Visconti di Modrone (1930, 1931, 1932, 1959, 1964), S. D.

Ernst Prinz Solms (1930), Georg Szell (1927, 1947), Generaldirektor Dr. Flick, Berlin (1927), Michael D'Oyly Carte, London (1927/28), Walter Gieseking (1950, 1951), Thomas Mann (1950, 1954), Frau Thomas Mann in 1911, with her parents; possibly also in 1929), Erika Mann (1957), Alberto Moravia (1951), Patrick Sauvage, Comédien, Paris (1952), Peter Rybar (1944, 1952), Baron N. de Montesquiou (1952), Sign. Franco Cortese, race-car driver (1952), Prinz Rupprecht Ludwig Ferdinand zu Löwenstein-Wertheim-Freudenberg (1955), H.S.H. Princess Löwenstein, London (1927), Prinz Udo zu Löwenstein-Wertheim-Freudenberg (1913, 1914), John Kenneth Galbraith (1955), Theodor W. Adorno (1955, 1956, 1957, 1958, 1959, 1960, 1961, 1962, 1963, 1964, 1965, 1966), M. Alberto Pirelli, Milan (1913, 1929), Mr. & Mrs. v. Siemens (1929), Prince et Princesse U. Poniatowski, Paris (1930), Princesse Aspasia de Grèce et sa fille, Pr. Alexandra (1931), Frau von Hindenburg and children, Berlin (1931), Swiss Federal Councillor R. Haeberlin (1925, 1932, 1934, 1938, 1941, 1942, 1943, 1944, 1945, 1946), Prinz Konrad von Bayern (1933), Swiss Federal Councillor Haab (1933, 1934, 1935, 1936, 1937, 1938, 1939), O. Reinhart, Winterthur (1934), Mary Lavater-Sloman (1964), The Marquis and Marchioness of Bristol (1925), NR Georges André Chevallaz (1966), Swiss Federal Councillor Rudolf Friedrich (1925 ff.), Swiss Federal Councillor Kurt Furgler (1963 ff.), Marc Chagall (1966, 1973), Swiss Federal Councillor Ludwig von Moos (1966), Werner Wollenberger (1967), Fürstin Rosemary Colonna, Rom (1968), Sir Michael Redgrave (1967), Fernanda Prinzessin von Thurn und Taxis (1968), Swiss Federal Councillor Hans-Peter Tschudi (1970, 1974), Madame la Présidente Félix Houphouet-Boigny, Côte d'Ivoire (1969), Otto-Ernst Flick (1973), Peter Lukas Graf (1973), Vittorio Klostermann (1972/73 and ff.), Ulrico Hoeppli (1950, 1969, 1970, 1971), Hans Brockhaus (1926), S. Fischer (1914), André Deutsch (1971), Dr. Franz Ullstein, Berlin (1925), Helmut Kindler (1976, 1978), Klaus Piper (1949), Andri Peer (1964, 1973), Fridolin Tschudi (1964), Men's Choir Concordia Wil (1966), Matthias von Spallart (1966), Mr. and Mrs. La Roche, Basel (1939), Karl Geigy-Ronus (1930), Fritz Thomy, Langenthal (1945), Rolf Bühler, Uzwil (1976 among others), Mrs. Hoffmann-La Roche with 2 sons and servants (1915), Mrs. Burckhardt-Burckhardt, Basel (1942), Karl Böhm (1944), Theodor Heuss (1947, 1957), Franz Kardinal König (1957), Giuseppe Kardinal Siri (1956, 1957), Richard Tauber (1925), Carl J. Burckhardt (1957), Willi Daume (1958), Swiss Federal Councillor Ph. Etter (1958), National Councillor Walther Bringolf (1960), Swiss Federal Councillor Paul Chaudet (1960, 1963), Ilona Herzogin zu Mecklenburg (1962), Andor Foldes (1963, 1967), the Swiss national men's ski team (1964), Primo Levi (1966, 1967, 1968), Prince et Princesse Marco Borghese (1908),

Mme. la Vicomtesse de Gontant-Biron, née Princesse Troubetzkoy, Paris (1908, 1909, 1910, 1911, 1912, 1913), Prince A. Doria (1908), François Mauriac (1947), Swiss Federal Councillor E. von Steiger (1947), Hermann Hesse (1949, 1950, 1951, 1952, 1953, 1954, 1955, 1956, 1957, 1958, 1959, 1960, 1961), Gottlieb Duttweiler (1949, 1951, 1952, 1953, 1959), André Rothschild, Paris (1972, 1973), Rod Stewart (1973), Rafael Kubelik (1975), Laurance S. Rockefeller (1975), Eric M. Warburg (1975), Thomas Bernhard (1977), Marc Andreae (1970/71 ff.), Mr. & Mrs. Morton Otis, USA (1927), Frau Schindler (1945 ff.), August von Finck (1973 et al.), Prof. Gottfried von Haberler (1973), Prof. Lewis Thomas, New York (1976), Erik Ode (1975/76), Gert Westphal (1976 ff.), Alfred Kälin (Ski Marathon, 1977), Maximilian Schell (1967, 1969, 1972, 1977 ff.), John Knittel (1944, 1945), Paul Sacher (1945, 1946, 1947, 1953, 1958; Frau Maja Sacher also 1971), Wilhelm Backhaus (1944, 1945, 1946, 1948), Arthur Honegger (1945, 1946), Dinu Lipatti (1946, 1947, 1952), Clara Haskil (1946, 1951), Princesse H. de Ligne, Bruxelles (1946), Fred C. Iklé (1961, 1967/68, ff.), Bronislaw Huberman (1928), Yehudi Menuhin with family (1932, 1933), Father Peter Lippert (1926, 1928), Generaldirektor Dr. Carl Bosch (1931), Inge Borkh (1971), Rollo May (1971), S. A. la Princesse Aicha Aziza Hassan avec 2 fils, Le Caire/Zürich (1926, 1927, 1928, 1929, 1930, 1931, 1933, 1934, 1935, 1936, 1937, 1938, 1942, 1943, etc.). M. et Mme. Léon Blum, Paris (1927), Albert Einstein (1927), Ahmed Ihsan Bey, Stamboul (1928), Friedrich Fürst von Hohenzollern-Sigmaringen and Fürstin Margarete von Hohenzollern, Herzogin von Sachsen, Schloss Neukirch (1928, 1929, 1930, 1931, 1932, 1934, 1935, 1936, 1937, 1939; she alone: 1946, 1947, 1961, 1962), Bruno Walter (1926, 1928, 1929, 1931, 1932, 1934, 1935, 1937), Rabindranath Tagore (1928), Rudolf Baumgartner, Lucerne (1945), Artur Schnabel (1946, 1947, 1948), Victor Reinshagen (1944, 1952, 1960), Josef Szigeti (1947) and Marcus Wallenberg, Stockholm (1950, 1957).

"To be continued."

The generations

An overview of the family members who play a role in this history

Generation I

Josef Giger[1] (1847–1921) ∞ Amalia Giger[2], nee Nigg (1849–1924)

Sister of [2]: Marie Bon, nee Nigg (1854–1944) ∞ Anton Bon[3] (1854–1915)

Sister of [1]: Maria S. Bon, nee Giger ∞ Primus Bon (1858–1936), brother of [3]

Generation II

Amalia and Josef Giger's children:

Amalia "Mali" Wolflisberg, nee Giger (1873–1952) ∞ Josef Wolflisberg (1873–1963)

Fanny Lutz, nee Giger (1876–1963) ∞ Gebhard Lutz (1875–1946)

Gustav Giger (1878–1957)

Helen Kienberger, nee Giger (1882–1959) ∞ Oskar Kienberger (1879–1965)

Oskar Kienberger's siblings: Josef (1874–1950), Alfred (1875–1944), Marie-Therese (Keller; 1880–1942), Martha (Müller; 1882–1916), Johanna (Rageth; 1887–1970)

Generation III

Helen and Oskar Kienberger's children:

Helen Kienberger (1912–1979)

Oskar Kienberger (1913–1999)

Rolf Kienberger (1917–1994) ∞ Rita Kienberger, nee Müller (1926–2006)

Gertrud Kienberger (1919–1995)

Amalia "Mali" and Josef Wolflisberg's children:

Helen Candrian, nee Wolflisberg (1904–1969) ∞ Albert Candrian (1904–1985)

Hans Wolflisberg (1906–1973)

Alfred "Fredy" Kienberger (1907–1983), Josef and Hedwig Kienberger's son

Generation IV

Rita and Rolf Kienberger's children:

Urs Kienberger (1952) ∞ Nancy Kienberger, nee Wiedeman

Maria Dietrich, nee Kienberger (1953) ∞ Felix Dietrich[4] (1950)

Claudia Claudia Klotz, nee Kienberger (1956) ∞ Peter Klotz

Jürg Kienberger (1958) ∞ Claudia Carigiet

[4] son of Hedy Dietrich, nee Mäder (1913–2010) and Josef Dietrich (1907–1998)

Generation V

Maria and Felix Dietrich's children:

Claudio Dietrich (1977) ∞ Cornelia Dietrich, nee Ryser

Franca Nugnes, nee Dietrich (1978) ∞ Rino Nugnes

Patrick Dietrich (1980) ∞ Ursina Dietrich, nee Planta

Sandra Palli, nee Dietrich (1980) ∞ Frédéric Palli

Carla Lehner, nee Dietrich (1983)

Claudia and Peter Klotz's children:

Beatrice Kintzinger, nee Klotz (1979)

Manuela Heuri, nee Klotz (1982) ∞ Michael "Michi" Heuri

Claudia Carigiet and Jürg Kienberger's daughter:

Lena Kienberger (1986)

Waldhaus Generation VI: Elias with Rafael, Lara with Dimitri, Selena, Flavia, Gion Mattia, Fabrizio and Christian (Photo: Stefan Pielow, January 2019)

Generation VI

Children of ...

- Franca and Rino Nugnes: Lara (2003) and Fabrizio (2008)
- Ursina and Patrick Dietrich: Elias (2013), Selena (2015) and Rafael (2017)
- Sandra and Frédéric Palli: Gion-Mattia (2012), Flavia (2014) and Dimitri (2018)
- Carla Lehner and Roman Lehner: Christian (2010)
- Beatrice Kintzinger and Josh Kintzinger: Ashton (2007) and Lindsay (2008)
- Manuela and Michi Heuri: Elina (2011) and Annica (2013)

Other family shareholders

As of May 2019:

Heidi McEvoy and Ariel Miller (Hans and Tommy Wolflisberg's daughters) and Irène Schilling (Helen and Albert Candrian's granddaughter), as Mali and Josef Wolflisberg's descendants;

Georg Kienberger = son of Alfred and Ursula Kienberger and grandson of Josef Kienberger of "Generation II";

Monika "Rishu" Lutz as the granddaughter, and her daughter Samira Lutz as well as Dario Dörig as the great-grandchildren, of Fanny and Gebhard Lutz

Managers

1908 –1913	Josef and Amalia Giger
	Gustav Giger
1914 –1917	Gustav Giger
	Amalia Wolflisberg
1918 –1924	Oskar Kienberger
	Gustav Giger
	Amalia Wolflisberg
1925 –1949	Oskar and Helen Kienberger
1950 –1960	Oskar and Helen Kienberger
	Rolf and Rita Kienberger
1960 –1977	Rolf and Rita Kienberger
1977 –1987	Rolf and Rita Kienberger
	Felix and Maria Dietrich
1987 –1989	Felix and Maria Dietrich
1989 –2010	Felix and Maria Dietrich
	Urs Kienberger
2010 –2014	Claudio Dietrich
	Patrick Dietrich
	Urs Kienberger
2015 –	Claudio Dietrich
	Patrick Dietrich

The "pop-up managers" from outside, at Oskar Kienberger's side, during the first, truncated postwar winter seasons:
in 1955–56, Konrad Illi, manager of the Kurhaus St. Moritz; in 1956–57, Alfred "Fredy" Giger (1904–1968); a nephew of Josef Giger's, hotelier at the Stolzenfels in Davos and earlier the Beau-Rivage in Lucerne; 1957–58 to 1962–63, Alfred Berthod (1912–1983), manager of the Parkhotel Giessbach.

Founding partners, "Giger & Co."

See p. 32, "Capital matters."

The first board of directors of Waldhaus, Inc. in 1918

See p. 115 f., "Capital, revisited."

Anton (Sebastian) Bon, Chairman; Gustav Giger, Gebhard Lutz

The board of directors in 2019

Patrick Ghielmetti, Chairman (board member since 2017)
Claudio Dietrich (since 2018), Maria Dietrich (since 1999), Patrick Dietrich (since 2018), Benedikt Germanier (since 2018), Urs Kienberger (since 1975)

Chairmen

1918 – 1924	Anton (Sebastian) Bon
1924–approx. 1930	Rudolf Bon
approx. 1930–1958	Anton Bon; absent abroad from 1939–1945, during which time Josef Kienberger-Suenderhauf was acting chairman
1958 – 1965	Oskar Kienberger
1965 – 1983	Alfred "Fredy" Kienberger
1983 – 1994	Rolf Kienberger
1994 – 2018	Urs Kienberger
2018 –	Patrick Ghielmetti

Anton (Sebastian) Bon (1881–1959), Fritz Bon (1889–1953) and Rudolf Bon (1887–1979) were three of the five sons of Suvretta founders Marie and Anton Bon.

Until 2018, board and management were always entirely in the hands of the family, often without any clear separation between management and the board. This has served the Waldhaus well, but was not without risks in terms of corporate governance. Our approach has always posed a certain risk of our becoming too inward-looking and of lacking organizational rigor.

We have come to the conclusion that in today's ever more challenging environment, it is essential to be more disciplined and focused, precisely because we treasure our independence and tradition of personal, hands-on management. In response, we have now added two experienced personalities from outside the family to the board. We were not simply looking for suitably qualified experts. We wanted to have somebody at our side with experience of the wide world, but willing and able to maintain a specific Waldhaus perspective: he or she would have to be deeply in tune with our values and with the Waldhaus. And we lucked out!

In the case of Patrick Ghielmetti (1960), you can see what we mean on p. 317. Benedikt Germanier (1968), too, has known and valued Sils and the Waldhaus since student days, when he came to Sils as a ski instructor. After a career in international banking, the marketing wiz deliberately took on a challenge with some surprising parallels to the Waldhaus: he is the CEO of a small, exquisite and ambitious ski manufacturer, "zai."

With what they are and know, the two Gs will hopefully help us maintain and strengthen the Waldhaus as a fiercely independent, family-managed operation for many years to come.

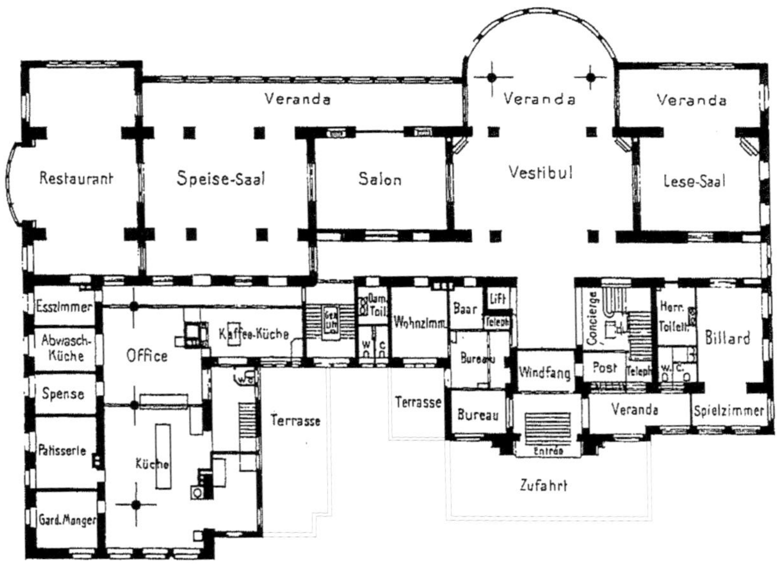

Main floor—1908

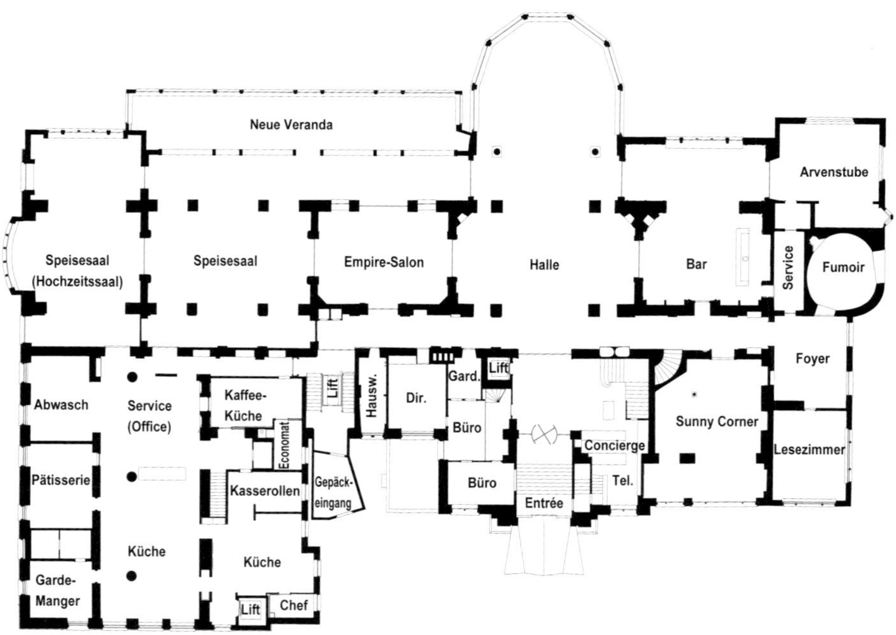

Main floor—2019

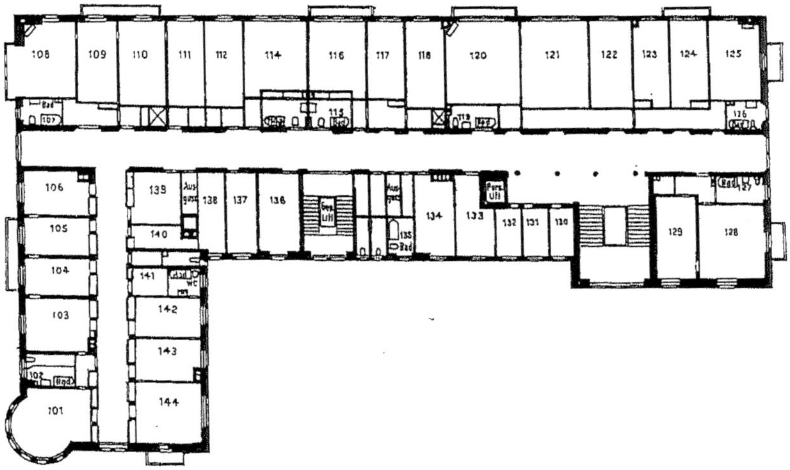

First floor—1908

"You have to think twice before tearing down just any old wall at the Waldhaus."
(Beat Birchler, p. 41)

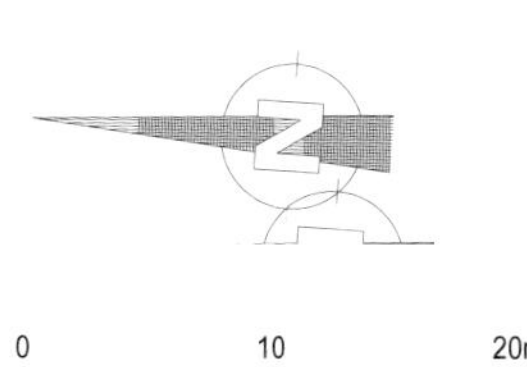

First floor—2019

The authors

Andrin C. Willi (*1976) grew up in the Posthotel Löwen in Mulegns, a legendary inn on the other side of the Julier Pass. He was a commercial apprentice at the Waldhaus from 1993 to 1996 and graduated from the Lucerne Hotel School in 2000. From 2004 to 2012 he worked as an editor for RTR Radio e Televisiun Rumantscha. Concurrently, he was editor in chief of *Vinum* until 2006 and then, until 2019, of Marmite, a gourmet and restaurant magazine, where he initiated numerous events and activities. Living and working in Zurich, he is active today on many fronts as a communicator, publicist, speaker, moderator, jury member, and provider of ideas in tourism and the hospitality industry. "If you have an interest in wining and dining in Switzerland, there is no way around Andrin C. Willi." (*Annabelle*, Dec. 31, 1982).

Stefan Pielow (*1959), as photographer, together with writer Zora del Buono, was the author of the book about the Waldhaus centennial in 2008, *Waldhaus Sils. A Family Affair since 1908*. He grew up in northwestern Germany and found his way to photography early on, beginning as a photographer's assistant. During his studies at GHS University in Essen, where he majored in communication design with a focus on photography, he had already published some lead stories in prestigious magazines such as *ZEITmagazin* and *stern*. Since 1990, he has worked as a freelance photographer for international magazines, companies and agencies and has won praise for a variety of books and projects. His specialty is carefully staged portraits, be they of people, places or objects. Stefan Pielow (see www.pielowphoto.com) lives in Starnberg, Bavaria, with his wife and two daughters.

Urs Kienberger (*1952) was born in Davos and moved to the Waldhaus (which his great-grandparents built and his parents ran for many years) when he was one month old. During and after his bilingual (German and French) education at a high-school/ junior college in Fribourg and degrees in economics from the University of St. Gallen and the University of Illinois in Urbana-Champaign, he travelled and worked on various continents, read innumerable books and was engaged for six years as a bank economist at a major Swiss bank in Basel—laying the groundwork for what followed next: his life as a hotelier at the Waldhaus, first alongside his sister and brother-in-law and then his nephews. He is happily married to Nancy Kienberger, who has translated this book into English.

Imprint

Concept: Urs Kienberger and Andrin C. Willi
Texts: Urs Kienberger et al.
Chapter photographs: Stefan Pielow
Drone pilot and assistant: Thilo Härdtlein
Translation into English: Nancy Kienberger
Proofreading: Louise Stein
Design concept: Anita Lussmann
Typesetting: Sabine Hahn, grafikdesign, Berlin; Livia Locher, marmite Verlags AG, Zurich
Scans and image editing: Widmer & Fluri GmbH, Zurich
Printing and binding: DZA Druckerei zu Altenburg GmbH, Thuringia

This book is available in English, French and German editions.

Verlag Scheidegger & Spiess
Niederdorfstrasse 54
8001 Zurich
Switzerland
www.scheidegger-spiess.ch

Scheidegger & Spiess is being supported by the Federal Office of Culture with a general subsidy for the years 2016–2020.

ISBN 978-3-85881-831-7

German edition: ISBN 978-3-85881-634-4
French edition: ISBN 978-3-85881-841-6